Presented To

Barb

Compliments of

Imperial

Travel

LENAWEE COUNTY

"Partners in Progress" by
Frederick G. Eaton and
Mary Ward-Eaton

Produced in cooperation
with the Lenawee County
Chamber of Commerce

Windsor Publications, Inc.
Chatsworth, California

LENAWEE COUNTY

A Harvest of Pride and Promise

An Illustrated History
by Charles N. Lindquist

Windsor Publications, Inc.—History Books Division
Managing Editor: KAREN STORY
Design Director: ALEXANDER D'ANCA
Photo Director: SUSAN L. WELLS
Executive Editor: PAMELA SCHROEDER

Staff for *Lenawee County: A Harvest of Pride and Promise:*
Manuscript Editor: DOUGLAS P. LATHROP
Photo Editor: PATTY SALKELD
Editor, Corporate Biographies: MELISSA WELLS
Production Editor, Corporate Biographies: DOREEN NAKAKIHARA
Proofreader: MARY JO SCHARF
Customer Service Manager: PHYLLIS FELDMAN-SCHROEDER
Editorial Assistants: KIM KIEVMAN, MICHAEL NUGWYNNE, MICHELE
OAKLEY, KATHY B. PEYSER, SUSAN SCHLANGER, THERESA J. SOLIS
Publisher's Representative, Corporate Biographies: GREG GAURILIDES
Layout Artist, Corporate Biographies: BONNIE FELT
Layout Artist, Editorial: MICHAEL BURG
Designer: ELLEN IFRAH

Windsor Publications, Inc.
ELLIOT MARTIN, Chairman of the Board
JAMES L. FISH III, Chief Operating Officer
MAC BUHLER, Vice President/Sponsor Acquisitions

Library of Congress Cataloging-in-Publication Data:
Lindquist, Charles, 1939-
  Lenawee County : a harvest of pride and promise : an illustrated
    history / by Charles Lindquist. Partners in Progress / by Frederick
    G. Eaton and Mary Ward-Eaton. —1st ed.
  p. 216 cm. 22x28
  "Produced in cooperation with the Lenawee County Chamber
    of Commerce."
  Includes bibliographical references.
  ISBN 0-89781-337-5
  1. Lenawee County (Mich.)—History. 2. Lenawee County (Mich.)—
Description and Travel—Views. 3. Lenawee County (Mich.)—
Industries. I. Ward-Eaton, Mary. II. Eaton, Frederick G. Partners in
Progress. 1990. III. Lenawee County Chamber of Commerce. IV. Title.
F572.L5L55   1990   90-12158
977.4'31—dc20   CIP

FRONTISPIECE: S.W. Temple operated a thriving lumber mill in Tecumseh during the last half of the nineteenth century. Courtesy, City of Tecumseh

THIS SPREAD: This 1894 image depicts Monument Square in Adrian. Courtesy, Lenawee County Historical Museum

PREFACE: A youngster fishing at Round Lake in northern Lenawee County waits patiently for an afternoon catch. Courtesy, Lenawee Tomorrow

CONTENTS

PREFACE

Not since 1909 has a countywide history of Lenawee been published. In that year Richard I. Bonner completed the third history of Lenawee that he had worked on, and presumably decided that he had finally got it right. He and several collaborators had worked on county histories over the previous 30 years, but strangely, no more would be written for the next 80 years.

One reason for this may be Bonner's own *Memoirs of Lenawee County*. This book was very thorough on the history of every township, village, and city, with special chapters on lawyers, doctors, the banks, the schools, the churches, the military, farmers, and the press. Maybe people really did think that there was nothing more to write about.

Something else was at work, too. For one thing, Lenawee was bogged down in an economic slump which lasted for 60 years. In 1870 Lenawee's population was 45,000, the county was—and had been for years—one of the most important in the state, and prospects for new growth seemed bright. By 1930, however, the population had barely reached 50,000, and no one really wanted to know where the county stood in relation to the rest of the state. Writing a history of the county at the time could only advertise Lenawee's stagnant condition, and who wanted that?

For many years, furthermore, few local histories were produced anywhere in the country. Local history seemed uninteresting or insignificant when compared to events in Washington or the rest of the world. Beginning in the 1960s, though, historians and others came to realize that, as important as Washington was, it could work only with those local institutions which were already in place. Much of our history now took place in places like Boston, Selma, and Detroit, with Washington merely reacting. Increasingly, then, historians returned to studying local history and culture.

Meanwhile, in Lenawee, it was obvious during and after the Second World War that something remarkable had happened here. The county was full of energy, big plans, and hope for the future. People felt good about the society that had been established here, and the time seemed ripe to write another history of Lenawee. This is an attempt to write that history. It may be that, as with Bonner, it may take several attempts and 30 years to get it right. If so, it is high time to get started.

In working on this history, I am grateful for the previous work done by many writers. Many are named in the bibliography, but some are not. They are the editors and reporters for the county newspapers who, over the years, have filled their columns with interesting accounts of people, places, and events. Thanks to one person—the late Madge Millikin, who kept up a subject index to the *Daily Telegram* for many years—I have been able to learn (and borrow) from many of these stories. When it came to collecting photographs or works of art, I have to thank all those who have donated their pictures to the Lenawee County Historical Museum so generously for years. Also, every institution and individual I have contacted about copying their pictures for this book have cooperated wonderfully, and I would like to thank them all.

Finally, there is no question that I should thank my family for their patience during this project. History is fun, but it is time-consuming. When my fifth-grade son was asked by his teacher what he wanted for Christmas, one of the things he mentioned (not major, but still . . .) was that he hoped his Dad could shoot some hoops again some time.

CHAPTER ONE

THE PIONEER PERIOD

1 8 2 4 - 1 8 4 0

By 1815 America's second war against the British was over. Britain's power over the Northwest Territory—Ohio, Indiana, Illinois, Michigan, and Wisconsin—was gone. The Michigan Territory still bordered the British colony of Canada, however, and territorial governor Lewis Cass believed that the best way to secure this land was to fill it quickly with American settlers. The territory had to be surveyed and platted first, and so Cass arranged for U.S. Surveyor-General Edward Tiffin to send a survey party north of Ohio. Unfortunately, the party began in the region—between the Maumee River and the River Raisin—where Lenawee County would soon emerge.

For years to come this area would be known as part of the great cottonwood swamps extending for miles inland from the western shores of Lake Erie. Tiffin's party never went beyond the swamps, and Tiffin concluded his report on Michigan by describing the land as "so bad that there would not be more than one acre out of one hundred, if there would be more than one out of one thousand, that would admit of cultivation." Tiffin's report set back the settlement of Michigan for some years.

Cass was unhappy with Tiffin, but he never questioned Tiffin's assessment of what would become part of Lenawee County; he said only that not all of Michigan was that bad.

The first settlers of Lenawee, who showed up in 1824, came down from Detroit or straight west from Monroe instead of through the swamps, and the land did not seem as bad as Tiffin had said. All around them forests stretched for miles, the tall trees often forming canopies over open spaces in some areas. Called "oak openings," these clearings were desirable because logging was not necessary before farming could start. While the land was dry in the northern and central parts of the county, it had plenty of water from numerous springs and streams, and the major stream, the River Raisin, was strong enough in places to run a watermill. As for the soil, it surely could support farming if it could sustain tremendous forests of such quality trees as whitewood, oak, and maple.

Other parts of Lenawee appeared just as attractive in terms of soil and water when the pioneers pushed a little further west in the 1830s—especially the valley of Bean Creek, running south from Devil's Lake through Rollin, Hudson, Medina, and Morenci. In addition,

The wide-open countryside of Lenawee County afforded residents acquiring land to build beautiful homes like the one seen here. This home was owned by I.S. Hamilton, M.D., of Tecumseh. Courtesy, City of Tecumseh

the pioneers discovered a number of small lakes nestled in the rolling hills of northwest Lenawee.

Some early settlers tried to make something of the cottonwood swamps in southern and eastern Lenawee, but they had little success. Thirty years after settlement began, maps of the county still showed much of Ogden, Riga, Blissfield, and Ridgeway townships as mostly swamp.

The second consideration for the pioneers, after the nature of the soil, was the native peoples. The settlers knew the War of 1812 had broken the Indians' power in this region, but one never knew what might happen in any particular place. As it happened, the native peoples in this area, the Potawatomi, were well aware of the need to get along with the whites. There were several Indian villages in what would become Lenawee, including the village of Meteus on the shores of Round Lake. Other native peoples also maintained hunting rights to land along the southern border of Riga. Given the wet nature of that region, no one would contend their rights for years.

According to archaeological evidence, native peoples had lived and hunted in Lenawee for thousands of years. By historic times, however, few major settlements were left. A number of burial mounds throughout the county and an important council ground near Tecumseh (possibly from the Hopewell Indians, who lived 1,500 to 2,000 years ago) were here when the first settlers arrived. Unfortunately, farmers plowed up and erased most of these signs of Indian civilization.

Evans, Brown, and the Settlement of Tecumseh

One might think that chopping down trees, farming, building homes, and laying roads would have taken all the pioneers' time and energy. What one finds, though, is that they had brought with them all the values, inter-

ests, and characteristics of the New England and New York State regions from which they had come. Almost as soon as they got here, these settlers were going to church, sending their children to school, making business deals, getting involved in politics, and even having a bit of fun—as if they were living in Palmyra, New York, instead of Palmyra, Michigan.

The people who first settled in Lenawee typify that. These people were from New York, and their leader was Musgrove Evans. A surveyor, Evans came to the county in

1823 to look the land over, and noticed a substantial flow of water where a creek (now called Evans Creek) flowed into the River Raisin. He knew the first settlers would need a sawmill and then a gristmill, and he thought a mill could be built there.

After his survey of the land, Evans returned to Monroe and talked things over with Austin Wing, his wife's cousin. This conversation indicates how far removed they were from the common image of pioneers as simple, rustic poor folk. Wing, a lawyer who wanted to get elected to Congress, thought

that if Evans could go back to New York and arrange for a large number of settlers to return with him, they might vote for Wing. He pointed out the importance of having a good miller and farmer to lead the party. Evans was no farmer, but happily, a brother-in-law of Evans, Joseph Brown, was both a miller and a farmer. Moreover, Brown's older brother, Jacob, was Chief of Staff of the U.S. Army. It seemed possible that some military road surveying contracts might come to Evans if he could talk Brown into joining the party.

General Joseph Brown (1793-1880) was the most important and significant pioneer of Lenawee County. As a farmer, miller, explorer, and genial innkeeper, he was at the center of Lenawee's first settlement in Tecumseh. As a commander of troops, he led Michigan's militia in the 1835 Toledo War and was later appointed associate judge of Lucas County, Ohio, by the Governor of Ohio in 1848. It was said of General Brown that he was "practical and thorough, generous and hospitable, shirked no duty, feared no responsibility, and commanded the respect and confidence of all citizens." Courtesy, Tecumseh Area Historical Museum

When Brown agreed to join the venture, Wing drew up the papers for the partnership of Wing, Evans and Brown, and began to buy land suggested by Evans. The upshot was a successful venture in town building, a narrow victory for Wing over Gabriel Richard in the next congressional elections, two military road contracts for Evans, and a wonderful life for Brown in Lenawee County. He became, easily, Lenawee's most esteemed pioneer leader. He built the first grist and sawmill in the county, did the first farming and ground the first wheat, built the first frame house in Tecumseh, established the first stage-based mail route between Detroit and Chicago, became a noted explorer of the Michigan Territory, served as Lenawee's first judge, commanded Michigan's militia in the Toledo War, and ran a first-class inn in Tecumseh for years.

There were about 20 people in this first group of settlers, including Ezra Blood, George Spafford, and the Turner Stetsons. Stetson was a blacksmith which made him especially useful to this pioneer community. By the end of 1824 there were about 50 people in this Tecumseh group, and they were all busy. While Evans platted the village, naming it after the noted Shawnee warrior, Tecumseh, Brown had an interview with Governor Cass in Detroit during which he argued for Tecumseh's becoming the county seat. Others worked on roads, houses, a dam, and a sawmill located up by the Fall (along with a rough-log schoolhouse in which Mary Spafford taught school that first winter).

The next year the settlers began to build a gristmill, and plowed and planted the few acres they had cleared the previous year. Cornelia Brown, Joseph's wife, also arranged for the Presbyterian minister from Detroit to come down and hold a religious service in her husband's new inn, the Green Inn. By the next year a Methodist parson, the Reverend John Braghman, was holding regular bi-weekly services in Tecumseh.

On the Fourth of July 1826, the villagers held a great celebration featuring plenty of gunpowder and a French fiddler from Monroe. Lest all this seem too jolly, it should also be noted that the normal work routine was exhausting, and the Evanses had lost a child who drowned in the river. About this time Captain Merritt of Tecumseh was asked where he lived. "Tecumseh," he said. "Where is that," he was asked. "It is thirty miles from Monroe and forty miles beyond God's Blessing," was the answer.

Through constant effort, Tecumseh continued to grow. By 1830 the population of Tecumseh Township stood at 771, about the same as that of the other two townships in Lenawee, Logan (in which Adrian was located) and Blissfield.

Other Settlements

The second community founded in Lenawee was Blissfield. Here, too, the quality and energy of the early settlers were impressive. For Harvey Bliss and family, their move into

Michigan's interior in 1824 was just a move farther up the River Raisin. They had been living ten miles up the Raisin from Monroe since 1819, and trekking another 20 miles upstream did not deter them even though the land they took up had extensive swamps to the south and east. Also, the forests along the river were almost impenetrable all the way to Petersburg.

Some others, like Gideon West and George Giles, joined the Blisses the next year. Natural obstacles were severe, though, and growth was slow. By 1830 only 150 lived in this entire eastern and southeastern part of the county. Even so, a schoolhouse went up in 1827, and the Methodists and Presbyterians were holding religious services in members' homes by the same year. In addition, Mrs. Giles was a fine nurse and doctor, supplying medical assistance to the entire area from Adrian to Petersburg for 14 years.

Adrian was the third community to be settled. It came along in 1826 thanks to 23-year-old Addison Comstock. In 1825 Comstock bought 640 acres where Adrian now stands, with the goal of developing the land into a profitable community. By the end of 1826 he had a sawmill up and running, and by 1829 he and his father-in-law, Isaac Deane, had built a gristmill. In 1828 he laid out and platted the village, called Adrian by his wife, Sarah, in honor of the Roman emperor Hadrian. Comstock was helped considerably in all his efforts by his father, Darius, who had come to Lenawee in 1825 and had settled about four miles north of Adrian along Valley Road. Educated, well-to-do, considerate, and highly-thought-of by everyone in the area, Darius was just as determined as Addison to develop the region.

By 1830 Logan Township had a population of 500, and Comstock campaigned to have the county seat moved from Tecumseh to Adrian. Adrian, he argued, was more centrally located even though it was smaller and

younger.

Besides the major communities, a number of other settlements were taking shape by 1830. North of Tecumseh, Alpheus Kies began Clinton in 1829, naming the village after Governor Clinton of New York. Thanks to the busy Chicago Road, which ran through the village, Clinton's future was assured. In 1826 William Kedzie founded a settlement in the midst of a forest on the River Raisin a few miles downstream from Blissfield. Kedzie died in 1828, but his little community of Kedzie's Grove lived on. In 1836 the name

Sarah (Deane) Comstock (1805-1872) was the daughter of Isaac Deane, the first innkeeper in Adrian. In 1826 she married the founder of Adrian, Addison Comstock. In 1828 she proposed that the new community be named after a Roman emperor, Hadrian, who was known for his exceptional governing skills. Her idea was accepted. This photo dates to around 1855. Courtesy, Lenawee County Historical Museum

of the village was changed to Deerfield after the great number of deer in the area, and also because it reminded some people of their original home, Deerfield, Massachusetts.

Some smaller settlements were founded about this time as well. The Penningtons and the Millses helped to get Macon going, and the Bradishes became synonymous with the history of Madison Township.

By 1830 Lenawee was off to a good start, with a population of more than 1,400 and a number of able leaders. The county acquired the name "Lenawee" in 1822. Lewis

Although Tecumseh, great war leader, never resided in Michigan, he was very much admired by the people of north-eastern Lenawee County, who payed homage to the great Shawnee Native American by naming their town Tecumseh. From 1808 to 1809 Tecumseh rode across the Midwest uniting the Indian tribes against the encroaching white man. Courtesy, City of Tecumseh

Cass, the territorial governor, was responsible for the name, which came from the Shawnee word *Lenawai*. To the Shawnee, the word meant "men" or "the people." Cass probably used it as a way of showing interest and respect for one of the tribes the whites were supplanting in the Old Northwest.

In the 1830s the county grew even faster. By 1834 the population was up to 7,911. Three years later it had grown to 14,878, and still they came. By 1840 Lenawee had a population of 17,889, making it the fourth largest county in the state. Only Wayne, Washtenaw, and Oakland counties were larger.

Stories abound in the old county histories concerning the exciting days of the 1830s. All over the county settlers poured in to scout the land, buy it, attack the forests, put up their first little log cabins, and plant crops. These pioneers came mostly from New York and New England. Place names like Palmyra, Cambridge, Deerfield, Woodstock, Medina, Clinton, Canandaigua and Seneca helped to remind the pioneers of places "back home."

Hiram Kidder and Beriah Lane, two of the most significant pioneers in western Lenawee, helped to establish Hudson in 1833. Kidder was the original founder, and Lane came in 1834. Hudson, the second largest city in the county in the second half of the nineteenth century, was first called "Lanesville" in recognition of Lane's efforts. Lane put up the first mill and helped to organize the township politically.

Roads and Railways

Wherever the pioneers settled, they knew that they had to improve the roads; it was just too difficult to take goods to and from market along the primitive Indian trails. In the task of developing roads, Musgrove Evans of Tecumseh was preeminent. He was a surveyor, and he worked on the first two significant roads in the area. The first, the Chicago Road (now U.S. 12), was laid out in 1826 to run between Detroit and Chicago along the age-old Indian path called the Sauk Trail. Once established, the Chicago Road became one of the most heavily traveled roads in the nation. Inns were established every fifteen miles or

so to accommodate the thousands of travelers moving west. The Park House in Clinton (started in 1830 and now in Greenfield Village, Dearborn), the Davenport House on the north shore of Evans Lake (an 1839 successor to the original log cabin inn erected in 1834, and now called the Bauer Manor), and Walker Tavern about 10 miles west at Cambridge Junction (now a state historic site) all help to remind us of the surge of settlers who came during this time.

In its session of 1831-32, Congress appropriated money for a road from Monroe to the Chicago Road at Cambridge Junction via Tecumseh. Musgrove Evans was contracted to survey the route (now M-50), which was completed in 1835. In Lenawee, the Walker

Tavern reminds us of that time, as does the old Springville Inn, which can still be seen alongside the road in Springville.

Roads must have been a sore subject for the struggling community of Adrian around 1830. There were no government contracts to help build roads through that community, and since several extensive swamps lay between Adrian and Toledo, its natural port city to the east, travel was difficult except through Tecumseh. For Adrian to become more than a satellite of Tecumseh, something bold would have to be done.

A new form of transportation called a railroad had been developed in England in the 1820s, but there were no railroads in America any further west than New York. Neverthe-

Shawnee war leader, Tecumseh, founded a confederacy of Indians across the Midwest, including tribes from the Lenawee County area. He urged these tribes to preserve the Native American belief of man and nature working together under the authority of the Great Spirit, not of the white man. Courtesy, City of Tecumseh

Hooks' Mill was on Wolf Creek a few miles northwest of Adrian, about where Wolf Creek Highway and Country Club Drive intersect today. The mill dates back to 1836, which makes it one of the earlier ones in Lenawee. It took its name from its first owners, Edward and Thomas Hook. In the exciting days of the 1830s, settlers poured into Lenawee to scout out, buy, and clear the land in order to plant crops and erect log cabins and mills. Courtesy, Lenawee County Historical Museum

less, Addison Comstock, Darius Comstock, Calvin Bradish and a few others from the central part of Lenawee decided to form a railroad running from Adrian to Toledo. It would go through the swamps and open up the central and western parts of the county. Actually, the promoters of the line had a much more grandiose idea than simply to open up Lenawee. This line would run from Toledo to the navigable waters of the Kalamazoo River, enabling freight and passengers to be transported by water and rail all the way from Buffalo, New York to Chicago, Illinois. To emphasize the purpose of the line, it would be called the Erie and Kalamazoo Railroad.

The whole idea was almost too bold. Imagine the capital demands of such a venture! It was almost comical to dream of engineering a railroad through the Black Swamp. Few knew what a railroad passenger car even looked like. And wherever would they find a railroad steam engine? All the same, the Comstocks put up money themselves, as did Brad-

ish and others, and they found enough capitalists in Toledo and back in New York State to finance the venture. For engineering, they found a talented man named George Crane to help lay out the route through the swamps. As for transportation, they began with horses and then got a Baldwin locomotive, and their passenger cars looked very much like stagecoaches.

The first train ran along newly laid strap-iron rails from Toledo to Adrian in November 1836, the first railroad in America west of Schenectady, New York. In all of Lenawee history, nothing else approaches this achievement in terms of its daring, success and significance for the county.

In the short run, the Comstocks and others used the opening of this line to get the state legislature to move the county seat from Tecumseh to Adrian in 1837. Tecumseh might be the fourth largest city in the state, but Adrian was already sixth and getting its steam up.

Tecumseh was hurt in this rivalry after

its founder, Musgrove Evans, organized a group of settlers from Tecumseh and moved to Texas in the mid-1830s. Evans lost a son at the Battle of the Alamo, whereupon he signed up and fought in the victorious Battle of San Jacinto in April 1836.

The Toledo War of 1835

The other important founder of Tecumseh, Joseph Brown, remained in Lenawee, and it was a good thing that he did because he played a very important role in the birth of the state of Michigan. In 1835 Michigan met all the qualifications for statehood set by Congress. However, Ohio refused to allow Michigan to become a state until the boundary line between the two, running almost 70 miles from Maumee Bay west to the Indiana border, was settled to Ohio's satisfaction. The sticking point was the Maumee Bay area at the western end of Lake Erie, an area valued as a potential center of trade and transportation. The rest of the territory in question, including a 30-mile stretch along the southern part of Lenawee County, was wet wilderness. Clearly, though, Lenawee had a significant

The Reverend Henry Tripp (1783-1863) was one of the first settlers in the Irish Hills area. He brought the good tidings of the Gospel in a forthright way to the other Baptist settlers of the area. He was also considered the first abolitionist in Franklin Township. Courtesy, Lenawee County Historical Museum

interest in how the dispute between Ohio and Michigan came out.

With Michigan about to become a state in 1835, Ohio decided to assert its claim to this "Toledo strip," placing permanent markers along the claimed boundary line. This led to open conflict in April 1835, involving an Ohio surveying team caught at its work in Lenawee. Joseph Brown was the man in charge of the Michigan forces in this drama. A Brigadier General in the Michigan militia, Brown was ordered by Michigan Governor Stevens Mason to keep an eye on the Ohio surveyors. If they crossed into territory regarded by Michigan as its own, Mason wanted them arrested for trespassing. On April 25 Brown's scouts told him that the party of Ohio surveyors, plus some armed guards, were in Michigan territory about 15 miles south of Adrian. Brown alerted Deputy Sheriff McNair, who immediately formed a posse while Brown called up some of the militia to intercept the Buckeyes.

Once the Michigan forces had reached and surrounded the cabin occupied by the surveyors, McNair and Judge Blanchard of Tecum-

Beriah Lane (1880-1887) has been called the father of Hudson, and indeed, the community was first called Lanesville. He settled in what became Hudson in 1834 and worked the rest of his long life to make his settlement better. This is his portrait as it appeared in the 1874 Lenawee County Atlas. Courtesy, Lenawee County Historical Museum

One of the earliest inns along what would be called U.S. 12 was established in 1838 by Sylvester Walker at the intersection of the Old Sauk Trail (U.S. 12) and La Plaisance Bay Trail (M-50). A historic marker was dedicated to the inn at the time of this 1930 photo. Courtesy, Lenawee County Historical Museum

seh entered and told the Ohioans they were under arrest. When a few of the guards raised their firearms, McNair signaled to the men outside, who let out a mighty roar. The Buckeyes panicked, rushing for the door and taking to the woods, whereupon Brown ordered some of the militia to shoot their guns into the air as a warning to the Ohioans to stop. Some did, but others ran all the harder as they thought they were under attack.

Most headed east toward the village of

Maumee on the Maumee River. This meant traveling about 20 miles through meadows, forests and swamps infested with wolves, bears and snakes, but it was the nightmarish vision of angry Wolverines shooting at them which drove them on. When a number of them staggered into Maumee hours later, their stories of these dreadful Wolverines (this was one of the first times Michiganders had been compared to this foul-smelling, quick-tempered animal) inflamed all of Ohio. Ohio Governor

Robert Lucas immediately ordered up 10,000 more of the Ohio militia. Lucas had had enough. He meant to occupy Toledo and keep it.

Upon hearing of Lucas' action, Mason ordered Brown to take 1,500 Michigan militiamen into Toledo. Brown did as he was ordered, and all accounts say that his handling of his men as well as the villagers helped to keep tempers down.

Meanwhile, cooler heads managed to head off the impending conflict. A settlement between Ohio and Michigan was reached. Ohio would get the disputed territory while Michigan would get the rest of the Upper Peninsula (it was already slated to get the eastern part of that peninsula). For Lenawee

this settlement meant the loss of almost one-fifth of its territory. However, no one could say that Lenawee had not fought admirably and well even if the results were not to its liking. The county had served notice to the entire state that it was proud, pugnacious, and purposeful.

In fact, it could be said that both the development of the Erie and Kalamazoo Railroad and the actions taken by Brown and his militiamen showed that the people of Lenawee were moving out of the early stages of pioneer development. Both of these efforts required planning, organization and a fair amount of capital or manpower. Clearly, the people of Lenawee were moving toward a more complex and organized way of life.

This drawing of the first Erie and Kalamazoo train to be powered by a steam engine was created years after the Adrian-Baldwin locomotive arrived in 1837. Following the engine is the two-story coach, or "Pleasure Car," as interpreted by the artist who heard about but never saw one of these top-heavy cars. Courtesy, Lenawee County Historical Museum

CHAPTER TWO

THE GOLDEN AGE

1 8 4 0 - 1 8 7 0

Between 1840 and 1870 Lenawee's population grew from 17,889 to about 45,000, to become the third largest county in Michigan—growth due to developments in agriculture, transportation, and industry.

In Lenawee, almost the entire county was proved suitable for agriculture once the land was cleared and drained, roads built, and farming begun. By the 1870s much of the county had gone through this process, and as a result, Lenawee had some 250,000 improved acres involved in agriculture—a remarkable amount compared to other counties in Michigan. Agriculture was the basic growth industry in Michigan into the 1870s, and having so much good land gave Lenawee a rich base for its economy.

Several areas that caught more attention at this time than they had in the pioneer era were the Irish Hills and the swampy southeastern part of the county. In the case of the Irish Hills a great number of settlers had come from Ireland and England; some called the entire area "the Irish Hills," while the English settlers called the area where they lived "Little England." The more general term, "the Irish Hills," prevailed.

One settler, John Drake, recalled in later years how the land first looked when he took it up in 1839, buying 40 acres from Francis Dewey on Dewey's Lake. His farm lay between three lakes, and the view, he said, was enchanting in those days before the land was cleared and the lake drained, as it had been by the 1870s.

At the other end of the county, initial efforts to farm in the Blissfield area were anything but blissful. The swamps were too extensive for any one man to drain, since they were spread over the entire area. Help was on the way, however. In the early 1840s Guy and David Carpenter, two brothers from Blissfield, and their brother-in-law, Dr. Henry Wyman, figured out a way to tackle the swamps. Obviously, concerted action by all those owning a piece of a swamp was necessary, so why not develop drainage districts in a particular area, which would function the same way as local school districts? If all the property owners affected by a proposed drainage ditch could be brought into a district and assessed a fair amount of money to dig and maintain the ditch, the swamps could be drained. Wyman ran for the State Legislature

Depicted here is the third and final home of Addison Comstock, founder of Adrian. This Italianate house was located at the northwest corner of South Winter and West Church streets. It is probable that friends and neighbors gathered together to make this 1870s photo an interesting one. Courtesy, Lenawee County Historical Museum

in 1844 for the express purpose of getting legislation enacted to allow for the creation of such drainage districts. When passed, this legislation was the first in the nation, and progressive farmers and developers—like Roswell Knight of Riga and William Crockett of Ogden—began to promote drainage districts in their areas.

Beginning in the 1840s and continuing for a generation, a number of German immigrants began to settle in this area. As they did, they undertook the backbreaking job of chopping forests down, draining swamps, cutting roads, and doing some farming. By the later part of the century this land had become the most bountiful in Michigan. Today familiar names like Rodesiler, Knobloch, and Goetz remind us of this German immigration to the wetlands of Riga, Ogden, and Blissfield.

It should not be assumed that the only new developments were occurring in the north-

west and southeast parts of Lenawee. They were happening everywhere. By the 1870s Lenawee had about 20,000 people living in rural areas, most toiling on the more than 3,000 Lenawee farms. The changes taking place in farming at the time were remarkable. For instance, the number of oxen plummeted from 2,200 in 1860 to 367 in 1870, and by 1900 there was not one left in the county. Horses are more productive than oxen in the fields, and their numbers already exceeded 9,000 in 1860. By 1900 there were 18,000.

Farmers were discovering what really paid during this time too. Milch cows numbered 11,000 by 1860, and almost 90,000 sheep were grazing on good Lenawee farmland, increasing to 112,000 a decade later. The production of wheat also continually increased, though after 1880 the annual production dropped from a high of 1,250,000 bushels to 321,000 bushels by the turn of the century.

Just some of Lenawee's riches are the 100 or so Greek Revival buildings still in existence dating back to the 1840-1860 era. Perhaps the finest of these is the home at 401 West Chicago Boulevard, Tecumseh, depicted here in the 1950s. It was built in 1840 by Elijah Anderson, a local carpenter. The basic size and form of the house are in the Greek Revival style, as are the Doric columns and corner pilasters. Anderson later added a roof balustrade and an Italian belvedere in the Greek Revival style to top it off. Since 1937 this house has been recognized nationally for its architectural and historical qualities. Courtesy, Tecumseh Public Library

John Campbell (1825-1863) was general superintendent of the Michigan Southern and Northern Indiana Railroad as well as Mayor of Adrian at the time of his death. The facts surrounding his life tell the story of a self-assured and important man who was very much admired by the people of Adrian. Courtesy, Lenawee County Historical Museum

Dramatic changes such as these suggest that farmers were keeping very close watch on what turned a profit. One way they did was through the annual county fair—dating back to 1849—but they were clearly reacting to other indicators as well. These farmers lived close together, and news traveled fast, They even shared common feelings about what their houses should look like.

Architecturally, farmers during this period were leaving an abiding mark on the county. In the 1840s and 1850s the Greek Revival style was most popular. Houses in this style are usually fairly low, rectangular homes with little windows under the eaves, often with columns in front and a triangular pediment over the entrance. When this style is stripped of all ornamentation, it takes on a plain look, often referred to as a "Michigan farmhouse." Plain or fancy, these houses can be seen across Lenawee.

In the 1860s and 1870s the Italianate style became more popular in the county. These houses tend to be rather tall, somewhat boxy, with high, narrow windows, overhanging eaves, and fancy brackets under the eaves. As with Greek Revival, many of these houses remain, and they give the Lenawee countryside a real historic charm.

The Growth of a Railroad Town

During the pioneer period Lenawee witnessed the creation of the Midwest's first railroad, the Erie and Kalamazoo running from Toledo to Adrian. In addition, the Erie and Kalamazoo was involved in the construction in 1838 of a spur line from Lenawee Junction (a point on the Erie and Kalamazoo several miles north of Palmyra) to Tecumseh. Although the intent ultimately was to run this line to Jacksonburg (as Jackson was called then), Tecumseh remained the terminus of the line for the next 20 years.

The next significant development was the creation of the Michigan Southern Railroad, a state-owned and -operated railroad beginning in Monroe and running through the southern counties. Since Adrian was on a more direct line westward from Monroe than Tecumseh, the route was laid from Monroe through Deerfield to Adrian. To appease Tecumseh, the state agreed to subsidize the spur running from Lenawee Junction to Tecumseh.

Once it was clear that the line was going through Adrian, the next question involved the route it would take on its way to Hillsdale. The most level and direct route would have gone through Rollin in western Le-

nawee. That route did not suit a man named Augustus Finney, who had land in Lanesville (soon to be renamed Hudson), a few miles to the south of Rollin. At a meeting of the railroad commissioners in charge of routing, Finney drew attention to the remarkable waterpower on the Bean Creek at Lanesville. Soon, Finney said, Lanesville would become a thriving industrial community, and the railroad would benefit from all the freight generated. It is hard to resist a salesman in full sail, and it helped that Rollin relied only on its superior geography to make its case. As a result, the line was sent south to go through Hudson, and Rollin remained a quiet, rural place.

The Michigan Southern laid track as far as Adrian in 1840, and reached both Hudson and Hillsdale in 1843. There it stopped for some years. During this time the state lost enthusiasm for running the railroad, and so it sold the Michigan Southern to a private company in 1846. This company did little until 1851, when it got up a full head of steam and ran

the line all the way to Chicago. This was the first railroad to reach that growing city, though it beat the Michigan Central by only a few months. These Michigan lines provided the only railroad connection between Chicago and the east for some years, and it was a rich plum for both of them.

For farmers living near the railroads, the cost of shipping was reduced so much that Eastern markets were now open to them as never before. This also helped many smaller villages like Clayton, where produce would be brought to the line to be shipped. Having the railroads also helped industry by lowering costs of raw materials as well as the finished articles. This led to Adrian, Hudson, and Tecumseh becoming increasingly oriented toward industry.

For Adrian, the coming of the Michigan Southern meant even more. At first, control of the Michigan Southern remained in Monroe where the line had originated. After the sale of the railroad to private owners, though, the new owners began to focus on improving access not only to Chicago but to the east. Buying rights to the old Erie and Kalamazoo right-of-way provided access to Toledo (and soon to the Ohio coastline along Lake Erie) through Adrian. Management then was moved from Monroe to Adrian since Adrian was now the connecting point of the lines from Monroe and Toledo.

It made sense, too, to put repair shops for the line in Adrian. In the 1850s Adrian gradually became a railroad town wholly wed to the fate and fortunes of the Michigan Southern. In 1860 about 800 of Adrian's 6,000 residents worked for the railroad or related industries, and Adrian had become the third-largest city in Michigan. When you figure that many of these workers were married men with several children in each family, the railroad's impact on Adrian is easy to see.

New Centers of Manufacturing

As Lenawee developed between 1840 and 1870, it became one of the leading industrial centers in Michigan. By 1874 the county had the third highest number of manufacturing businesses, employed the sixth highest number

Henry Angell (1826-1914) came to Adrian in 1853 and set up a foundry to manufacture railroad car wheels. In the 1860s Angell expanded into building railroad cars, especially freight cars, for railroads like the Northern Pacific. His firm was the largest in Adrian during that time. Angell is portrayed here in 1888. Courtesy, Lenawee County Historical Museum

of people in industry, and ranked sixth in the value of its manufactured products.

Although Adrian led the way in manufacturing, it was by no means the only center of industry. In 1874 Adrian had 22 manufacturing businesses employing over 800 men. Tecumseh was second with 207 industrial workers, while Hudson was third with 195 workers. Blissfield and Clinton also had some industry, with 90 workers each, and Riga was not far behind with 80 workers—presumably working in the lumber mills. Once those cottonwoods were all gone, that was the end of Riga's manufacturing.

In Adrian the Michigan Southern railroad yards were the largest employer. Next came Henry Angell's railroad car factory works. Angell came to Adrian in 1853, probably lured by the business generated in the repair shops. By the late 1860s, though, Angell's company made boxcars, passenger cars, and specialty cars, selling them to railroads across the country. Angell employed hundreds of workers at his Adrian Car Company by the 1870s. Toward the end of this period another large railroad manufacturing company settled here. The company had been founded in Chicago, but Adrian interests bought it and

From 1905 to 1935 Frank Navin, a man born and raised in Adrian, was principal owner of the Detroit Tigers Baseball Club. In 1923 his nephew, Charles Navin of Adrian, who was secretary of the club, arranged for the team to come down to Adrian right after the season ended. At Franklin Field the Tigers played a good semipro local team, the Adrian Independents. The ballpark was packed as the Tigers beat the Independents 17 to 3. Despite the score, the Adrianites enjoyed the only game the Tigers played in Lenawee county. Courtesy, Lenawee County Historical Museum

Francis Stebbins (1818-1829) was one of Lenawee's most talented, public-spirited men in the nineteenth century. He was an expert builder of cabinets, and ran a fine furniture factory and store in Adrian from 1841 until 1892. He loved to write and served as editor of a local newspaper from 1850 to 1860 as well as writing many articles dealing with local history and travel. He also served on many public committees, including the Adrian School Board, for which he designed the attractive Central School constructed in the late 1860s. Stebbins is seen here in a portrait from 1880. Courtesy, Lenawee County Historical Museum

FACING PAGE: In the late 1860s the 100 block of West Maumee in Adrian was still being dressed in brick buildings. This photo prominently features the Masonic Temple, built in 1867, and the Lawrence Hotel on the right-hand side of the street. Courtesy, Lenawee County Historical Museum

brought it here. Called the Illinois Company, it employed 100 to 200 people making railroad locks, keys, and lanterns.

In addition to the men employed in repair and construction shops, other men from Adrian were employed by the Michigan Southern as conductors, engineers, detectives, ticket agents, telegraphers, and managers.

Many of those who worked in the shops, on the tracks, or in the trains were of German or Irish heritage. During this period Adrian's Irish neighborhood, Corktown, began to emerge on Erie and Frank streets close to the parish church of St. Mary's. One young fellow, Frank Navin, came out of Corktown some years later and moved to Detroit, where he wound up owning the Detroit Tiger baseball team for 30 years. The German immigrants in Adrian settled on the east side, in or near the factory district. In their case, Tecumseh Street became a second "downtown" for what was called "Dutch Hill."

Aside from the railroad industries in Adrian, other factories and shops in Lenawee were related to the needs of local residents. America did not yet have mass industries, except for its textile and railroad concerns. Thus, if you wanted a piece of furniture, a

carriage, an engine, or an agricultural machine, you went to the local furniture, buggy, machine, or blacksmith shop, which made something for you. Brewer's machine shop in Tecumseh was a good example of this. The mills had larger markets, though, and Hayden's grain mill in Tecumseh, the Clinton Woolen Mill, and Kellogg and Buck's mill in Morenci grew accordingly.

In Hudson, of course, Augustus Finney had foreseen tremendous growth because of the formidable waterpower of the Bean Creek. Nothing ever came of that, but Hudson nevertheless grew and flourished thanks to the railroad. Sitting in the midst of a fine farming area, the town became a solid commercial center. The Boise family began as merchants in the 1840s, and by the 1860s had moved into banking. The Thompson banking firm was founded in the 1860s. Then there was the wholesale trading firm started by Louis Frensdorf around 1860. The firm dealt in local agricultural products such as wool, which Frensdorf would buy from local farmers and then ship by rail to buyers in the East.

In Adrian the Hurlbut carriage works and Francis Stebbins' furniture factory and shop had good reputations for their products, and a "funeral-furniture man" like Joseph Eveiss was there to help you at several times in your life. About the first significant person in Morenci was Silas Scofield. He made and sold various things, but was especially known for the new kinds of hardware he had invented for caskets. Another Morenci business of this period was Allen's Jewelry Store. John Allen opened the store in 1853, and his granddaughter, Mary Jane Weber, was still running it in 1989.

The Beginning of Lenawee Banking

In addition to industry, banks began to emerge in this period. The first Michigan banks—the infamous "wildcat" banks—came along after achievement of statehood in 1837.

These banks were given the right to print their own money, which they handed out freely as loans to farmers and other businessmen. At that time not much was known about how the banks should be controlled, but everyone could see there was an urgent need for new money. The money was secured only by the ventures the banks were supporting. Thus, when business became shaky in the late 1830s, the money was worthless, and the banks all failed. For some time the reputation of banks and bankers was very low.

Not until 1850 did anyone dare to organize another bank in Lenawee. That bank was organized by Ira Bidwell and William Waldby in Adrian. Bidwell bowed out right away, but Waldby persisted, and in 1857 his firm put up offices at the corner of Main and Maumee. That bank (and the bank it merged with later on, the Lenawee County Savings Bank) stayed at that corner until 1987. Also in the 1850s the Erie and Kalamazoo Bank, the one sound Lenawee bank of the 1830s, was revived. Addison Comstock, the man

who founded Adrian in 1826 and had done so much since then, was heavily involved in this bank, and its failure within a few years brought Comstock to ruin. He was still trying to pay off debts when he died in 1867.

Two more banks trace their origins back to the 1850s. One was the Tecumseh Bank, founded in 1855. Lucius Lilley, the bank's teller, would become synonymous with banking in Tecumseh over the next 60 years or so. The Tecumseh Bank was closed down in 1860, but Lilley then helped organize a new bank called P. Bills & Company. After several more closings and reorganizings, this bank reopened as the Lilley State Bank in 1893. In Hudson, too, 1855 was the year when the town's first bank, the Exchange Bank, was opened. Both John and Henry Boies were associated with the Exchange Bank, and under the management of the Boies family it lasted well into the twentieth century. As everyone knows, the bank established in 1867 by W.B. Thompson and G.I. Thompson is still going strong. In 1892 it was reorganized as the Thompson Savings Bank.

Hudson was also the home of the most infamous banker in Lenawee history, William H. Treadwell. He was owner and manager of the People's Bank from 1862 to 1864, when he stole about $66,000 of the bank's money. He was soon caught, but he managed to transfer the money to his wife and father-in-law. Treadwell was convicted on July 1, 1864, but he escaped from jail with a horse thief named John Cowell. Cowell killed him for the money, but, of course, Treadwell did not have it. When the trail led to Treadwell's father-in-law, the creditors sued him. Large sums were eventually realized, but it is said that most of it went to lawyers.

Adrian saw one more new kind of bank come into being in the 1860s. This was the Lenawee County Savings Bank, incorporated in 1869 and opened for business in 1870. The significance of this "savings bank"

was that it sought to attract the funds of small depositors, planning to use the money to finance home mortgages. The idea worked, and that bank is still very much with us as Bank of Lenawee. Since its early days, of course, it has expanded its sources of capital and what it finances.

Lenawee Goes to Press

Like the banks, newspapers also began to flourish during this period, and then found ways of enduring for long periods of time—some of them to the present day. R.W. Ingalls founded the first newspaper in Lenawee in 1834. It was called the *Adrian Gazette* at first, but Ingalls soon changed the name to the *Adrian Watchtower*. Like most papers of the time, it openly espoused one brand of politics, in its case the politics of the Democratic Party. Ingalls ran the paper until 1863. In 1865 General William Humphrey bought the paper, changed its name to the *Adrian Daily and Weekly Times,* and made it an organ of the Republican Party.

Before the 1850s the other major political party in America were the Whigs, and in 1843 the *Michigan Expositor* was founded in

William L. Greenly (1813-1883) was a Democrat who served at the highest levels of state government in the 1830s and 1840s when Michigan was a strong Democratic state. In 1845 he was elected lieutenant-governor. When Governor Alpheus Felch resigned in early 1847 to take an appointment as U.S. Senator, Greenly became Governor of Michigan for the rest of the year. He returned to local politics and legal work after that. This photo was taken in 1858 when he served as Mayor of Adrian. Courtesy, Lenawee County Historical Museum

Adrian to state that party's views. In 1869 Humphrey bought this paper too, merging it into the *Adrian Daily Times*. The new paper, called the *Adrian Times and Expositor*, lasted into the early twentieth century.

Outside Adrian several newspapers appeared which would have even more staying power than the *Times and Expositor*. The first was the *Tecumseh Herald*, which began publication in 1850 and is still publishing the news of Tecumseh and the surrounding area. In Hudson several shortlived papers gave way in 1858 to the appearance of the *Hudson Gazette*. Under the able leadership of W.T.B.

Schermerhorn, it became a popular, strong paper with leanings toward the Democrats. In 1862 a Republican-oriented paper, later called the *Post*, began publication. Many years later these two papers would merge into today's *Hudson Post-Gazette*.

The Emergence of "Downtowns"

With the growth of major and minor industries, banks, and wholesale and retail businesses and shops, the various communities in Lenawee saw a great deal of building going on to house new commercial businesses. Beginning in the 1850s downtown buildings began to be built of brick in the commercial Italianate style. These buildings tended to be three stories high, with distinctive cornices at the top and arches over round-topped windows. These were handsome buildings, far more resistant to fire than the older wooden buildings. As a result, many of them are still with us. When people today speak of the handsome downtowns in Adrian, Hudson, Tecumseh, and Clinton, it is these nineteenth-century buildings they are referring to.

In the residential areas, meanwhile, people were building homes in the popular Greek Revival and Italianate styles of the time, and many of these homes remain as well. Blissfield, Adrian, Tecumseh, Hudson, and Clinton all have an uncommon number of these lovely old homes, which give those communities much of the historic charm and character they have today.

Political Change

Because of Lenawee's population and continued growth, the county was represented very well at the state level from the 1830s into the 1870s. The county always had a state senator who represented just Lenawee, plus four representatives in the state legislature from 1837 to 1863. From 1863 to 1873 the county had five.

Lenawee County started out Democratic, as did the rest of the state. After achiev-

ing statehood under the Democrats in 1837, the state embarked on an ambitious program of improvements, with the emphasis on railroads. Lenawee's state senators from 1837 to 1845 were Anthony McKay, William L. Greenly, and John J. Adam. They all helped to bring the Michigan Southern through their district—especially McKay, who was state senator when the route was being worked out. Greenly was a leading Democrat in the State Senate in the mid-1840s. In 1846 he was elected Lieutenant-Governor, which led to his becoming Governor in 1847 when Governor Alpheus Felch resigned to take a job in the U.S. Senate. Greenly is one of two governors to come from Lenawee.

In the 1850s the Democrats lost their hold on the state. The slavery issue was gaining importance across the country, and Michigan was no exception. Lenawee was firmly opposed to the existence of slavery, and as early as the 1820s some abolitionists in Lenawee began to speak out against it. Perhaps the first was Elizabeth Margaret Chandler, who began to write poems, essays and letters against slavery as early as 1826, when she was only 19 and living in Philadelphia. After moving to Raisin Township in 1830 with her

brother, Thomas, she continued to write for the national movement. She is considered the first woman poet in America to use her talents for this cause.

Near the Chandlers lived other Quakers, such as Charles and Laura Haviland. In 1832 the ladies among them, led by Elizabeth Chandler, organized the Logan Female Anti-Slavery Society, the first women's antislavery society in the Old Northwest. As the 1830s wore on, other Protestant churches also became involved, and all denominations split over the issue. In Lenawee, the Havilands and other antislavery Quakers were forced to leave their church because of their stand. This led to their joining a fervently antislavery group of Methodists called the Wesleyans, where they carried on their fight.

In 1837 the Havilands, in one of their most significant antislavery activities, founded the Raisin Institute. The first integrated school in Michigan history, the Raisin Institute opened its doors to blacks, women, anyone who wanted to learn. The Woodstock Man-

Fernando Beaman (1814-1882) was mayor of Adrian in 1856 when this portrait was taken. As a lawyer and politician, Beaman was active in antislavery politics in the 1840s and 1850s. In 1860 he was elected to Congress as an antislavery Republican, and he served his district, which included Detroit and Monroe as well as Lenawee and Hillsdale, throughout the 1860s. Courtesy, Lenawee County Historical Museum

In 1880 Governor St. John of Kansas said "God never made two nobler, grander women." He was referring to Laura Haviland of Raisin Township, left, and Elizabeth Comstock of Rollin Township, conductors on the Underground Railroad before the Civil War. After the war they continued to work for the freed slaves. In 1880 they were helping black refugees to start their lives over in Kansas. These freed peoples called Comstock "Mrs. Cornstalk" for her practical help while they called Haviland "Mrs. Heavenly." Courtesy, Lenawee County Historical Museum

ual Labor Institute, another integrated school, was founded in 1846 by a black man from Ohio, Prior Foster. Near the Quaker community just north of Addison, the school was one of the first in the nation founded by blacks for blacks. White children were welcome, too, and they attended.

By the 1840s an illegal, though well-organized movement called the Underground Railroad had been established in the North to help fugitive slaves find their way to Canada, where slavery was illegal. Lenawee had more than its share of people opening their homes to runaway slaves, even though they were breaking the law in doing so. The Quaker communities in Raisin, Rollin, and Woodstock townships seemed to have been much involved. I.N. Hathaway, Asa Sutton, Laura Haviland, Aaron Comfort, Samuel Satterthwaite, and John and Elizabeth Comstock all were involved, as were others such as George Crane of Palmyra, Warren Gilbert of Cambridge, and Stephen Allen of Madison. At least two Lenawee citizens acted as "conductors"—undertaking the hazardous task of guiding fugitive slaves from one station to another along the "Freedom Trail." Laura Haviland did this work in Ohio, while Warren Gilbert was active in Michigan.

In addition to the operators and conductors on the Underground Railroad, others in the county supported the antislavery movement in their own ways. Some, for instance, became involved in the formation of the Republican Party because of its strong antislavery stance. Three Lenawee lawyers helped to organize the party in Jackson in 1854: David Carpenter of Blissfield; Charles Croswell of Adrian, who served as secretary of the Jackson convention; and Fernando Beaman, also of Adrian, who served as one of the vice presidents of the convention.

Compared to the Democrats, who could not resolve the issue of slavery within

their own ranks because of the strength of the South in their party, the Republicans offered a clear choice on this vital issue. By 1860, as a result, Lenawee had moved away from the Democrats and into the ranks of the new party. As had happened earlier with the Democrats, a number of Lenawee Republicans soon made themselves known at the state level. Fernando Beaman was the first, and one of the most important. In 1860 Beaman was elected to the House of Representatives from the district that included Lenawee. In 1862 the district lines were redrawn to include the more-populous Wayne County, and Beaman still won. Throughout the tumultuous 1860s he served in the House, supporting the Republican policies of union and reconstruction designed to keep the country united and to provide civil and political rights to the former slaves in the South.

On the state level Lenawee's four representatives and one senator all tended to be Republican. Men like John K. Boies of Hudson supported the war effort unceasingly, while Charles Croswell began to move up in state politics. As a state senator in the 1860s, Croswell clearly supported the radical, antislavery wing of the party.

Broadening Educational Opportunities

Once communities were organized, they began to build schools for the children. Public education was seen as a charter right in all the states formed out of the Old Northwest, and funds were set aside for such education in the Northwest Ordinance of 1787. After Michigan became a state, a primary school fund was set up from the sale of lands in one of the sections of each township. This money

renamed the Will Carleton School.

Some districts, however, felt a need to provide more than an ungraded education. In 1843 the state passed legislation allowing school districts to merge, forming "union schools." In 1859 the state went further, allowing any district with more than 200 students to establish a high school. Tecumseh, East Blissfield, West Blissfield, Adrian, Clinton, East and West Hudson, Addison, Britton, Clayton, Deerfield, Morenci, and Palmyra all eventu-

Perhaps the most striking aspect of this 1870 photo of Adrian College students playing croquet, is how prominently female students figure in the scene. These were still relatively early days for young women to attend college, but Adrian College was all for this

was given to local school districts, which also were granted the power to tax. All over Lenawee small school districts were established; Raisin had 12 districts, Medina had 13, and so on. Eventually, Lenawee had 196 school districts, 179 of which were single one-room schools where students of all ages and educational levels were taught by a single schoolmaster or -mistress. In Hudson Township, Michigan's beloved state poet, Will Carleton, attended the same one-room school at which he later taught. In his honor, the school was

ally had graded schools which measured up to state standards.

During this period several private schools opened as well. The Raisin Institute and the Woodstock Manual Labor Institute have already been mentioned. In 1850 the Raisin Valley Seminary was founded at the quarterly meeting of the Friends of Adrian at the home of that good Quaker, Darius Comstock. This school was open to all, irrespective of religious belief, and it provided a solid education for many until it closed in 1908. A fourth

development. The handsome campus had been constructed along Madison Street in Adrian just before and during the Civil War. All of the buildings depicted are gone now except for Downs Hall, second from the left. Courtesy, Shipman Library, Adrian College

private school, the Medina Academy, lasted for years after its founding in 1853.

Finally, Adrian College must be mentioned. The school was founded in 1845 by the Wesleyan Methodists in the small town of Leoni near Jackson. By the late 1850s the school's trustees, seeking to ease chronic financial problems, planned to move to a larger town. At the time Adrian was the second largest city in Michigan, and the pastor of Adrian's Plymouth Congregational Church, Asa Mahan, believed that Adrian was ready for a college. Mahan, who had served as Oberlin College's first president from 1835 to 1850, was also a staunch antislavery man, and he admired the Wesleyans' stance on this issue.

Mahan showed Adrian's interest, as well as his own leadership abilities, by getting 20 acres and $30,000 committed to the college within six weeks in 1859. The college opened in Adrian that same year with Mahan as president. The first decade for Adrian College began well, with an impressive campus and faculty and several hundred students (including many women). The Wesleyans could not provide the financial support they had promised, however, and before long the school once again had serious financial problems. In 1867 Adrian College turned for help to the Methodist Protestant Church, another liberal Methodist denomination, which was looking for a college in the Midwest. Unfortunately, Adrian College was on the northwest edge of this denomination's area of influence, and it proved difficult to attract money or students from the Methodist Protestants. That the college endured was largely due to faculty, alumni and community.

Religion

The churches of Lenawee's pioneer period had grown out of the religious traditions of the original settlers from New York and New England. With the arrival of German and Irish immigrants, who brought their own traditions with them, Lenawee's religious life was considerably enriched. Since the county thrived economically during this period, many handsome churches were built. Many of these churches are still with us, and they help to provide the traditional atmosphere

This photo of East Maumee street in Adrian looking east shows three churches around the Broad Street intersection. The photo was taken between 1863, when the Methodist Episcopal Church on the left was built, and 1866, when the Adrian Central School burned to the ground. The large three-story Central School building with a white cupola was located behind the wooden Christ Episcopal Church at the corner of East Maumee and Broad streets. On the far right is how the First Presbyterian Church looked before radical change was undertaken in 1869. Courtesy, Lenawee County Historical Museum

that is so strong in this area.

In Hudson the big, lovely Congregational church dates back to this time, as does the Greek Revival-styled Presbyterian church in Blissfield. In Adrian the Presbyterians, Episcopalians, Methodist Episcopalians, and Congregationalists all built lovely churches in various styles between 1840 and 1870 while the First Baptists actually began their church earlier, in 1836. Two of those Adrian churches, the Baptist and Presbyterian, are still with us. In Clinton, meanwhile, the Episcopalians, Methodist Episcopalians, and Congregationalists all built attractive churches in the 1830s and 1840s, all of which are still with us.

As the Germans and the Irish took root in Lenawee, they began to build churches as well. Adrian is fortunate still to have St. John's Lutheran Church (built in 1862) and the old St. Stephen's Lutheran Church at the corner of Front and Center as examples of these early immigrant churches.

Roman Catholics in Adrian, many of whom were Irish, built the Romanesque St. Mary's Church in 1869. By the 1860s German-speaking Catholics desired their own parish, and the result was St. Joseph's, built in 1879.

Many Irish settled in Hudson and the surrounding countryside, leading to the construction in 1866 of the large and beautiful Sacred Heart Church. The original Sacred Heart was torn down in 1906 to make way for an even larger, more beautiful church. St. Joseph's Shrine in the Irish Hills dates back to 1854, and St. Dominic's Catholic Church appeared in Clinton in 1867 to accommodate the Catholics of northeast Lenawee.

Christians who come from the heritage of the New England Puritans have never believed that their sole mission is to pray for the individual's salvation. They have always believed that their mission, at least in part, is to reform the world, and this was never more true than just before the Civil War. Probably the cause with the greatest participation was the temperance movement. The campaign against alcohol would continue through the century until the issue finally was resolved in the next century. The second great cause of the old New England churches was the antislavery movement. This movement originated on the national level with the Quakers, and with Quaker communities in the Raisin and Rollin areas, it is not surprising that Lenawee became so active in this movement. Other Protestant denominations, including the Wesleyan Methodists, Congregationalists, Presbyterians, and Baptists, also provided support and sympathy.

The Civil War

As the North and South went to war, Michigan stood by its president, and no county in Michigan exceeded Lenawee in its support of the Union. Whether in numbers of volunteer soldiers, money raised in fund drives, or even numbers of civilian groups rolling bandages, Lenawee's record was second to none in the state.

Although Lenawee soldiers served in regiments across the North, certain regiments had whole companies composed of Lenawee soldiers. Two infantry regiments, in particular, had a strong Lenawee flavor: the 18th Michigan Infantry and the 4th Michigan Infantry. Five of the 18th's companies came from Lenawee: Company A from Hudson, Company E from Tecumseh, and the rest mixed though each had large contingents from Adrian. The 4th was the only regiment actually organized and trained in Lenawee. Commanded by Colonel Dwight Woodbury of Adrian until he was killed in battle in 1862, it included the Hudson Volunteers, the Adrian Volunteers, and the Tecumseh Volunteers. The men trained at Camp Williams in Adrian (actually the Adrian College campus) in May and June 1861. When they marched through town to the waiting railroad cars on June 20, everybody in town turned out to see them off. If all the soldiers were dressed like the Tecumseh Volunteers, they must have been a sight; the Tecumseh soldiers wore blue coats, red pants, red capes, and shiny black shoes.

In the next three years the Michigan 4th fought many battles in Virginia, Maryland, and Pennsylvania. The regiment had a shining record of courage, but the cost was high. Three of its colonels died, and many men from every town joined them in death. After the war, when army veterans organized posts for the Grand Army of the Republic, the posts in Adrian and Tecumseh were named for fallen heroes of the 4th: Colonel Dwight Woodbury of Adrian and Lieutenant

Jeptha Beers of Tecumseh. The GAR post in Hudson was named for Captain Samuel DeGolyer, who served in Battery H of the artillery and died in 1863 after being wounded in the siege of Vicksburg.

Communities, too, showed their pride and sense of loss for the slain Civil War soldiers by erecting monuments. The Civil War shaft in Tipton Cemetery was dedicated to the memory of the 31 Franklin Township soldiers who died in the war—a considerable number for a rural township. The monument was dedicated on July 4, 1866, the second such monument erected in the North after the war. Other Civil War monuments were put up in later years in Adrian, Lime Creek, Tecumseh, and Ogden.

The Era Draws to a Close

By the 1870s some of the surviving pioneers had begun to think about the accomplishments of the last 50 years. One result was the formation of the Lenawee County Pioneer Society. In the fall of 1877 the Pioneer Society met in Hudson, and General Joseph Brown, Lenawee's first citizen, was invited to attend.

As the general traveled through the Irish Hills on his way to Hudson from Tecumseh, his mind went back to an exploratory trip he had made in 1826 from Tecumseh to Niles. The entire land west of Tecumseh had been unbroken wilderness with unspoiled forests and lakes. Now, he said, he saw mile after mile of thriving farms with solid barns and comfortable houses. Where once there had been only a few Indian trails, now there were good roads bordered every few miles by churches and schools. Where the lakes had been desolate, one now could see dozens of pleasure boats, enough picnic tables for 500, and even a ballroom on Devil's Lake. This transformation made him, and all the pioneers, very proud, and they must have wondered what the next 50 years would bring.

CHAPTER THREE

LENAWEE MATURES

1 8 7 0 - 1 9 1 4

A funny thing happened to Lenawee County between 1870 and 1914: it stopped growing. By 1910 the county's population was 47,907, compared with 45,601 in 1870. Actually, however, even the slight growth shown by 1910 is quite misleading, since the county's growth during this period occurred largely before 1890. In that year the county's population reached its nineteenth-century high of 44,448. The decline was extremely gradual, to be sure (48,406 in 1900, 47,907 in 1910, and 47,767 in 1920), but it was unmistakable. For 30 years, from 1890 to 1920, the county slipped backward.

Part of this lack of growth was related to significant losses in Adrian industry during the 1880s. In 1880 itself, actually, the industrial situation seemed rather bright. The railroad shops of the Lake Shore and Michigan Southern (the name of the Michigan Southern after 1869) were going strong, and the Adrian Car Works of Henry Angell produced freight and passenger cars for railroads across the nation. In addition, local businessmen P.L. Swords and Henry Hart had bought a potentially lucrative new firm in Chicago called the

Illinois Company and then moved it to Adrian, where it made railroad lanterns, locks, and keys for the booming railroad industry. The Illinois Company employed 100 or more in its three-story building by the railroad tracks in the industrial district, and the Adrian Car Works employed several hundred.

With activity like this in the industrial district, Adrian was indisputably one of the leading industrial centers in Michigan, let alone in Lenawee County. Suddenly, though, the railroad industry in Adrian went into decline. For one thing, the Lake Shore and Michigan Southern laid off about one-third of the men in its car shops. From 330 employees in 1876, the company was down to about 270 by 1884, and then it laid off another 80. The company's work force, although still sizable, was significantly smaller than it had been. In part, the reductions at Adrian had to do with temporary depressions, though the basic reason was that Adrian was no longer along the main route between Toledo and Chicago. The route now ran through northern Ohio and Indiana, and a new repair and service center was established at Elkhart, Indiana (where the route

One of Lenawee's most attractive buildings is the Masonic Temple constructed in 1867 on W. Maumee in Adrian. In 1893 the building suffered a major fire, which led to the removal of its wonderful mansard roof. However, the rest of the building was maintained. In 1908 the Adrian State Bank moved into this building, and it has been there ever since. In 1987-88 the bank thoroughly restored the exterior. This photo dates to 1867. Courtesy, Lenawee County Historical Museum

intersected the Old Line coming down from Michigan on its way to Chicago). Elkhart, there-fore, supplanted Adrian to some extent as far as the Lake Shore was concerned.

Losing the 400-plus jobs from the Lake Shore and Michigan Southern was a heavy blow for a town of 8,000 to handle, and more losses were at hand. The Adrian Car Works had run into financial difficulties in

the late 1870s, and early in the 1880s the busi-ness was sold to Detroit interests and moved there. Then, the Illinois Company closed as well. All told, Adrian lost a minimum of 500 railroad-related jobs by the mid-1880s. More than that, however, the city had lost all hope of remaining a vital and important center of the railroad industry.

The effect on the town and county was

As for the City of Adrian itself, it hardly seemed to notice that its historic heart, the railroad industry, was dwindling away. In 1883 the city allocated funds for a municipal waterworks system, and in 1885 funded a new street lighting system. Also in 1885, the city built a handsome new city hall on the south side of the business district to balance the new courthouse on the north side. Plunging on, in 1888 Adrian became the first city in Michigan to approve an electric street railway system. Obviously, neither business nor governmental leaders lacked confidence in the

not very noticeable at first. Two of the fine public buildings most identified with Adrian—the Lenawee County Courthouse and the Adrian City Hall—were built during this period. If those buildings showed anything, it was an optimism of spirit.

Lenawee County had struggled along without a courthouse ever since the first one burned down in 1852. In the early 1880s the county commissioners decided to centralize the courts and offices of the county, and as long as they were building a courthouse, they figured, they might as well build a dandy. When the new courthouse was completed in 1886, rising 140 feet into the air on top of a small hill, the entire county took pride. The style combined Romanesque-style rounded arches over the entrances with Classical-style columns rising all the way to the tower, and the use of colored tiles and sculptured bas-reliefs of an Indian chief and the Goddess of Agriculture gave the building the type of rich, decorated surface that Victorians loved so much. Certainly more than any other building in the county, the courthouse demonstrates the wealth, pride, and exuberance of the people of Lenawee during this period.

BELOW: The Lenawee County Fair is one of the oldest fairs in Michigan, beginning in 1839. The fairgrounds were in the center of Adrian until 1879, when the Agricultural Society of Lenawee County decided to take up new and more spacious grounds on the east side of Adrian where the fair has been held ever since. Courtesy, Lenawee County Historical Museum

In the last quarter of the nineteenth century Lenawee's farm-based economy was booming. By 1900 there were 5,500 farms across the county and Lenawee was considered one of the nation's top ten counties in terms of agricultural production. Farmers helped reach these new levels by using workhorses instead of oxen and by leaning toward dairying with increased numbers of dairy cows. Courtesy, Stair Public Library, Morenci, Michigan

future of the community.

Even the state government stepped in to help. At this time state government was not known for providing services or aid, but in 1884 the State Industrial School for Girls was opened on the north side of Adrian. While not a large institution, the school played its part in sustaining the local economy. There was more to the school than this (as we shall see when discussing Governor Charles Croswell), but its economic importance could not be ignored.

From Farm to Dairy

Why were people so confident in the face of serious losses and what we now know was the beginning of 50 years of decline? The basic reason, no doubt, was that the Lenawee economy was based on farming, and farming was still expanding. It must have seemed in 1870 as though agriculture could hardly grow

any more. The county already supported 3,500 farms and had 262,000 improved acres. Nevertheless, by 1900 farmers had found another 90,000 acres to put into production, and the number of farms had grown to 5,500.

Farming did not grow simply in terms of acreage or number of farms. Lenawee farmers continued to specialize and improve productivity. As a result, by 1900 a good case could be made for Lenawee as one of the top 10 counties in the nation in terms of agricultural output. Looking at Michigan farming alone, there was no question that Lenawee was the leader. One township, Riga, clearly was the richest rural township in the state, and Ogden was second. This indicates how thoroughly the region's farmers had ditched and drained the swamps away. Overall, Lenawee farmers produced well over $6 million worth of farm products in 1900— more than was produced by the leading industry of the day in Lenawee, the wire fence industry.

Lenawee farmers reached these levels in part through the improvement and change of types of livestock on their farms. Of 2,200 oxen in the county in 1860, none were left by 1900. Meanwhile, the number of work-horses rose from 9,500 in 1860 to 18,000 in 1900. Horses are much more productive than oxen, and so this in itself made farming more efficient. Another farm animal that saw its numbers go down was the sheep. From a high of 116,000 in 1880, their numbers dropped to 80,000 by 1910. Meanwhile, the number of milk cows rose from 11,000 in 1860 to over 20,000 in 1910.

As these numbers show, Lenawee farmers were moving away from the production of wool (though it continued to be important) and toward dairying. Actually, the county already had begun to produce dairy products by the middle of the century. In 1860 Lenawee was second only to Oakland County in the production of butter with almost one million pounds. By 1900 individual family farms had doubled production to over 2 million. Another million pounds of butter were produced in various commercial creameries throughout Lenawee, which produced millions of pounds of cheese as well.

In cheese production, the Horton family of Fruit Ridge in Fairfield Township was particularly well known. After Samuel Horton came to Lenawee in 1851, he began producing a distinct kind of soft cheese that his wife, Lucina, had learned to make in New York. In 1866 Horton built the first cheese factory in Michigan. Samuel and Lucina were succeeded in business by their son, George, who became the most famous, successful, and influential farmer in Lenawee history. By 1900 George Horton was the largest individual cheese manufacturer in the United States, with cheese factories all over the southern part of Lenawee producing 2 million pounds

This 1910 caricature of George B. Horton captures many of his interests, including farming and making cheese in his many cheese factories. Horton was head of the Lenawee County Fair Board from 1878 to 1912 and first to begin campaigning to save the primeval trees of Lenawee and Michigan. He was considered to be, without a doubt, the foremost farmer in Lenawee. Courtesy, Lenawee County Historical Museum

of cheese annually. With farmers like George Horton, it was no wonder that Lenawee led all Michigan counties in the production of cheese and butter.

Another farm product, sugar beets, also had become important by 1900. Farmers in eastern Lenawee found this new crop rewarding. The Continental Sugar Company then constructed a processing plant in Blissfield, encouraging farmers in the surrounding townships to keep producing this crop. Many sugar-beet laborers from Moravia (in present-day Czechoslovakia) immigrated to plant, cultivate, and harvest this difficult crop in the first decade of the century, and today names such as Holubik, Brablec, and Fojtik can be found throughout the eastern half of Lenawee.

The constant growth and change in Lenawee farming did not just happen. After the Civil War Lenawee farmers developed quite an elaborate means of information and socialization based on a new farm organization called the Grange. George Horton began the first grange in 1873, and soon Lenawee had more of them than any other county in the state.

On July 22, 1871, the community of Morenci celebrated the breaking of ground for the roadbed of the Chicago & Canada Southern. The town was already a thriving community, but the coming of the first railroad furthered its development. On June 20, 1872, the steam cars reached Morenci for the first time, and passenger service lasted until 1938. The handsome Morenci Exchange Hotel was built in 1847 but was destroyed by fire many years later. Courtesy, Stair Public Library, Morenci, Michigan

By the turn of the century there were 34 granges in Lenawee with an active membership of 3,500 to 4,000. To some extent the granges were religious, patriotic, and politically oriented, but they also were a reason for farmers to gather every two weeks to discuss the weather and to learn about the issues of the day. The grange halls also served as meeting places for more formal learning exercises called "farmers' institutes." They were held in the winter when farmers were not so busy.

Unhappily, as productive as Lenawee farming was, there was a limit to the amount of land available. Aside from the marshy ground between Deerfield and Britton, not much more could be drained in the eastern part of the county. Lenawee farmers would continue to produce more, but by using fewer men and more machines.

Signs of slowdown in the early twentieth century can be seen in population figures for rural townships. Between 1910 and 1920, for instance, the population of Macon dropped from 1,013 to 952, that of Ogden from 1,698 to 1,450, that of Rome from 1,057 to 1,033, and that of Woodstock from 1,531 to 1,473. These were not big losses, but they showed that the day of growth for Lenawee farmers was over. The fact that Lenawee was down to 5,080 farms in 1920 (compared to 5,500 in 1900) tells the same story. More significantly, it also helps to explain Lenawee's overall declining population during the late nineteenth and early twentieth centuries.

Railroads Cover the County

Lenawee's solid relationship with the nation's arteries of commerce and industry, the rail-

roads, also gave reason for confidence. Between 1840 and 1870 only one railroad came into Lenawee, the Michigan Southern. In the next era no fewer than six new lines were built through the county. The business alone generated by the construction of these lines must have helped the economy considerably, though their long-term impact was based on what they brought to every area they touched. Every community knew what the railroads could mean to them, and the initial news that a railroad might come through an area always elicited excitement, as well as offers to do all that could be done to smooth the way for the new line.

The first new railroad was the Chicago and Canada Southern. It was built in 1872 on a route running diagonally from Deerfield southwest through Blissfield, Jasper, Weston, and Morenci on its way to its terminus in Fayette, Ohio. Morenci in particular was helped by this railroad since it put that community on a line for the first time.

The second new railroad to come into the county, the Wabash, arrived in 1880. This railroad ran from St. Louis, Missouri, to Detroit, and every community in between vied for the chance to be on the line. The financier who controlled this line, Jay Gould, had an infamous reputation, and it became known that any town that wanted to be considered should help construction with a "bonus."

The Ohio and Michigan Railroad, built in 1884, and which ran east-to-west through the northern part of the county, stimulated business and the farm economy in small towns along the rail line. One such town was Onsted, depicted in this 1978 painting by Helen Hartman based on a 1917 postcard. Courtesy, Lenawee County Historical Museum

Adrian did not hesitate. E.L. Clark, Adrian's richest man, donated $10,000, and others coughed up another $26,000. That $36,000 "bonus" not only guaranteed that the railroad would come to Adrian, but even brought the great man himself, Jay Gould, to town for three hours. Running north and east of Adrian toward Detroit, the Wabash opened up northeast Lenawee. The railroad stop of Britton was developed for farmers in the area. South of Adrian, the Wabash cut southwest through Sand Creek (largely creating that community), Seneca, and North Morenci before entering Ohio.

A third line built in 1884, the Ohio and Michigan Railroad, ran east-to-west through the northern part of the county. With stations in Britton, Ridgway, Tecumseh, Pentecost, Onsted, Devil's Lake, and Addison, the line later became part of the Lake Shore and Michigan Southern system. The Ohio and Michigan stimulated the farm economy of this area and helped to begin a seasonal tourist business in the Sand Lake and Devil's Lake area.

The same was true of the fourth line built into the county, the Cincinnati, Jackson and Mackinaw (later the Cincinnati Northern). It ran from north to south through the western part of Lenawee from Hudson through Addison on its way to Jackson. The line

The Page Woven Wire Fence Company found a number of ways to advertise its products. This image from the 1900s not only shows how Page fences kept people away from the railroad tracks, but it also shows a Lake Shore and Michigan Southern passenger train eastbound on the trestle over the River Raisin, east of Adrian. Courtesy, Lenawee County Historical Museum

was built in 1887. A fifth line, the Lima Northern, was built in Lenawee in 1898, cutting through Adrian on its way to Detroit from Lima, Ohio. Later called the Detroit, Ironton and Toledo, the Lima Northern gave the county a second connection to Detroit. Without a doubt these rail connections to Detroit were worth many times the bonus paid to secure the Wabash in 1880.

The early twentieth century saw the construction across the country of short electric interurban railroads, including the Toledo & Western. One line was opened between Toledo and Adrian in 1901, and in 1902 a second line was opened between Toledo and Morenci.

Commerce and Banking

Just as agriculture and transportation did their part to sustain—and, hopefully, to push forward—the local economy, so did the local merchants and bankers. The best examples of this were the collective efforts by community businessmen to attract new railroads. A number of long-lived businesses—including quite a few financial institutions—took root

during this period as well.

The Commercial Savings Bank of Adrian (renamed to Trustcorp Bank-Lenawee in 1988 and to Society Bank in 1990) was founded in 1888 in response to a new state law allowing banks to have both commercial departments, which dealt with businesses, and savings departments, which dealt with small savers and home purchasers. In 1889 the Adrian Building and Loan Association was organized for the latter purpose. In 1893 the Adrian State Savings Bank was founded in response to another law allowing the formation of state savings banks. In 1907, as soon as the Lenawee County Savings Bank (now the Bank of Lenawee) moved out of the Masonic Temple on West Maumee where it had been for 30 years, the Adrian State Savings Bank moved in. It has been there ever since. In 1909 the National Bank of Commerce set up shop in a handsome building on East Maumee.

Tecumseh, although it had no luck in achieving a stable, enduring bank until 1893, has had no trouble since then. In 1893 two savings banks were organized, the Lilley State

Vernon Hoxie, plant manager for Lamb Fence Company, was interested in developing overhead conveyors to move his inventory. It is said that he was responsible for attaining the building seen in this 1905 photo. It is believed that this structure was originally the Horticultural Building at the Pan American Exposition of 1901 in Buffalo, New York. Hoxie had the building disassembled and moved to Adrian where it served as a warehouse for Lamb Fence Company. Courtesy, Lenawee County Historical Museum

Savings Bank and the Tecumseh State Savings Bank. Both of these banks would endure until 1931, when, in the depths of the Great Depression, they merged to form the United Savings Bank of Tecumseh. In Hudson, two banks founded in the 1850s and 1860s continued to provide good service. They were the Exchange Bank (which became Boies' State Savings Bank in 1892, after several name changes in the intervening years) and the Thompson Savings Bank.

In Morenci, the rising trade of that

town in the 1860s led to the organization of the private bank of Charles Wakefield in 1868. Wakefield was still at the helm in 1898, when it was converted into the Wakefield State Bank of Morenci. A second private bank, the Bank of Morenci, was reorganized as the First National Bank of Morenci in 1900. Blissfield also saw two state banks—the Blissfield State Bank and the Jipson-Carter State Bank—organized in the 1890s out of earlier private banks. Still other state banks were organized in Deerfield (1906), Addison (1905), and Onsted (1907).

As it went with banks, so it went with newspapers. Several papers founded during

Running a millinery shop was an important line of work for women in the later nineteenth and early twentieth centuries. It could be profitable, too, considering how important hats were in ladies' fashion. Seen here is Josephine Killin, right, and Carrie Murfitt of Killin's Millinery Shop wearing two of their special creations. Courtesy, Stair Public Library, Morenci, Michigan

this time are still doing business. The best-known, the *Daily Telegram* of Adrian, began publication in 1892. In 1893 it was bought by newspaperman David Grandon, who proceeded to make headway against the established daily, the *Adrian Daily Times and Expositor*. In 1907 Stuart Perry bought it and continued the struggle until 1914, when its competition ceased publication. Since then the *Daily Telegram* has been the only major daily newspaper in Lenawee.

A number of other familiar newspapers also were born during this period. The *Blissfield Advance* was founded in 1874, the *Morenci Observer* in 1875, and the *Clinton Local* around 1885.

Several other retail businesses familiar today got their start in the late nineteenth century as well. One was founded by Archimedes Stevenson, who came back to Lenawee and became a farmer after trying his luck out west in the 1840s. An interest and aptitude for the lumber business led him to found the Stevenson Lumber Company in 1873. A number of funeral homes started up after the Civil War, and one, the Everiss-Wagley Funeral Home founded by Joseph Everiss in 1867, is still with us today.

The late nineteenth century saw such familiar utilities as gas, water, and electricity get their start. Several of the businessmen involved became extremely successful in developing these services. Will Foote was one such businessman. Foote, born in 1854, attended public schools in Adrian, and during the 1870s and 1880s worked at several power mills in the city. In 1885 his mill furnished the power necessary to run an electrical generator, which convinced him to enter the new field of electrical power. In 1886 Foote built a new power plant on Pear Street furnishing power for an electric light company in Adrian. The plant was a success, and Foote, ready for newer and larger horizons, moved to Jackson. Here he began the process that even-

tually would lead to the development of one of the largest electric power companies in the United States, the Consumers Power Company. In Adrian, meanwhile, Captain J.H. Fee bought Foote's power plant on Pearl Street, beginning his family's very successful venture in the utilities field on the local level.

In the 1880s Hudson produced its own power magnate in the new field of electricity. His name was George Avis. In 1889 Avis took over the Hudson Electric Light and

Power Company. Through that company and others, Avis brought power to many towns in Michigan and Ohio until Consumers Power eventually swallowed him up. In Tecumseh, services like electricity, telephones, and water were developed in the 1890s.

New Manufacturing

As we have seen, Adrian hardly seemed to suffer from the loss of its major industries in the early 1880s. Major new city, county, and state buildings came along at that time, and the city was in the forefront nationwide when it came to developing utilities such as water and power. Meanwhile, the rural economy—as well as business and industry—was doing fine. Add to that the railroads being built through the county, and an overall slump would have been difficult to achieve.

Then, at the end of the 1880s, Adrian received another significant boost in the area of manufacturing in the form of a brand new

into it if the farmer did not want it to sag. It was time-consuming and irksome to tighten fence constantly. What farmers needed was fencing that would bounce back even if a bull ran into it.

Page invented a loom for weaving "bounce-back" fencing in 1884 on his farm in Rollin. After experiments showed that it worked and was economical, he set up a small shop in Rollin and then in Hudson. In 1888, needing more capital and space, Page

Many of Lenawee's attractive downtowns date back to the Victorian era. Here is the north side of E. Chicago Boulevard in downtown Tecumseh in 1894 after a considerable snow. The view looks east, and the decline toward the valley of the River Raisin can be distinguished some distance down the street to the east. Except for the building that housed the Oyster Bar, that section of the boulevard doesn't look much different today. Courtesy, Tecumseh Public Library

product invented by Lenawee's first homegrown industrial magnate, J. Wallace Page. Page, a farmboy born and raised in Rollin Township, went back to farming after serving in the army during the Civil War. He had a strong flair for mechanics, and he began to see the need for a new type of fencing. The destruction of the forests was dooming wood fences. There was wire fencing on the market, but it had to be retightened every time a horse or cow ran

moved to Adrian and took over some of the buildings that had housed the railroad industry. Page's company was incorporated as the Page Woven Wire Fence Company in 1889, and for the next 25 years or so its growth was steady. Eventually 600 men were employed at the plant in Adrian, with another 700 employed at a steel plant in Monessen, Pennsylvania.

While Page was able to sell his woven wire fence at a low price, one of his assistants, Walter Clement, also generated some of the most interesting publicity of the era, with advertisements featuring clever writing and amusing cartoons. Then there was the black baseball team, the Page Fence Giants, which the company sponsored in the mid-1890s. By this time racism had driven blacks to form their own baseball league, and Page sponsored what became the best team of the 1890s. Page also provided a railroad passenger car so the team could travel in

early twentieth century Adrian was calling itself the wire fence capital of the world. The second largest of these new concerns was the Lamb Wire Fence Company organized in 1897 by Hiram Lamb. That same year several Adrian businessmen, including William Burnham, Charles Hart, and B.L. Shaw, bought Lamb's patents and experimental machines and moved the enterprise from Tecumseh to Adrian—the same procedure used by another Hart, Henry, to get the Illinois Com-

Several hundred Murray cars were assembled in Lenawee between 1902 and 1903. The imaginative management at the Church Company, which built the cars, tried in several ways to show how sturdy and efficient their little Murray was. In December 1902, for instance, the Adrian post office agreed to let a Murray be used instead of the regular horse and buggy over the rural routes, which were in bad condition during the winter months. William Blaine of the Church Company drove while a regular carrier, W.C. Moran, bundled up alongside him. According to the company, delivery times were cut in half, but this successful experiment was not enough to save the car. Courtesy, Lenawee County Historical Museum

style and not have to worry about finding accommodations in towns where they played. Of course, the railroad car featured Page's name.

One significant effect of a new invention or manufacturing process is that it can lead to the development of other products or processes. Such was the case with the woven wire fence business. Between 1890 and 1914 a number of fence companies joined Page in manufacturing wire fence in Adrian. By the

pany to Adrian back around 1870. By the turn of the century Lamb Fence was selling a considerable amount of fence, especially in the Mississippi Valley. Other large companies, such as Monarch Fence and Adrian Fence, also had their own lines and territories.

Outside Adrian there was significant new industrial growth in this period—though, again, it would be hard to tell from the population figures. Much of the new industry was related, like the wire fence industry, to

Lenawee's special understanding of the needs of farmers. In Hudson, for instance, the Bean-Chamberlain Company began manufacturing plows and pumps around 1890. This company also made some popular bicycles, particularly the "Hudson" and the "Lenawee." In 1903 the Hardie Manufacturing Company was founded to build a new type of pump Harry Hardie had invented for spraying orchards. Then, in 1909, the Helvetia Milk Condensing Company built a large plant in Hudson to take advantage of the dairy industry surrounding the city. Pet Milk later owned and operated this plant.

In Tecumseh the Brewer Foundry remained the community's largest industry throughout the early twentieth century. Although it only had about 25 employees making clay-working machinery, new and larger shops were built around 1910 on the south side of town. In Blissfield Herbert Hathaway established the Home Canning Company in 1898 to can tomatoes and squash, and Richland Furs got started in 1899 as the Blissfield Robe and Tanning Company. In 1900 the Continental Sugar Company set up a mill to process sugar beets, and in 1913 the National Bundle Tyer Company was founded to manufacture bundle-tying machines.

Something should be said for other manufacturing in Adrian besides the fence industry. The Clough and Warren Company, for instance, made pianos in Adrian for about 20 years. In 1900 George and Ladd Lewis came to Adrian and purchased the Adrian Knitting Mills. The mill, which concentrated on making children's heavy cotton underwear, was so successful that by 1903 it employed 100 people. The Bond Steel Post Company, also founded in 1900, manufactured steel posts (which it thought would replace farmers' old wooden fence posts). Yet another company, the Gilliland Company, owned a large plant next to the county fairgrounds, where it

made parts for the nation's growing electrical industry.

No matter how successful, though, none of these companies were likely to push Adrian and Lenawee out of the economic doldrums they began to find themselves in around 1900. As we now know, one industry might have had an enormous impact on the county if only it had become established. That was the automotive industry. If Lenawee did not become a major center of production in this field, it was not from lack of trying.

Adrian businessmen, well aware of the potential in this area, got in on the ground

Charles Croswell (1825-1886) was the most eminent political leader to come out of Lenawee County. After serving many years in a variety of important local and state positions, he was elected and served two terms as governor of Michigan, from 1877 to 1881. This photo was taken in 1862 when Croswell served as mayor of Adrian. Courtesy, Lenawee County Historical Museum

BELOW: In 1909 Henry Bowen and a group of Adrian investors chose the former Lion Fence plant as the location for the new Lion Motor Company. Production and sales of the first car, the Lion 40, went well in 1910 and 1911. Unfortunately in 1912, a devasting fire forced the plant to close down. In this 1911 photo, Henry Bowen's daughter, Elise, is at the wheel of the big, five-passenger Model K. Courtesy, Lenawee County Historical Museum

floor. The first company to try its hand was the Church Company (so named because it was located on Church Street near the Wabash tracks). As the twentieth century began it was building gasoline engines, but in 1901 its ambitious management decided to manufacture a car. The key person involved was Wal-

ter Clement, who had been at Page Fence in the 1890s and was also head of Bond Steel Post. Charles Hart also was an important investor, in addition to serving on the board.

The car would be called the Murray in honor of its designer, Willis Murray, who had worked for America's most successful manufac-

turer of cars, Ransom Olds. Several hundred Murray cars were assembled between 1902 and 1903, but the company was too small and inexperienced to succeed in so complex a business. Although the Murray seems to have been a sound car and quite inexpensive at $600 (a price $50 less than Olds' most popular car), the capital needs were too great. In 1904 the Church Company tried again with another car, the Lenawee. Only 12 of these larger cars were made before the company closed down production.

In 1909 Detroit interests, along with local men like William Burnham, organized the Lion Motor Car Company in Adrian. This firm produced several styles of Lions in the next few years. Like the Murray, these cars were well-received. In 1912, however, the factory suffered a devastating fire from which the company never recovered. That was it for Adrian-made cars.

Politics

Even as the economy of the county began to slow down, Lenawee continued to provide political leadership at the state level, particularly between 1870 and 1890. Clearly the most significant politician ever to come out of Lenawee was Charles Croswell.

From 1854, when he served as secretary at the convention at Jackson which organized the Republican Party, to 1880, when he was completing his second term as governor of Michigan, Croswell was a major force in the state. Using his influence to make government more humane and efficient, Croswell gave constant support to the war effort against the South during the Civil War, worked against the imposition of the death penalty, led Michigan to abolish slavery by ratifying the 13th Amendment to the Constitution,

and served as Secretary of the State Board for the supervision of the charitable and penal institutions of Michigan in which he worked to help the unfortunate. His popularity with the people is shown by his twice being elected as governor.

Croswell served as governor from 1877 to 1881. During that time he opened a new prison at Ionia and a mental institution at Pontiac, while also reducing the public debt. In Lansing he is best-known for being governor at the time the new state capitol was completed and dedicated. In Lenawee he is known for listening to Laura Haviland's call for the state to attend to the care and education of young girls whose home life was nonexistent or deplorable. The result was the establishment of the State Industrial Home for

Girls at Adrian in 1881.

If there is one statesman from Lenawee who could rival Croswell in influence or reputation during this time, it would be one of Croswell's old law partners in Adrian, Thomas M. Cooley. Cooley was a scholarly lawyer who built his early reputation by compiling all the laws of Michigan in only nine months.

FAR RIGHT: In the early twentieth century the Adrian attorney, John E. Bird (1862-1928), was one of the state's most prominent Republicans. He served as attorney general of the state from 1904 to 1910, and then served on the state supreme court from 1910 until his death in 1927. Using old photographs from around 1910, Jacques Egan, a well-known Adrian artist, created this painting in the 1970s. Courtesy, Lenawee County Historical Museum

The Honorable Thomas M. Cooley (1824-1898) was considered at the turn of the century to have been the most eminent man who ever lived in Lenawee County. In 1858 he became one of the first law professors at the University of Michigan, and in 1864 he became a member of the state supreme court, serving until 1885. During this time the court became distinguished on a national level for the quality of its opinions and decisions—many of them written by Cooley. This portrait was made in 1880. Courtesy, Lenawee County Circuit Court

In 1858 he moved to Ann Arbor after being chosen as one of the University of Michigan's first law professors. In 1864 he won election to the State Supreme Court, where he served as chief justice for 20 years. While on the court he became known nationwide for the intelligence, scholarship, and vigor he put into his decisions. Today Judge Cooley is remembered in two significant ways. The

prestigious annual law lectures at the University of Michigan Law School are called the Cooley Lectures, and a private law school in Lansing is called the Cooley Law School.

Both Croswell and Cooley were Republicans—something to be expected of political figures from Lenawee. From the Civil War to the present, Lenawee County has voted Republican in almost every election. That party's early identification with antislavery sentiment captured the support of Lenawee citizens, and after the Civil War the party held their support through constant attention to Protestant moral concerns such as temperance. In a county filled with thousands of small businessmen toiling on their farms or in their shops, the Republican Party suited

them fine.

Several important political figures came from western Lenawee County in the early twentieth century. One was John E. Bird of Adrian, who served as State Attorney General from 1904 to 1910, and then served on the State Supreme Court until his death in 1928. He was joined on the bench by Grant Fellows of Hudson. He too served as Attorney General, and then served on the Supreme Court from 1916 until his death in 1929. From 1922 to 1929 he served as Chief Justice of that distinguished body.

Journalists, Poets, and Churches
The western half of Lenawee gave birth to three eminent journalists who came of age during this period. The best known, Will Carleton, was born and raised on a farm a few miles east of Hudson. He later became the editor of the *Brooklyn Eagle,* a leading New York newspaper. Carleton was much better known, however, for his poetry, writing book after book of poems based on his Midwestern rural experiences. Recognized officially in Michigan as the State Poet, he has been called America's best-loved poet of

Justice Bert Chandler (1869-1947) was born and raised in the Rollin and Hudson area. After studying law with Grant Fellows, he became his law partner in 1890. The partnership continued until 1917 when Fellows joined the state supreme court. Bert Chandler also became a member of the state supreme court in 1936, serving until 1943. In Hudson he is remembered as an exceptionally kind and compassionate man as well as an extremely able lawyer. Chandler is depicted here around 1940. Courtesy, Lenawee County Circuit Court

FAR LEFT: The Honorable Grant Fellows (1865-1929) was born and raised in the Hudson area. He began practicing law at the young age of 21 in Hudson, where he formed a partnership with his lifetime friend and fellow Hudson lawyer, Bert Chandler. From 1912 to 1916 Fellows served as attorney general of Michigan, and then was elected to the state supreme court. He was Lenawee's third distinguished lawyer in that body, where he served until his death in 1929. He is depicted here around 1925. Courtesy, Lenawee County Circuit Court

the late nineteenth century. In 1919 the state legislature designated Carleton's birthday, October 21, as Carleton Day and directed all teachers of grades five and above to read one of his poems to their students on that day. His most famous poem, "Over the Hill to the Poor-House," lamented the neglect and indifference Americans had for their aged poor.

James Schermerhorn came out of Hudson in the 1890s to seek his fortune in Detroit. After working on both the *Detroit News* and the *Detroit Free Press,* he founded the *Detroit Times,* serving as president and general manager of that newspaper for 21 years. Meanwhile, Edward D. Stair bought the *Free Press* in 1906 after a successful career as developer of a nationwide chain of theaters. Stair owned and operated the *Free Press* until 1940, when he sold it to John Knight. Stair was a regular visitor and a generous benefactor to his old hometown through the years.

In religious affairs, the most significant development was the founding of the Con-

gregation of Adrian Dominican Sisters. It began as a request in 1884 to a small congregation of Dominican nuns in New York City from Father Casimir Rohowski, pastor of St. Joseph Catholic Church in Adrian, that some sisters be sent to Adrian

to establish a hospital for the elderly. After eight years the new leader of the group, Mother Camilla Madden, realized that the mission was bound to collapse from lack of support from parishes in the Detroit diocese. However, she also saw a need to provide a Catholic education for girls.

To begin a new school in the diocese, Mother Madden needed permission from Bishop Foley of Detroit. Foley was not sympathetic. The Detroit diocese already had a fine school at Monroe, the Sisters of the Immaculate Heart of Mary (IHM), and so he said no to Madden. Being Irish himself, the bishop should have realized that this Irishwoman had just begun to fight. Within two years she had enlisted Dr. Charles Reilly of St. Mary's Church in Adrian to help her campaign. Reilly was considered the finest orator in the Detroit dio-

cese. Also, Madden had figured out how to keep her tuition fees low enough to keep from competing with the IHM school and yet high enough to keep her own sisters from starving entirely. Foley finally consented to the new school in 1895, and in 1896 St. Joseph's Academy, a boarding school for girls, opened.

The new school was a success from the start, and soon some of the girls became interested in becoming members of the Adrian Dominicans. Madden was aware that many Detroit parish schools needed teaching sisters, but again, Foley was reluctant to undercut the IHM sisters. Denied access to the Detroit diocese, the Adrian Dominicans sent their sisters to schools in Chicago, Cleveland, the Southwest, and finally Florida. By the 1920s the Adrian provincial house had become so large, with such a complex mission in so

The establishment of St. Joseph's Academy in 1896 gave the Dominicans in Adrian a purpose with a real future. A number of students later became members of the Adrian Dominicans, and then went on to teach in parochial schools across the nation. This photo shows eight of the students at the school during the second year, two of which became Dominicans. Courtesy, Adrian Dominican Archives

many parts of the country, that it seemed best to make it into an independent congregation. That remarkable woman, Camilla Madden, was still in charge, but now with the title of Mother Superior.

The first decade of the century also saw efforts to expand the educational mission at Adrian itself, in order to train the many sisters needing a college education before they could teach in parochial schools. Thus, in 1919, the Adrian Dominicans opened St. Joseph's College to exist alongside St. Joseph's Academy. In 1939 the name was changed to Siena Heights College to distinguish it from the Academy, but it otherwise retained its educational mission.

The period before 1914 saw a number of new churches built. Two very attractive fieldstone churches in Hudson, the Methodist Episcopal Church (built in 1901) and Sacred Heart Roman Catholic Church (built in 1906), were perhaps the most significant architecturally.

An Architectural Legacy

From 1870 to 1914 two architectural styles, Queen Anne and Classical Revival, were especially popular. In Hudson and Adrian, the

two most bustling cities of the period, these styles are particularly evident. Lovely homes in Hudson, such as the Thompsons' and the Frensdorfs', were built in the fanciful Queen Anne style—with towers, balconies, stained-glass windows, and other decorative features. The same was true in Adrian, where J. Wallace Page, Leslie Robertson, David Metcalf, and Charles G. Hart built outstanding homes in this style. In the countryside George Horton built perhaps the loveliest and most impressive home in Lenawee history in this same style. The designer and builder of many of these homes was Adrian architect and contractor C.F. Matthes.

The Classical Revival style lent itself to dignified buildings such as bank offices, a marvelous example of which was built by the Lenawee County Savings Bank in downtown Adrian in 1908. In 1917 the Wakefield State Bank in Morenci built a similar building on a smaller scale.

Meeting the Needs of Lenawee's Children

Between 1870 and 1914 most of the important innovations in education took place at the secondary level. Most communities had built a central or union school by 1870, and in the next generation they proceeded to show what kind of education justified keeping a child in school after the normal leaving age of 14.

What happened in Adrian would serve as an example for the rest of the county. In the 1880s schools began to offer a number of commercial courses, as well as courses in science and American history. The move toward more modern and practical courses accelerated during the 1900s. Classes in music, manual training, domestic science, physical culture, and agriculture were offered for the first time between 1900 and 1914. Adrian schools began providing medical examinations in 1910, and in 1919 a cafeteria was added to the junior high.

With such useful and interesting courses—taught increasingly by professional teachers—more students began to stay in school past eighth grade. Moreover, students started coming in from rural districts, where education ended after eighth grade. Enrollment in Adrian rose from 1,180 in 1890 to 1,850 in 1906, while the number of graduates rose more modestly, from 10 to 39.

All these changes in the high schools made the old union or central schools seem inadequate, and new high schools were built all over the county. Addison and Clinton started the ball rolling in 1905. The school in Addison burned down in 1924, but a new school was soon built. In Clinton, the new school served the community until 1971, when the current school was built. Morenci followed with a new school in 1907. In Adrian, a new high school opened in 1908, and Hudson followed suit in 1913. Finally, in 1918, Tecumseh closed this era of new school construction with a high school of its own. By and large, these early-twentieth-century high schools would serve their communities for the next 50 years or so.

LEFT: By the time this photograph was taken, around 1900, Lenawee had a number of schools with children separated into different grades. This photo from the Morenci area suggests education was a pretty serious affair. The teacher, Lillie Anderson, is wearing a rather formal costume, and the fixed desks, schoolbooks held at attention, and the steady gazes of the students all suggest a no-nonsense academic atmosphere. Courtesy, Stair Public Library, Morenci, Michigan

CHAPTER FOUR

GEARING UP

1 9 1 4 - 1 9 3 5

In the quarter-century between 1910 and 1935, Lenawee's population hovered around the 48,000 mark attained in 1880. In 1920 the county had 47,700 people, down from 48,400 in 1900. In the 1920s things began to change, however, with a small gain to 49,800 by 1930. That was only 2,000 more people, but it must have been heartening after 40 years with no growth.

Unfortunately, the Great Depression lay dead ahead. As might be imagined, Lenawee experienced difficult times in the early 1930s, but the statistics indicate that, on the whole, the county continued to grow during this decade. In fact, it even grew at a slightly faster pace than it had in the 1920s. This seems remarkable considering the state of the American economy during the 1930s, but this growth actually came from seeds sown in the previous era.

The growth statistics for Adrian during this period indicate where Lenawee's future lay—in the cities, not the countryside. In the 1910s the city grew by about 1,100 people while the county as a whole lost 140. In the 1920s Adrian gained another 1,100, so that by 1930 Adrian had 13,000 people. Mean-

while, the rural townships continued to lose population as the number of farms declined.

One reason for Adrian's growth involved the prosperity of the fence companies. As a national center for the manufacture of wire fencing, Adrian benefited from the boom in American farming from 1914 to 1918. Those were the years of the First World War, and the people of Europe needed more food than they could produce. Thus, they turned to American farmers. The farmers then bought more fencing for the larger and better farms being developed. As a result, Page Fence, Peerless Fence (the name taken by Lamb Fence in the early 1910s to avoid confusion with another Lamb Fence in Canada), Adrian Wire Fence, and other fence companies all prospered.

The fence manufacturers were joined in this display of manufacturing prowess by other companies which had come along before the war, including several with the traditional closeness to the soil of nineteenth-century Lenawee firms. Acme Preserve is an example. Acme began in 1904 to can many of the vegetables produced on Lenawee farms. Another firm, the Gibford-Weiffenbach

Lenawee farmers began to switch to tractors during and after World War I. By 1930, at the time of this photo, there were almost 1600 tractors on Lenawee farms. One of them was the Case tractor owned by Trevor Smith of the Morenci area. Courtesy, Stair Public Library, Morenci, Michigan

The Ohio Dairy Company came to Morenci in 1902. Similar companies were opening elsewhere in Lenawee at this same time. Farmers welcomed these new companies that paid more money for their dairy products than the old-style creameries. A sign of the times was the closing of all the Horton creameries but the one on the home farm, by 1912. At its peak the Ohio Dairy in Morenci produced 180,000 pounds of milk per day. Production ended at this plant in 1950. Courtesy, Stair Public Library, Morenci, Michigan

Company (founded in 1900), relied on leather to produce the shaving strops for which it was known.

Beyond these, however, there was a significant new development after 1910. Several companies began manufacturing articles for the dynamic auto industry in nearby Detroit. Schwarze Electric (which became Faraday in the 1940s) was founded in 1904 to manufacture the electrical bells invented by its founder, Carl Schwarze. When American businesses began installing fire alarm signals in their factories to make them safer, they turned to Schwarze. By 1916 Carl Schwarze had invented 30 different kinds of bells, ranging from little one-pounders to 300-pound alarm bells. Schwarze also was moving into the car business, inventing an electric horn and an electric generator controller. By 1916 Schwarze was producing 600,000 horns and circuit breakers

annually for cars.

In the 1920s the company built three additions to its Adrian plant plus a branch in Blissfield. In 1928 Schwarze Electric took on new owners when the two top officials at Peerless Fence, W.H. Burnham and Vernon Hoxie, bought into the company. They could see how things were going. In the depths of the Depression Schwarze continued to prosper, paying a dividend in 1930, hiring more help in 1931 and 1932, and coming out with a new product, window defrosters, in 1931.

Edd Oliver, a university-trained engineer, founded Oliver Instrument in Detroit in 1913, moving it to Adrian in 1915. Oliver was known for designing and engineering assembly-line machines for companies like Ford and Buick.

Outside Adrian the county almost held its own in terms of population, and new industry developed here as well, much of it related to the agriculture of Lenawee. In 1911 the Quaker Oats Company built a plant in Tecumseh to produce macaroni noodles. Even earlier, in 1900, a plant to make sweetened condensed milk was opened in Morenci. In 1902 the Ohio Dairy Company bought the plant and built a new one in 1905. This plant was an important part of Morenci's life until it closed in 1950. The Helvetia Milk condensing plant in Hudson has already been mentioned. Helvetia (which later changed its name to Pet Milk) kept this plant going through the 1930s. In fact, in 1938 it expanded the plant, making it one of the largest of their 50 plants across the country. By 1948, 110 employees worked there processing 300,000 pounds of milk per day. When the plant was finally closed in 1956, it had processed 5 billion pounds of raw milk and had shipped 50 million cases of Pet Milk.

Adrian had two dairy-oriented plants of its own in the early part of the century. Van Camp opened a plant on West Beecher around 1910 to produce condensed milk.

Then, in 1922, the Michigan Producers Dairy Company opened a plant which made butter, ice cream mix, powdered milk, and sweet cream. This company has been an important part of Lenawee's economy ever since.

Lenawee still produced a lot of wool, and the leading industry in Clinton, the Clinton Woolen Mill, used much of it. The mill kept on producing in the 1930s, and in the early 1940s reached its height of production making wool coats for the U.S. Navy during World War II.

These companies held the Lenawee economy together and produced a steady market for local farmers. Something new would be needed, however, if the county outside Adrian were to resume growing. This was particularly true after World War I. The demand for farm products declined in the 1920s, but the farmers' debt—taken on during the prosperous war years—did not go away. The result was that hard times for many American farmers began in the 1920s, not the 1930s. Signs of decay could be seen in Lenawee. The number of farms declined, for instance—from 5,080 in 1920 to 4,186 in 1940. As the number of farm families declined, so did the

Felix Witt (1894-1977), depicted here in 1910, was born in Illinois, but grew up in the Fairfield area in Lenawee. He could be considered a prototype for modern farmers in his high regard for the importance of education. He strived to learn all of his life, and it showed in such successes as being the first farmer in Michigan to begin growing hybrid corn. In 1965 he was honored as one of the 12 outstanding farmers in North America. Courtesy, Lenawee County Historical Museum

FAR LEFT: In 1904 Carl Schwarze (1860-1918) began applying his knowledge of electricity to the invention and manufacture of bells and horns for automobiles, factories, and other locations. His great invention was a non-arcing bell, which meant there would be no spark between the contact points. Every mine operator could see the merit in that, and Schwarze Electric Company was on its way. After many years in Adrian, his firm, now known as Faraday, moved to Tecumseh in 1961. Courtesy, Lenawee County Historical Museum

Sand Lake in the Irish Hills has been a favorite summer place for Lenawee residents since the 1880s. This 1894 photo shows the Hotel Putnam, which was built in 1882. In those days, for $2 a day, visitors could live at the hotel and enjoy the fishing, the view, and the boating. Courtesy, Lenawee County Historical Museum

communities that existed to serve them. Villages like Clayton, Cadmus, Macon, Riga, and Rollin suffered along with the farmers.

The slumping and changing farm economy was bound to hurt the larger towns too. In Tecumseh two of the larger employers were Brewer's, which made clay-working machinery for drain tile, and Heesen's Foundry, whose main product was iron stock-feed cookers. Neither of these companies would survive the hard times of the 1920s and 1930s. In Adrian, most fence companies found farmers quite reluctant to buy more fence after the war. As a result, Page became much more involved in the auto business while Adrian Wire Fence became just a wholesale dealer in fence by the end of the 1920s. Monarch, Michigan and Bond Steel shut down completely.

Peerless was the only fence company that kept going after the 1920s. It was sold to another firm, Brown Fence, but that did not hurt production in Adrian. While Peerless laid off many of its employees in the early 1930s, it was back up to 200 workers by 1933. During World War II Brown had 500 employees, and still employed 120 when it closed on January 1, 1947. That marked the end, finally, of the second industrial era in Adrian.

Signs of New Growth

In the 1920s the pace of mechanization and industrialization quickened. In agriculture, for example, Lenawee farmers went from owning 17,500 horses in 1920 to 8,370 in 1940. The fact that Lenawee farmers in 1930 owned 4,453 cars, 959 trucks, and 1,591 tractors shows how thoroughly and rapidly they were mechanizing. Farmers also began to develop new organizations to help them understand and cope with changes in agriculture. In 1914 the Cooperative Extension Service was established to bring new ideas straight from the labs and experimental fields of Michigan State

to farmers in their fields. Then, around 1920, the Farm Bureau was organized.

One new crop that aroused interest in the 1930s was soybeans. Actually it was that well-known industrialist, Henry Ford of Dearborn, who became one of the first to experiment with them, buying several thousand acres in the Tecumseh-Macon area and hiring local farmers to grow them. Ford was not interested in this crop for its food value, but rather for its potential as a raw material that could be used to make things like car steering wheels. Real farmers—like Felix and Joseph Witt of Fairfield—got interested in soybeans

as a basic foodstuff, however, and began to pioneer the development of varieties suitable for growing in Michigan.

Something also should be said for that small but socially significant segment of agriculture in Lenawee, sugar-beet farming. Before World War I sugar-beet farmers relied on Moravian immigrants to help with the work needed to grow and harvest this crop. This source of labor was cut off by the war and the subsequent dislocations in Europe, and after 1919 Mexican-Americans in the Southwest were recruited to work crops in the Midwest. By 1929 some 4,000 acres of

sugar beets were being farmed, with 39,000 tons of sugar beets harvested. In time, some migrant workers began to live year-round in the Blissfield area.

Even with all the changes in farming, the basic pattern for Lenawee farmers into the 1930s was still the small general farm of less than 90 acres (up from the traditional 80 acres). Just about every farm had some livestock—cows, chickens, horses, pigs—plus fields devoted to different crops. The five or six cows per farm were especially important; in 1929, 19,700 cows were being milked on 3,800 farms, and by 1940 Lenawee farmers were milking 23,200 cows on 3,600 farms. Pet Milk, Ohio Dairy, Van Camp, and Michigan Producers ensured plenty of demand for all this milk.

In the cities—Adrian especially—more auto-related companies came along in the 1920s. Page Fence, which was sold to American Chain in the late 1910s, had already developed auto-related lines, and in the 1920s these became its basic products. Page made bead rings, car window lifters, and emergency brakes, but its specialty was car bumpers. In

Outside of Adrian, a welcome harbinger of things to come in the 1920s was the Parker Rust Proof Company of Detroit. Willard Cornelius, a lawyer born and raised in Adrian, bought control of this failing company in 1918. After he infused it with capable businessmen, lawyers, and a professor from Lenawee, the company became quite profitable. In 1927 Parker built a plant in Morenci to produce a new rustproofing product, called "Parco Powder," invented by Elmer Jones, a chemistry professor from Adrian College. In

the early 1930s Page had to lay off several hundred men, but the company slowly increased production again. By 1935 the company had 500 employees hard at work.

Yet a fourth auto-related industry to come along in Adrian in the 1920s was the Raymond Garage Equipment Company. Samuel Raymond (whose wife was related to Henry Ford), the guiding force in the company, was the inventor of the visible gasoline pump that his company built. The firm lasted for almost 10 years.

1928 Parker won a lawsuit against the Ford Motor Company for patent infringement, and from then on Parker had the market for this product pretty much to itself. Over the next 60 years Parker Rustproofing would grow into one of Morenci's leading companies, and when it finally closed its Morenci plant in 1989, it was one of the year's sadder events.

Other Kinds of Industry

After the war, in addition to pursuing auto-related companies, Adrian made a commitment to bring in other kinds of companies as well. It was almost as though the town realized there were perils in being so committed to one kind of industry, as it had been to railroads and wire fencing. By 1923 Adrian was a town with 33 significant companies making everything from artificial ice to woven-wire fence—with things like bead rings, bread, castings, concrete burial vaults, knitted goods, drawing tables, suspenders, paperboard, and steel posts in between.

This movement toward diverse industry could not just happen. There had to be an active chamber of commerce to recruit new firms. A.H. Billings was at the center of this for years, and local capitalists like W.H. Burnham and Charles G. Hart were willing to venture funds to support new firms.

Ollie E. Mott was one of the new businessmen in town. In the 1910s he purchased patent rights to a new method of making suspenders. In 1919 he came to Adrian with his company, called Nu-Way Strech, and in the 1920s bought a Chicago tie company and moved its manufacturing operations to Adrian. Nu-Way Strech lasted into the early 1960s. Another company, the Ervin Foundry, settled in Adrian in 1925, where it has been ever since. Also in 1925 the Simplex Paper Corporation set up shop at the corner of Treat and Wabash to manufacture case linings, box board, corrugated paper products, and automobile panel board.

The list could go on—and it should because what was happening was significant. Adrian was regearing its industrial base for the third time in its history. The Economy Drawing Table Company was part of this restructuring. Founded in Adrian in the 1910s, it was sold in 1926 to the Kewaunee Manufacturing Company of Kewaunee, Wisconsin. Soon Kewaunee was expanding operations in Adrian. The company made metal laboratory furniture for schools, hospitals and colleges. Through 1931 and

1932 Kewaunee added workers or new shifts, and started new lines of metal furniture. For 60 years the company would be a vital part of Adrian.

It is a long stretch from craft kits to machinery designed to make concrete forms, but Adrian did it in the 1920s with two other new firms. One was Fireside Industries, a crafts firm that made up the kits in Adrian and then sold them through stores or directly to consumers from 1924 to the middle of the century. The concrete-form machinery came in when Gene Olson set up the Consolidated Concrete Machinery Company here in the mid-1920s. For the next 50 years Olson's firms would produce machinery to make concrete forms used in the construction business. The names of the firms changed, but the business stayed the same.

Commerce and Banking

Between 1914 and 1935 Lenawee merchants began to adapt to the new world of automobiles and mass merchandising. One sign of the times came in 1923 when the historic Comstock Hotel in Hudson was razed to make way for a gas station built by the Moreland Oil Company. Moreland did the same in Tecumseh when it tore down the old table factory on West Chicago to put up a gas station (from which Mayor Harold Easton pumped gas and ran Tecumseh later in the century). The creation of businesses catering to the auto, truck and tractor driver was extensive in every community. New and used car agencies, service stations, tire centers, car washes, and other auto-related businesses appeared in droves during the 1920s. Those businesses which had been part of the horse-and-buggy days quietly slipped away. The harness makers, blacksmith shops, wagon shops, buggy and carriage works, and stables closed down one by one. The change was enormous, and every town, village, and farm participated in it.

FACING PAGE: Throughout its history Clinton has been well known for the fact that the historic highway between Detroit and Chicago, based on the Indians' Old Sauk Trail, ran through town. This photo shows U.S. 112 (now called U.S. 12) in downtown Clinton around 1917, a few years before the highway was paved through the village. Standing on the left at the end of the street, is the Clintonian Hotel. The Lancaster Hotel (which was razed in the 1960s) is on the right behind the bandstand. Courtesy, Lenawee County Historical Museum

In addition to selling and servicing cars, businessmen saw a way to boost the tourist business in Lenawee by catering to the auto. Tourism had gotten its start in Lenawee during the 1880s when the Cincinnati, Jackson and Mackinaw Railroad began scheduling special trips to Devil's and Clark lakes. The Lake Shore did the same with a branch running along the northern side of Lenawee. By the 1910s hotels and amusement parks in the Irish Hills were doing a remarkable business during the summer. The Lake View Hotel and Dance Pavilion were especially popular.

From 1915 on, many of the lakes in the Irish Hills saw development all around

Captain Charles Cole (1875-1957) was an aerial high diver who occasionally performed his stunts for the Irish Hills tourists. From the mid-1890s to 1927 he thrilled crowds across America with, first, his balloon ascensions and free-fall parachute descents and, second, his high dives into a small net from a 100-foot ladder. He did these acts from 1906 to 1927 and amazingly, only once, in 1912, did he suffer a serious injury. This photo shows him in mid-dive from the ladder on July 31, 1909, at Edon, Ohio. One of his last dives was off the top of the "original" Irish Hills Tower into a net below in 1927. Courtesy, Lenawee County Historical Museum

their shores thanks to the increasing use of the automobile by the middle-class family. Then, in the 1920s, several roads were widened and paved—including U.S. 112 (now U.S. 12), M-50, and M-223 (now U.S. 223)—making the Irish Hills accessible to the growing urban populations of Detroit and Toledo looking for pleasant day trips to the country.

Many tourist spots were developed to capture visitors' fancies. They included the Twin Towers on U.S. 112, the Swan Tower and golf course on M-223, and most of all, the many amusement places around Manitou Beach on Devil's Lake and along U.S. 112 in the Irish Hills. Overall, thanks to the auto, the Irish Hills tourist business was becoming an important industry on its own.

Otherwise, downtowns were in their heyday during this period. The streets were paved and lighted; the traffic and parking problems still seemed manageable; and the lovely three-story Victorian commercial buildings were filled with stores, offices, and lodges from top to bottom and from day to night. Certain kinds of stores were especially popular, including department stores like Albig's, McConnell's, and A.B. Park's in

Adrian, and dime stores like Kresge's and Ben Franklin's. Going downtown on Saturday night became enormously popular in the 1920s. Farmers would drive in to shop and visit, and the local residents would drive or walk downtown. Going shopping, taking in a movie, and stopping for ice cream at a parlor like Fox's in Adrian or Pete Spadafora's in Hudson was a regular custom for many.

As far as banking was concerned in this period, only a few important developments occurred before the trauma of the Depression. The most significant was the merger in 1915 of Adrian's two oldest banks, Waldby & Clay's and the Lenawee County Savings Bank (whose name the new bank continued to use). In 1919 the bank sold the grand bank building it had constructed in 1907 and moved to the corner of Main and Maumee, where Waldby & Clay had been since 1857. Another bank merger occurred in 1927, when the First National Bank of Morenci and the Wakefield State Bank consolidated into the First State Savings Bank of Morenci. The new bank moved into the handsome Classical Revival building constructed by the Wakefield Bank in 1917.

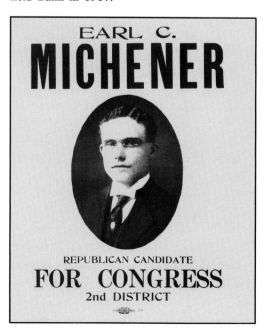

FAR LEFT: From 1888 to its close in 1971, the A.B. Park store was Adrian's leading dry goods store. It was located for most of that time at 115-119 S. Main. This caricature of Ambrose B. Park (1852-1915), top, and two of his employees appeared in the 1910 "Men of Affairs in Adrian" booklet taken from the Adrian Daily Telegram. *Courtesy, Lenawee County Historical Museum*

Earl C. Michener (1876-1957) served in Congress longer than any other congressional representative from Lenawee. As a Congressman for 28 years, he served on the powerful Rules Committee and for two years chaired the Judiciary Committee. Michener's honesty, hard work, and conservative stand were valued by the Second Congressional District and led to his repeated reelection. Based on his conservative stand, the name "Michener" became synonymous with "Republican." Michener is seen here just prior to his 1920 election. Courtesy, The family of the late Earl P. Michener

The Great Depression

The Depression did not hit Lenawee County like a bomb, hurting rich and poor alike. The effect was more like the stalk of the wolf, hitting the young, the weak, and the poor first and foremost. Many people with marginal farms and shops, or working at marginal occupations in factories, were the ones hit hardest. For the rest it was a dreary bad time, but if they buckled down, they were able to endure it. Happily, considerable resources in Lenawee enabled most people to do just that. Most farms, for instance, were general farms. If the main source of income was reduced, supplemental sources like eggs or butter could be sold. Also, most farm families had large gardens and canned much of their food. Many people in the villages and towns also canned and stored foodstuffs they had produced themselves.

A second resource in Lenawee was the variety of industry built into its economy during the 1910s and 1920s. The local industries tied into food production—like Van Camp or Home Canning in Blissfield—kept going, which not only helped their own laborers but farmers too. A third resource for Lenawee in the mid-1930s was the comeback of the auto industry after a few years of hunkering down. Considering the many Lenawee plants related to Detroit, this resurgence had an immediately positive effect. Finally, a fourth resource was the individualistic grit and the sense of family and community possessed by so many people in this area. All those old Yankee, black, German, Irish, and Moravian families knew how to save, make do, and be ready to pounce on something better if and when it came along.

Tecumseh, in particular, needed all the grit and sense of community it could muster. Its major long-time industries like Brewer's and Heesen's were closed, the bank was closed (as we shall see), and there was no good news in the offing. Tecumseh was the quintessential old country town, and it was in trouble.

By 1931 things were so bad in Hudson that the Exchange Service Club and several Women's Clubs served almost 6,000 meals to the children of the unemployed during the winter of 1931-32. Overall, the number of men laid off from their factory jobs numbered in the thousands.

One particular kind of commercial business, banking, also was in serious trouble. All over the nation borrowers were having a hard time paying back loans. In addition, the banks were hurt by some of their own investments in other banks or companies which were closing down. Starting in 1929, banks began to close their doors, and Lenawee banks felt the squeeze. The first sign of bad trouble came in Tecumseh when the Lilley State Bank closed in November 1929. In August 1931 the two banks in town, Lilley State and Tecumseh State, merged to form a new bank, the United Savings Bank of Tecumseh. The merger only made matters worse. On October 31, 1931, this new bank was forced to close. For all those holding deposits in this troubled bank during the 18 months it was closed, this must have been an anxious, irritating time. The bank reopened on April 15, 1933, however, and this time things went much better. United Savings gained strength each day and has never looked back.

In February 1933, although no other banks in Lenawee showed such signs of trouble, Governor William Comstock suddenly closed all the banks in the state. He called it a "bank holiday," but no one felt like celebrating. Comstock had been told that some big banks in Detroit were about to collapse, and that they would take with them many smaller banks which had money invested in them. Then, in March 1933, newly-inaugurated President Franklin D. Roosevelt closed every national bank in the country for the same reason. There was no federal deposit insurance at that time, so it is easy to imagine how Americans felt if they had any money still left in their banks by 1933.

While the banks were closed, federal bank examiners looked at the books of all the banks in the Federal Reserve system. Once deemed sound, they were allowed to reopen beginning in the summer of 1933. Every bank in Lenawee except one passed this test, and when the banks reopened, bank officers were greeted with flowers and happy depositors. Surprisingly, most depositors did not withdraw their money—although deposits slipped by as much as 25 percent over the next year in some banks.

The one bank that had trouble reopen-

ing was the National Bank of Commerce in Adrian. Requirements were very strict for national banks. After reorganization, financing by the government, and a renaming, it was allowed to reopen later in 1933 as the National Bank of Adrian. At first this bank rebounded well under its president, W.F. Jacobs, but in 1939 he was arrested and convicted of theft from the bank. This had to hurt depositors' confidence. Finally, in 1942, the Lenawee County Savings Bank bought the assets of the bank, and it went out of business. In the 1950s the Commercial Savings Bank bought the former offices of the old National Bank on East Maumee, which became their new central office.

Lenawee's first hospital was founded in 1908 in Morenci by Dr. Charles Blair. The basic charge was $15 a week for room, board, dressings, and the services of the nurse, Ethel Rae Morgan, who lived on the premises and worked 24 hours a day, 7 days a week. This 1912 photo shows the hospital on the right and Dr. Blair's home on the left. Courtesy, Stair Public Library, Morenci, Michigan

Politics: Opting for Stability

In the period between 1914 and 1935, Lenawee shared—along with the rest of America—a decidedly mixed reaction to the major social forces and events of the time. For example, the United States managed for three years to stay out of the First World War. The U.S. was happy to sell arms and food to the Allied Powers, Britain and France, but it did not see the need to get in-

assure their fellow Americans of their loyalty. However, cheap accusations and cowardly midnight destructive raids against barns and shops owned by German-Americans still occurred occasionally. This was not a good time to be different from the majority.

It is better to think of someone like Maurice Spear from Morenci. Spear was so eager to join the Army in April 1917 that he could not bear the thought of waiting until

The Emma L. Bixby Hospital in Adrian opened in 1911. A former resident, William Bixby, gave $25,000 to the city for a hospital, and in appreciation the city named the hospital after his mother, Emma, who had been one of Adrian's community leaders for years. With the $25,000 the city bought the old E.L. Clark house at the corner of E. Maumee and N. Locust, renovated it, and also built the addition shown to the left in this 1911 photo. Bixby Hospital was at this site until 1957. Courtesy, Lenawee County Historical Museum

volved in the war to a larger extent.

When the country finally did declare war in April 1917 against the Central Powers of Germany and Austria-Hungary, Lenawee rallied to the flag reasonably quickly. The first bond sales and enlistment did drag almost everywhere except in Hudson, but once the war effort was on, Lenawee got more involved. In some instances, in fact, Lenawee citizens got overly involved by suspecting the worst of some. Lenawee had many citizens of German descent, for instance, and they went to great lengths to

after graduation in June. Thus, the school board gave him and a few others special permission to graduate early so that they could enlist right away. After a fine service record, Spear returned to Lenawee and became a lawyer, later becoming a probate judge. The Maurice Spear Campus, a Lenawee juvenile detention center, is named for the judge.

After the war two long-time political movements came to fruition, and as in the case of the war, Lenawee had mixed feelings about them. One was the movement to give women the vote. The other was the movement to prohibit the sale of alcoholic beverages. Lenawee Protestants had campaigned at least since the 1840s to limit or end the sale of liquor, and so the coming of Prohibition was hailed in this county as a great triumph. Giving women the vote was something else. Lenawee was conservative politically, and had never seen much agitation for women's rights. So, women's suffrage was simply accepted without much comment and no rejoicing—at least not publicly.

One political development after the war that just about everyone liked was the emergence of a politician named Earl Michener. In 1918 Michener was elected to Congress from the Second Congressional District, which included Lenawee, and the people just kept on electing him. From 1918 to 1950 he served as Lenawee's man in Congress (except for 1932, when not even he could avoid defeat at the hands of the Democrats). No other congressman in the history of this district has ever had such a solid hold on his seat as Michener. He was conservative—a vital requirement—hardworking, personable, modest, and bright. The combination made him unbeatable and a unique phenomenon in Lenawee's political history. Lenawee has not sent anyone to Congress since Michener retired in 1950.

While Lenawee was quite conservative during this period, it had little interest in any movement further to the right. This was shown in the mid-1920s, when the Ku Klux Klan made a serious effort to organize chapters in Lenawee and exert influence on local politics. The KKK at this time was not only antiblack, but also anti-Semitic, anti-Catholic, and antiliberal. After several marches and rallies in Tecumseh and Adrian drawing thousands of spectators, the Klan went to work organizing a chapter in Adrian. This chapter remained active in Adrian from 1924 until 1933. After Congressman Michener and

Harry Fee (1868-1955), seen here in 1950, ran Citizens Light and Power Company, in Adrian until it was sold in 1923. Mr. Fee retired and spent much of his time developing a 227-acre farm in the Irish Hills, Hidden Lake Gardens, into a beautiful park. In 1945 he gave Hidden Lake Gardens to Michigan State College (now a university), but he continued actively in the park's further development. With endowments from Mr. Fee and others, Michigan State University has continued to run the gardens as one of the loveliest parks in southeastern Michigan. Courtesy, Hidden Lake Gardens, Michigan State University

most other local leaders denounced the Klan, however, its efforts to exert influence on the county's political life failed. The people of Lenawee may have been aware of some problems and weaknesses locally and nationally, but they were in no mood to support a movement that thrived on hatred, fear, and violence.

Advances in Health Care

In the early part of this century the field of health care was fully involved in the movement toward more technical knowledge and equipment. As doctors became better trained and more proficient with modern equipment and conditions of cleanliness, they preferred working in hospitals. Here the sanitary conditions and the equipment could be kept to higher standards. In Lenawee this led to the formation of four hospitals in the first quarter of the twentieth century.

In 1908 Dr. Charles Blair opened the first hospital in Lenawee, a private hospital in Morenci. It closed in the late 1920s, but in 1935 Dr. James Blanchard opened another private hospital in the Gateway Community. In Adrian, a generous gift of $25,000 to the city for the hospital from a former resident, David Bixby, made possible the opening in 1911 of the second hospital in Lenawee. In appreciation for Bixby's gift, the Board of Trustees named the hospital after his mother, Emma L. Bixby, a long-time community cultural leader. By the 1930s the hospital needed more space, and in 1940 (thanks this time to aid from the federal government) another addition was opened. After the hospital was moved to a new location in the 1950s, this addition was converted into the Charlotte Stephenson Home for senior citizens.

Dr. Bowers Growt opened the third Lenawee hospital in Addison in 1921. It, too, had to be expanded by 1940. Finally, in 1924 Ellen Thorn of Hudson willed her home to the City of Hudson for a hospital, which was named Thorn Hospital in appreciation. In 1927 the City built a $27,000 addition, and this expanded hospital served the community into the second half of the century.

Leisure Activities

The first part of the century saw the emergence of new forms of leisure and entertainment based on inventions like the motion picture and the automobile. The movies, in particular, dealt a serious blow to the older forms of live entertainment. The conversion in 1921 of the Croswell Opera House, built

in 1866, into the Croswell Moviehouse was an example of how entertainment was changing. In 1909 the opening of the Mauntauk Theatre in Hudson was part of this same trend. Other communities in the county also saw movie theaters open during this era.

Another important new development in leisure-time activity in the early part of the century was the development of parks. A nice example was Riverside Park in Morenci. In the 1920s local businessmen donated time, labor and money to develop this park along Bean Creek on the north side of town—putting in drives for autos, a baseball

From the 1920s to 1955 Harry Fee was active in developing Hidden Lake Gardens. This view was taken in springtime on Juniper Hill in the late 1940s and looks eastward across the north end of the lake. Any time of year, lovely views of hills, meadows, woods, and the lake can be seen in the park. The arborvitae in the foreground are examples of the interesting plantings Mr. Fee did for years. Courtesy, Hidden Lake Gardens, Michigan State University

diamond, electric lights, wells, and picnic tables and benches. They even dammed up Bean Creek to make a swimming hole.

Meanwhile, in the Irish Hills, it seemed as though the whole area was being turned into one vast recreation area. Two very different, but very lovely parks were established in the 1920s. Hayes State Park, on the shores of Wamplers Lake, had a bathing beach, picnic areas, and camp sites. The other park had none of those things. It was an entirely private project by an Adrian businessman, Harry Fee. Fee loved nature, plants, and landscaping, and he began to

develop some 220 acres along M-50 in Franklin Township in the 1920s. Gradually he introduced different plants, built walking trails through the hills and around the little lake—called "Hidden Lake"—and made the entire area into a showplace of nature. This would be called Hidden Lake Gardens. In the last decade of his life, between 1945 and 1955, Fee donated the property and much of his wealth to Michigan State University. The understanding was that the university would maintain Hidden Lake Gardens as a treasure for the public to enjoy, and the school has done just that.

CHAPTER FIVE

ON THE MOVE AGAIN

1 9 3 5 - 1 9 5 5

By 1935 Lenawee's life had spiraled downward a long way since the onset of the Depression in 1929. The valuation of taxable property in Lenawee County shows just how much. In 1928, the last year before the Depression, Lenawee's taxable property was valued at $81,467,400. By 1934 Lenawee's property was assessed at $55,580,000, a loss of just over 30 percent. Six years later valuations were a mere $40,000 more. It would take the enormous pressure of World War II to raise the Lenawee economy to the level of 1928. By 1944 Lenawee's valuation was up to $75 million.

Although the local economy was considerably depressed during the 1930s, as property values indicate, other statistics suggest that society as a whole still had some vigor. The population, for instance, grew from 49,849 in 1930 to 53,110 in 1940, a 6.5-percent increase. While not much in itself, this was the largest increase in population in 70 years. Considering this came during the worst depression in American history, it sug-

gests a certain amount of strength. Of course, it can be argued that this population increase was a sign of just how weak the overall economy was. For many, many decades young people in Lenawee had left the county since there was so little opportunity locally. Now things were just as bad everywhere else; and so the young people had to stay home. That is a dismal thought, but there might be something to it. However, the evidence does indicate that after a few very hard years in the early 1930s, Lenawee resumed the process of establishing itself as a mid-sized center of manufacturing.

In part, the rebuilding of Lenawee's economy came about because of businesses already functioning locally. These included American Chain, Kewaunee, Simplex Paper, Peerless, Oliver Instrument, Schwarze Electric, Parker Rustproofing, Great Lakes Sugar, Michigan Producers, Van Camp, Helvetia, Hardie, and the Clinton Woolen Mill. From the mid-1930s onward, many of these companies began to add more workers as

It is widely known that Ray Herrick (1890-1973) was one of the most remarkable and significant individuals in the history of twentieth century Lenawee. Herrick, seen here in 1959 addressing employees at Tecumseh Products, was a "hands-on" person who communicated his thoughts and wishes directly and forcefully. Not only was he the primary reason for the extraordinary growth of Tecumseh Products into the nation's leading manufacturer of refrigeration compressors, but he was a remarkable philanthropist. The foundation he established, the Herrick Foundation, has lavished untold millions upon practically every nonprofit concern in Lenawee, as well as many others across the nation. Courtesy, Tecumseh Public Library

business picked up.

There were also some significant additions in the later 1930s, however, including Tecumseh Products, Stubnitz-Greene, Magnesium Fabricators, Hurd Lock, and Gerity Steel. While all of these would play an enormous role in helping to bring Lenawee back—and then to push it forward—the emergence of Tecumseh Products was certainly the most significant development of the decade. It can be argued, in fact, that this was the most significant development in Lenawee County in the twentieth century—after all, how many areas can boast one of the 500 largest industrial corporations in the nation? It was not even that, however, which made the emergence of this company so significant, but the remarkable community-minded character of the company's dynamic force, Ray Herrick. In 1949 Herrick set up a philanthropic organization, the Herrick Foundation, to help worthy nonprofit causes. Moreover, the company's second-in-command, William Sage, did the same. As the company got richer, so did the Herrick and Sage foundations. The entire county eventually would benefit from both the company and these two foundations.

While Ray Herrick was at the center of Tecumseh Products, other important men also were involved. From the beginning in Hillsdale William Sage brought his toolmaking and business talents to bear. Another machinist, Clyde Giltner, would become factory superintendent in Tecumseh after the move in 1934. Another man, Frank Smith, came to Herrick and Sage in 1932 to have them build a compressor he had designed. In 1933 Smith brought in Curtis M. Brown, another engineer from the world of refrigeration, to help him with the engineering and sales of these compressors. Finally, in 1936 the company (which had moved to Tecumseh) brought in one more very talented engineer, Jens Touborg, as an equal partner in the business, now called

the Tecumseh Refrigeration Engineering and Sales Corporation (TRESCO). All of these men would help Tecumseh Products become the giant in the industry of refrigeration compressors after World War II.

By the time of World War II, Tecumseh Products had a work force of 1,000 and several lines of compressors which TRESCO had designed. In addition, the company's community programs were well under way. In Tecumseh itself, the already substantial impact of this company had just begun.

The second new company to come to Le-

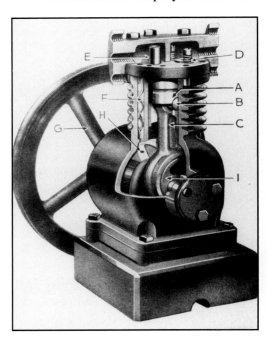

nawee in the mid-1930s was Stubnitz-Greene in 1935. Maurice Stubnitz was the prime mover in this company, which relocated here from Pennsylvania. Stubnitz-Greene made springs for car seats, and so it made sense to move closer to Detroit. The availability of factory space, plus good connections to Detroit and elsewhere, made Adrian a good place to settle. By the start of the war this company had become a solid member of the Lenawee business community.

Magnesium Fabricators came to Adrian in 1937. It too settled there because of the avail-

In the early 1930s Frank Smith of Hillsdale designed this compressor. He arranged with Hillsdale Machine & Tool (run by Ray Herrick and William Sage) to manufacture this model HP-14 compressor for them. In 1934 Hillsdale Machine & Tool moved to Tecumseh and changed its name to Tecumseh Products. Manufacturing this compressor and automotive parts for Ford helped Tecumseh Products to a successful start. Courtesy, Tecumseh Products Company

ability of labor, good rail connections around the country, and proximity to Detroit. An engineer named Les Brown was responsible both for the plant and for its coming to Adrian. With backing from Charles Bohn of Bohn Aluminum, Brown built a plant on East Maumee just east of the Wabash railroad tracks. A light metal like magnesium had many applications in the growing aircraft business, and soon Magnesium Fabricators was doing good business.

Another company which opened in Adrian in 1937 was Gerity-Adrian. James

made parts for the auto industry.

Meanwhile, Gerity-Adrian's business had become so successful that its plant on Logan was simply not big enough. To keep Gerity in town, a number of businessmen raised funds to build a new plant on East Beecher. Growth and change clearly were in the ascendancy as the 1930s ended.

As all of these companies, new and old, began to rebuild strength, they came to realize that there were new forces in the business world that they had to consider and cope with. These were the federal government

In 1940 Tecumseh Products had 800 employees, and was producing 160,000 conventional and hermetic compressors per year. By 1947, at the time of this photo, the company had over 2,400 employees and

Gerity, Jr., an ambitious businessman from Toledo, founded this company in a factory on Logan Street. Its business involved electroplating metal parts for the automotive and plumbing industries.

In 1938 Bohn decided to build a plant of its own just east of Magnesium Fabricators. The purpose of this plant, called Bohn #13, was to produce aluminum extrusions for other companies. It was open for business by 1939. That same year another company, Hurd Lock, moved into the old Adrian Knitting Mill on Michigan Avenue, where it

and the new industrial unions. The Wagner Act of 1935 strengthened the ability of industrial unions to organize, strike, picket, and have the federal government oversee the activities of both labor and management through the National Labor Relations Board. In Lenawee the United Automobile Workers of America became especially active. As early as 1937 locals were being organized at American Chain and Schwarze Electric. Management was not sympathetic, and the labor scene was quite lively through the rest of the 1930s. Gerity had disputes with labor, too, by 1939.

sales were reaching $35 million. Meanwhile, the community of Tecumseh was being transformed by this industrial giant growing on the south side of town. Courtesy, Tecumseh Area Historical Museum

Tom Frownfelder of Adrian served in the U.S. Army during World War II, and the Army Reserves upon his return home, where he achieved the rank of lieutenant colonel. He later went to work for Tecumseh Products serving as Credit Manager of the Service Division for many years. Courtesy, Lieutenant Colonel Retired Thomas Frownfelder

World War II

Between 1940 and 1945 Lenawee County would be asked to produce more and more for the war effort, until the county finally not only caught up to its 1929 level of activity, but actually surged ahead.

The most remarkable result of World War II and the postwar period was that Lenawee finally enjoyed a period of growth comparable to that of a century earlier. The statistics indicate how substantial the growth was. From 53,110 in 1940, the population grew to 64,629 in 1950—an increase of 28 percent, and the first time in 80 years that Lenawee had come close to the growth of

the 1860s. For once, too, the growth was not centered in Adrian. That city's population did grow from 14,230 in 1940 to 18,393 in 1950—a 29.3-percent increase—but the rest of the county grew at an equal pace. Tecumseh led the way here by growing from 2,921 in 1940 to 4,014 in 1950. One more statistical indication of Lenawee's growth in the 1940s was the jump in valuation of taxable property—from $56.6 million in 1940 to $120.5 million in 1950.

During the war a number of Lenawee companies were under considerable pressure to grow just because they were involved in critical war work. Hurd Lock was affected more than almost any other. In August 1942 Hurd Lock had 400 employees; by May 1943 it had grown to 1,600. A year later the company somehow managed to squeeze about 2,300 people into the old knitting mill on Michigan Avenue (of course, they did work three shifts around the clock six days a week). The basic operation of Hurd Lock was the manufacture of parts for antiaircraft shells, which it sold by the millions to the Navy.

Another company that produced antiaircraft shells was Tecumseh Products, whose number of employees grew to 1,600 by 1943. In addition to shells, Tecumseh Products produced parts for Rolls-Royce aircraft engines, tank armor-piercing shot, shells for the British armed forces, and depth-bomb parts.

A third major employer involved in war production was American Chain and Cable. Its work force expanded from 400 to 950 during the war. American Chain turned out heavy duty mechanical brake parts as well as brake assemblies for the armed forces.

As important as these companies and others were to the war effort, the roles of two others loomed still larger. They were Magnesium Fabricators and Bohn #13. Both of these plants were doing an excellent job making parts for the Air Force's medium- and long-range bombers, but as good as they were, the

Air Force needed more. Finally, the Air Force asked Bohn if it would run an even bigger aluminum extrusion plant if the government arranged to finance and build the plant itself. Who could turn down an offer like that? So, from April 1942 into the summer of 1943, the government's Defense Plant Corporation contracted the Krieghoff Company of Detroit to build a huge (750,000 square feet) state-of-the-art aluminum foundry and extrusion plant on East Beacher for $18 million. Once the plant was built, Bohn leased it from the Defense Plant Corporation, and its 1,200 employees built all sorts of parts for bombers like the B-17 and the B-29. At the same time Bohn #13 and Magnesium Fabricators on East Maumee had another 1,500 workers employed directly on all sorts of things for the War Department, especially for the Air Force.

Materials related to the war effort took on many forms, and so many Lenawee companies became involved. Michigan Producers in Adrian made powdered milk for the troops, while the 70 or 80 women at the Morenci Egg Dryers checked, cracked, dried, packed

and shipped 252,000 eggs per day. Meanwhile, the workers at the Clinton Woolen Mill kept on doing what they had been doing since 1902—making good blue woolen cloth for the Navy. Some companies hardly changed what they had been doing—they just did it all for the armed forces. Hardie Manufacturing in Hudson had been making high-pressure pumps for years. Now it sold its pumps to the Air Force for installation on airfields. Kewaunee did not change things much either; its labor force doubled from 250 to 500, but it otherwise kept on making lab

and hospital furniture.

All over the county, new and old plants went to extra shifts and hired new employees to keep up with the demand from the armed forces. The strain caused by this economic pressure led to the taxing to capacity of housing and dining facilities. The last time Lenawee had grown like this had been in the 1850s and 1860s when hundreds of Germans and Irish came here to seek good jobs. During World War II there was no access to foreign workers, so where did the thousands of new workers come from? Many of them

Victor and Maria Sanchez are considered to have been among the first Hispanics to settle in Adrian. Since the 1920s the Hispanic population has grown to about five percent of the total population. Much of this growth came after Bohn and other Adrian industries began employing Hispanics just before and during World War II. Courtesy, Lenawee County Historical Museum

FAR LEFT: James Gerity, Jr. (1904-1973) came to Adrian from Toledo in 1937 when he organized the Gerity-Adrian Manufacturing Corporation, a die casting business. Fellow businessmen in Adrian helped him to finance a new plant, and by World War II the company's 300 employees were busy producing armor plate, 20mm shot, and army cots. In 1956 Gerity sold his company to Hoover Ball and Bearing, and began a new career in the field of broadcasting. He is depicted here around 1937. Courtesy, Lenawee County Historical Museum

came from the households, offices, and restaurants of Lenawee. Wherever women could be found, they were sought out and exhorted to serve their country by doing war work. Hurd Lock alone employed 1,500 women. American Chain had well over 300, and 160 of Kewaunee's 500 employees were women. Actually, almost all the women who moved into war production served in Adrian factories. Outside Adrian the factories found enough men. Even Tecumseh Products, with its 1,600 employees, had only about 60 female workers.

Even with thousands of women going to work in the factories, Lenawee industries still needed more workers. As early as 1940 Magnesium Fabricators began to hire local

The armed forces claimed that the war plants could not operate if workers were not guaranteed adequate places to live and to eat. To its credit, the government did provide some new housing by constructing two new projects close to the Bohn factories. The largest of these was the Deerfield Temporary Housing Project on Mulzer Street just south of Beecher and east of Division Street. At first, only Bohn workers were permitted to live at Deerfield, but later all war workers and their families could live there. Before the apartments were demolished in the 1950s, a nice neighborhood had been established for a while at "the Project."

The second temporary housing project built by the government was a trailer camp

The Clinton Woolen Mill was a mainstay of the local economy from 1866 until it closed in 1957. During World War II, about the time this photo was taken, its 200 workers were producing good woolen cloth for the armed forces. Courtesy, Lenawee County Historical Museum

Mexican-Americans. This was the first time Mexican-Americans were hired for such jobs. Yet another source of wartime labor lay in the American South. A number of workers found their way to Michigan, and then to Lenawee, from Kentucky, Tennessee, and Alabama. After the war both the Hispanics and the Southerners stayed in large numbers, further enriching the local culture.

Locally, the pressure of the war years expressed itself mainly in the housing situation.

across from Simplex Paper at the corner of East Beecher and Treat Road. Eventually some 150 trailer units were located there. A third temporary housing project was built by Magnesium Fabricators. After bringing in Mexican-American families from Texas, room had to be found for them. So Magnesium Fabricators leased three buildings from the County Fair Board and housed a number of their workers at the nearby fairgrounds. The quarters here were crowded, poorly ventilated, and generally unattractive. Families moving to Adrian tended to get their start here, then to locate better housing on their own.

Somehow, with all the difficulty generated by the war, the people of Lenawee made it through—and wondered what would come afterward. What everyone dreaded was that, once the war ended, the good times would end, and the Depression would return.

The Postwar Period

For most Americans the decade after World War II turned out almost more prosperous than anyone had dared to imagine, and Lenawee shared in this prosperity fully. Again, the rise in assessed valuations (from $75 million in 1944 to $172.5 million in 1954) shows

how much the county was growing. Population figures for the 1950s tell a similar story, with an increase from 64,629 in 1950 to 77,789 in 1960. This 17-percent increase did not equal the 27-percent increase of the 1940s, but it was still remarkable for a county with Lenawee's long record of slow growth.

One interesting aspect to the increase of the 1950s was that much of it occurred outside Adrian. Adrian's population grew from 18,393 in 1950 to 20,347 in 1960, an increase of only 8.6 percent. It had been 120 years since the rest of the county had outpaced Adrian. Again, Tecumseh was responsible for much of the county's growth, rising from 4,014 in 1950 to 7,045 by 1960.

With all the difficulty generated by the Depression, residents of Lenawee continued to be creative in the enjoyment of their pastimes and careers. Caroline Loop Baldwin (1896-1981) was an avid gardener during her lifetime and was nationally known for her work in hybridizing delphiniums. She is depicted here around 1935 in her gardens in Adrian. Courtesy, Lenawee County Historical Museum

In 1946 Charles Hickman and Allen Goldsmith founded Brazeway, a refrigeration company. One of their manufacturing successes was the development of a self-centering core for a die which could be used to produce very small-sized, uniformly-shaped hollow aluminum tubing. By 1950 this die became the basis of their production for the refrigeration industry. In this 1963 photo, Goldsmith, on the right, holds a piece of extruded hollow aluminum tubing. Courtesy, David Hickman

Lenawee's growth and prosperity after the war were caused, in large part, by the considerable growth of two basic industries: automobiles and refrigeration/air conditioning. In the last year or so of the war, just about every company in Lenawee was aware of the pent-up demand for their normal peacetime products. Thus, when the war ended, they were ready to convert to peacetime production. American Chain and Cable, Kewaunee, Hurd Lock, and the agriculture-based industries all enjoyed growth after the war, as we shall see.

One company, Tecumseh Products, enjoyed spectacular growth. After the war orders poured into the company for refrigerator compressors, and Herrick took them all, plowing earnings back into the company and quadrupling the size of the plant between 1946 and 1950. By 1954 the company was producing 3.2 million compressors per year, almost 50 percent of all refrigeration compressors in the nation. In 1955, according to *Fortune* Magazine, Tecumseh Products was the nation's 248th-largest industrial corporation, with sales of $123 million, a net profit of $5.7 million, and more than 4,000 employees. Explaining how and why this company did so well, *Fortune* pointed to Ray Herrick: "He not only provided the phenomenal production skill and unrelenting drive of the undertaking, but he also is its outstanding entrepreneur."

Moreover, the company continued to look after its employees and its community. In 1948 Herrick announced plans to develop another housing subdivision with almost 200 lots. Each Products worker who qualified would get a lot for free and $200 to help finance his new home. Tecumseh Products and TRESCO, he also said, would give the Tecumseh School District $145,000 in cash to help build a new $400,000 high school if the district approved a bond issue and got the building started that same year.

In 1949 Ray Herrick formalized his philanthropic activities by establishing the Herrick Foundation. Since its fortunes were linked to the fortunes of the company, the foundation just kept growing until, by the 1980s, it was the fourth largest foundation in Michigan with assets well over $100 million. Since it gave a good share of its money each year to Tecumseh and Lenawee causes, practically every community would benefit in time from Herrick's generosity. The leading example in Lenawee would be Adrian College. It would receive $15 million during Ray Herrick's lifetime to redo and then enlarge the campus.

In addition to Tecumseh Products, several other companies involved in the refrigeration business developed in Lenawee after 1935. The first was Bohn Aluminum's Plant #13, which opened in Adrian in 1939, and whose purpose was to build refrigeration parts out of aluminum. During World War II employment grew to 500. After the war it benefited from the steady growth of the refrigeration business to such an extent that in 1950 Bohn decided to close down Magnesium Fabricators and convert that building into an extension of Bohn #13. By 1955 the combined plant employed 900 people, making aluminum refrigeration and air-conditioning products as well as aluminum extrusions.

A second plant, called REVCO (Refrigeration Engineering and Vending Company) opened in 1939. Two engineers, Howard White and Gregg Forsthoefel, began this company in Adrian after getting the financial backing they needed from the three owners of TRESCO, C.M. Brown, Jens Touborg, and

Frank Smith. REVCO was the first company to develop and market a vending machine for ice-cream cups.

The market for this vending machine was steadily growing when the war broke out. At this time the company moved into chilling and shrinking aircraft rivets. By 1943 REVCO needed much more space than it could find in Adrian, and so it moved to a 23,000-square-foot building in Deerfield. By this time the company was making refrigerated cabinets as well.

After the war the refrigeration business was good to REVCO. The company began to build chest freezers and then, in 1954, introduced a line of built-in refrigerators. This led to even more growth, and by 1962 REVCO had 650 employees. After that, however, business began to fade for the Deerfield plant, and in 1968 it was closed. All operations were consolidated in a plant in the South.

After World War II four more Lena-

In 1941 Alton McGehee and his partner, Max Sayre, began the M & S Company in Hudson. They produced automotive screw machine products, and over the next five decades the company continued to grow until it had 12 plants in Michigan and Ohio producing various screw machine products. As early as the 1950s M & S was becoming a mainstay of the Hudson economy with its many employees and its continuing support of worthwhile community projects. Sayre, left, and McGehee are seen here in 1955. Courtesy, Lenawee County Historical Museum

The Red Apple Restaurant in Morenci was a popular convivial dining spot. Seen here in the 1940s, this establishment served up meals for local residents, businesspeople, and farmers. Courtesy, Stair Public Library, Morenci, Michigan

wee companies got into the refrigeration business. Brazeway was one of them. It was founded in 1946 by Allan Goldsmith and Charles Hickman. They had been at Bohn #13, but in 1946 they began their own company to develop a discovery of theirs, which involved a new process for coupling copper and aluminum. Since its founding, Brazeway has been a mainstay of Lenawee's economy. The founders of the company also followed the path of Herrick and Sage by founding the Adrian Foundation in 1951. Since then the foundation has donated about $4 million to various community projects and organizations.

Another refrigeration company that began just after the war was Blissfield Manufacturing, founded by Orville Farver, former production manager at Tecumseh Products. This company made refrigeration units for air conditioners, dehumidifers, and bottle vending machines. Later Blissfield introduced another line of refrigeration units for egg cooling, dry cleaning, and medical equipment. Fire destroyed the plant in 1959, but a modern 230,000-square-foot factory was in place

within a year. By 1970 Blissfield Manufacturing had 230 employees.

The three owners of TRESCO—Brown, Smith, and Touborg—were responsible for the development of another Lenawee refrigeration company, called Primus, founded in Addison in 1949. V.C. Knight was brought in as part-owner and manager in 1951. In 1954 the name of the company was changed to Addison Products, and in 1955 the company expanded by building a new plant in Jonesville. In 1963 V.C. Knight bought out the original three owners.

Primore, another company in the Lenawee area involved in the refrigeration business, started out selling valves for refrigeration which were made by a company elsewhere. Soon the Adrian-based company began to manufacture air conditioners, and a related company, SEDCO, was set up to handle the engineering and sales involved. When Borg-Warner bought the manufacturing business, Primore continued to sell valves for refrigeration while SEDCO got into making pressure-relief valves for automobile air conditioners. These

In 1943 Orville Merillat was a U.S. Coast Guard ship's carpenter serving in the Pacific. In 1946 he and his wife, Ruth, took their wartime savings and started the Merillat Woodworking Company in Adrian. Over the next few years Merillat began to specialize in kitchen cabinets, and in 1953 the company built a much bigger plant designed to turn out each day enough cabinets for 14 kitchens. Courtesy, Merillat Industries, Adrian

two companies are still in business.

Although the refrigeration industries of Lenawee had become very important, the auto-related industries continued to hold their own as well. Schwarze Electric went through several different owners in the decade before 1955, finally changing its name to Faraday. American Chain, meanwhile, took on more

and more work, and by 1960 had over 1,000 employees in Adrian. Stubnitz-Greene also expanded during this period, as did Gerity-Adrian, Oliver Instrument, and Ervin Foundry.

In Hudson, M & S was founded in 1941 by A.B. McGehee and Max Sayre. By the end of the war their automatic screw machines had turned out millions of small parts, and the company had grown from 16 employees to 40 or 50. By 1955 M & S, with three divisions in Hudson and Morenci, had become a leading manufacturer.

Another auto-related company which began just before the end of the war, the Clinton Machine Company, was founded around 1944 when Don Thomas of Detroit moved his machine company from Detroit into the old electric light building in Clinton.

Rubber Products. This company closed down during the war due to scarcity of rubber, but from 1945 on enjoyed success and became the city's largest employer, with well over 200 employees. Even a disastrous fire in 1975 could not keep it down for long. With Parker Rustproofing, M & S, and Morenci Rubber all producing for the auto industry, it could be claimed that Morenci was more of a car town than Detroit!

No discussion of Lenawee's postwar man-

In 1955 Orville Merillat, right, put up an impressive display of his kitchen cabinets at the County Fair in Adrian. In the 1980s Merillat Industries boasted nine plants around the country and became the nation's leading producer of cabinetry for kitchen, bath, and home. Courtesy, Lenawee County Historical Museum

During the 1950s Clinton Machine (soon renamed to Clinton Engine) grew and prospered in spite of a 1953 fire that destroyed some of the plant. Its peak employment reached 800 before operations were moved to Iowa. In 1959 Thomas sold his plant to the Budd Company, and by the end of the 1970s Budd was employing 400 workers in Clinton, so the village retained its strong industrial character.

Yet a third auto-related manufacturing company founded in the 1940s was Morenci

ufacturing would be complete without noting what happened to the county's most impressive single factory—the 750,000-square-foot plant built by the Air Force in World War II for the manufacture of aluminum airplane parts. For a while after the war Bohn tried to manufacture aluminum window sashes there, but the plant was too big to operate profitably. Kaiser-Frazer took over part of the plant to use as a warehouse toward the end of the 1940s, but the Air Force was not satisfied with that. It decided to install some German extrusion presses, which it had received as war reparations, and Gerity-Michigan won a contract to manage the plant while the Air Force encouraged experimental work on heavy presses from around the country.

This never amounted to much, but then the Korean War got under way, and the Air Force realized it needed many more planes. Bohn got the contract to run the plant again, and in 1952 about 100 workers per month were added as Bohn tried to fill big orders for airplane parts. Bohn also added about 76,000 square feet on both ends and in front of the plant. The good times lasted as long as the Air Force needed more planes, but as soon as defense work slowed down toward the end of 1953, Bohn cancelled its lease. The government immediately looked for a new tenant, and at the end of 1953 it announced that Bridgeport Brass Company would take over the plant. Bridgeport ran the plant until the end of the 1950s.

In Hudson the Metalloy Foundry was founded in 1947. The Greater Hudson Industrial Group helped Richard and Nelson Berlin and Charles Gibbons get this company started. By the late 1950s Metalloy had 10 furnaces, 38 employees, and 73 solid customers for its aluminum, brass, and bronze castings.

Finally, one more small company should be mentioned. A carpenter named Orville Merillat came back from the war and decided to specialize in building kitchen cabinets. Between his savings and those of his wife, Ruth, they had $8,000, which they used to build a one-man carpentry shop on Springbook Avenue in Adrian. For eight years he remodeled Lenawee kitchens, and then in 1954 the Merillats decided to expand by building a new factory on West Beecher in Adrian. From now on they would do nothing but produce kitchen cabinets on an assembly-line basis. A manufacturer of prefabricated houses in Toledo would take all their cabinets, and so the 20 Merillat

employees would have plenty to do.

Not all of Lenawee's economic base thrived after the war, however. Hudson, for instance, lost two of its largest companies in the 1950s. The big Pet Milk plant closed down in 1956, and the Hardie Manufacturing plant followed in 1958. Happily, Metalloy bought the 110,000-square-foot Hardie plant in 1959 and announced plans to double employment within two years.

As for the railroads, the postwar period saw them withdrawing service. As early as 1936 the Cincinnati Northern was shrinking back from Jackson to Lenawee. All the railroads did big business during the war, but the 1950s were different. In 1954 the New York Central—successor to the Lake Shore and Michigan Southern—proceeded to end passenger service through Hudson (the last actual run was in 1956), and by 1963 the New York Central was tearing up its track west of Hudson. Five years later the tracks were gone west of Clayton. The lovely Hudson depot was torn down in 1970. Meanwhile, in Morenci the Ohio and Morenci line (formed from the old Toledo and Western) was abandoned in 1951. In 1956 the New York Central ran its last passenger train through Adrian. Since the Central's predecessor, the Michigan Southern, had been responsible for Adrian's growing in the first place, it truly seemed the end of an era.

Other industries that shrank during the 1950s were the agriculturally-based businesses. Pet Milk had been Hudson's largest employer as recently as 1949, but was gone by 1956. A few years later, in 1960, the historic Clinton Woolen Mill closed. In Morenci the United Milk Products Corporation closed in 1950, and in 1952 the Kellogg & Buck Feed and Grain Mill was turned into a grain elevator. Tecumseh was not immune to this development. The Quaker Oats macaroni plant closed in 1960 after 43 years of business. One agri-industry which kept on producing in

Lenawee during this time was the Michigan Milk Producers plant on East Maumee in Adrian.

Commerce and Banking

After the "bank holiday" of 1933, and through the rest of the 1930s, almost all of Lenawee's banks slowly regained strength. Commercial Savings Bank was typical. Its assets rose from $1.2 million in June 1933 to $2.7 million by 1940. Happily, during the 1940s and early 1950s all of Lenawee's banks grew much

the First State Savings Bank of Morenci to become the Bank of Lenawee County. Commercial Savings Bank of Adrian kept pace by absorbing the last private bank in the state, the Bank of Clayton, in 1953, and then consolidated holdings with the Bank of Addison. The Addison bank then became its first branch. Meanwhile, the United Savings Bank of Tecumseh was on its way toward becoming the largest bank in the county, and other banks were growing as well.

In the area of savings and loans, Ad-

While businesses were continuing to grow and thrive in the communities of Lenawee, businessmen enjoyed their time off by participating in various activities and clubs. This 1940s photo depicts the members of the Morenci Poker Club, a longtime institution that gathered together professional and businessmen in town. Courtesy, Stair Public Library, Morenci, Michigan

faster as the economy picked up. The postwar period saw a constantly-growing demand for consumer credit and mortgage loans. The housing industry boomed after World War II, and the banks (plus Adrian Federal Savings and Loan) could barely keep up with the demand.

In the early 1950s several financial institutions began to expand by adding branches or buying other banks. The Lenawee County Savings Bank started the county's first drive-in branch in 1953, and in 1956 merged with

rian Federal Savings and Loan Association (which had changed its name from Adrian Building and Loan in 1936) opened its first branch office in 1953. Tecumseh homeowners had been taking out mortgages with Adrian Federal since World War II, and so the first branch was opened in that community to accommodate Tecumseh customers. Over the next 25 years Adrian Federal would open five more branches in the area and change its name again. It would become 1st Federal Savings and Loan of Lenawee in 1969.

As for commerce, the 1940s and 1950s were the last good time for small family groceries like Westfall's on Comstock Street and Ramsay's on College Avenue, both in Adrian. The big chains like A & P, Wrigley's, and Kroger were too hard to compete with. Their parking lots, constant specials, wealth of merchandise temptingly laid out for the shoppers to select themselves, and mass advertising gave them a considerable advantage.

A new kind of communications business came along in the 1940s with the advent of a local AM radio station, WABJ, in November 1946. In 1965 WLEN joined the ranks with an FM station. It was at WABJ that Phil Donahue got his start in the broadcast business when, coming out of Notre Dame in 1957, he became news director in 1958. He stayed for about a year and then moved to Dayton, Ohio.

Local Government, Education, and Health Care

Not since the early part of the century had so many demands been made on professionals in education and health care as were made in the period after World War II. What was true for them was also true for those people trying to make local government workable, efficient, and fair. In all these areas the changes that came after 1945 were immense.

From the 1930s on, the increasing number of responsibilities faced by local governments—and the complexity and costs of these responsibilities—led communities to develop full-time professional staffs and to change their forms of government so as to allow professional managers to carry out their assignments under the supervision of elected councils. The community which moved farthest along these lines was Tecumseh. Between 1900 and the arrival of Tecumseh Products in 1934, that village had existed contentedly as a community of 2,400. The growth of the company led to the growth

of the village—to 4,000 by 1950 and 7,000 by 1960.

As far as Tecumseh government was concerned, all this new growth meant up to 40 miles of sewers and water lines, 40 miles of streets, and a new wastewater plant built in 1952. The police and fire departments also had to grow to service the larger town, and the people's rising expectations for government led to the growth of the recreation department as well. Ray Herrick helped here by buying the old Ford Mill on East Chicago in 1960 and giving it to the town for use as a community center.

To keep up with this growth, Tecumseh became a city in 1954, and that brought with it a new form of government involving a city manager monitored by an elected council. First Ed Nelson (1954-63) and then Cal Zorn (1963-85) served with distinction as city managers. Meanwhile, Harold Easton began serving as mayor in 1962, an office that he (with occasional absences) has occupied ever since.

Adrian switched to the council/city manager form of government in 1957, after 20 years of growth in city services had made it apparent that the old three-member city council (which included the mayor, chief of police, and director of public works) was no longer workable. This was due in part to the growth of utilities, which had begun in 1936 when the state ordered Adrian to build a sewage plant to curb pollution of the River Raisin. The quantity of water available also was a concern by 1940 due to the growth of the community. This led to the building of a dam on Wolf Creek in 1942 and a $300,000 water plant in 1943. After the war utility problems, including water pollution and sewer problems, continued to pester the city.

All of these concerns, and more, added to the work load and responsibilities of city government. Finally, in 1957 the people agreed to the manager-council form of government. Hudson had already adopted the new form of

In the 1930s Morenci's police force consisted of one friendly man, Peter Stetten, who had been a blacksmith for many years prior. This photo shows Green's Mobil Oil Station with a vintage gasoline pump and to its right the Morenci city hall fire station, built in 1888, with its distinctive towers. Courtesy, Stair Public Library, Morenci, Michigan.

government in 1956.

In education, consolidation of local school districts—one of the most significant postwar trends in American education—began in Lenawee in 1948, lasting until 1966. The development was complicated, painful for all those who loved the old one-room schools, and sometimes quite controversial. It helped that Lenawee's County Superintendent of Schools through this period was Milton Porter. A conservative man who loved the old schools, Porter nonetheless knew that larger schools had to be built for the sake of the children. In the end 187 separate school districts had consolidated into only 12.

Once the districts were bigger, they needed larger facilities for all the new children going to school. Also, since the whole point of consolidation was a higher-quality edu-

cation, these new facilities had to have good libraries, labs, and shops. Onsted was typical in having 21 one-room school districts join into the Onsted Consolidated District. The number of students increased from 368 in 1944 to 1,713 by 1976. With this many students, Onsted could offer commercial, technical, and college-bound programs, and could afford to acquire and maintain the necessary buses and lunch programs as well.

Again, Tecumseh probably provides the most dramatic example of change and progress during this time. By the mid-1940s the village had grown so much that classes were being held in the basement of the library and in several churches. In 1949 the voters of the village approved construction of a new high school. Then, in the mid-1950s, 19 rural districts merged into the Tecumseh School District. Voters soon approved an ambitious building program, and new elementary schools were built at Tipton, Herrick Park, Tecumseh Acres, and Macon while schools at Ridgeway and Patterson got additions. The old 1918 high school was converted into a junior high school in 1958 to improve the total program even more.

Adrian embarked on a similar program of growth during the 1950s. Three new elementary schools—Prairie, Michener, and Alexander—were built along with a new high school. In 1947, however, when Madison asked to merge into the Adrian system, Adrian had to turn down the idea because it was experiencing growth pains of its own. This led Madison to build a new grade school on Treat Road in 1949, and a new high school in 1957. Enrollment in the new Madison School District rose from 197 (kindergarten through eighth grade) in 1945 to 1,055 (through 12th grade) in 1960.

Health care was another area where Americans felt the need after the war for better facilities and better-trained experts. By 1971 Lenawee could boast of five new hospi-

In 1957, the health community welcomed the new 128-bed Bixby Hospital on Riverside Avenue in Adrian. In the days of the baby boom the old hospital often had 90 patients a day, but only 68 beds. Rapid technological changes in medicine over the years required Bixby Hospital to expand. In 1965 the Fisk-Palmer Wing was added to the facility bringing the bed count up to 254. Courtesy, Lenawee County Historical Museum

tals. Considering that the county's population was only 81,500 in 1970, having this number of hospitals was rather surprising. Two reasons for this spate of hospital construction were community pride and the generosity of Ray Herrick.

In Tecumseh, Herrick gave money and led the first fund drive to build a hospital in 1937. The hospital opened in 1938. In 1941 a new wing was added, and in 1950 Herrick donated $80,000 for another addition. Later gifts, of $81,000 and then $250,000, allowed the hospital to expand further during this decade. The community, in recognition of this generous man and his family, named the facility Herrick Hospital.

Meanwhile, in both Hudson and Morenci, the local hospitals were ordered closed by state authorities in 1960—for health reasons in the one and fire reasons in the other. In Hudson Herrick donated $250,000 for a new facility. After the community raised another $100,000 or so, Thorn Hospital opened in 1961 in a new limestone-clad building on North U.S. 127. In Morenci the story was the same, except that here Herrick gave $330,000 while the local community raised another $160,000. The result, a new 25-bed hospi-

tal, opened in 1961. In 1968 an addition of 12 rooms made this a 38-bed hospital.

A fourth Lenawee hospital to prosper after the war was Addison's. Its hospital dated back to 1921, when Dr. Bowers Growt got the first community hospital started in this small village. Further changes and additions came along in 1925, 1940, and 1958. Then, in 1971, a new 25-bed hospital was dedicated.

The story of the Emma L. Bixby Hospital in Adrian is quite similar to the story of the others. It expanded considerably just before World War II thanks to a grant from the Public Works Administration. This added new operating and delivery rooms, an emergency room, and 14 new beds. In 1942 a radiology department was added, and a new x-ray unit came along in 1952. By the 1950s, however, it was clear that the hospital was too small for all the demands placed upon it. Unfortunately, there was not enough room for expansion in its location near downtown. Thus, in 1955 a new building on Riverside Avenue was begun. The new hospital was completed in 1957. In 1965 a major new addition, the Fisk-Palmer Wing, was completed, bringing Bixby to a total of 254 beds.

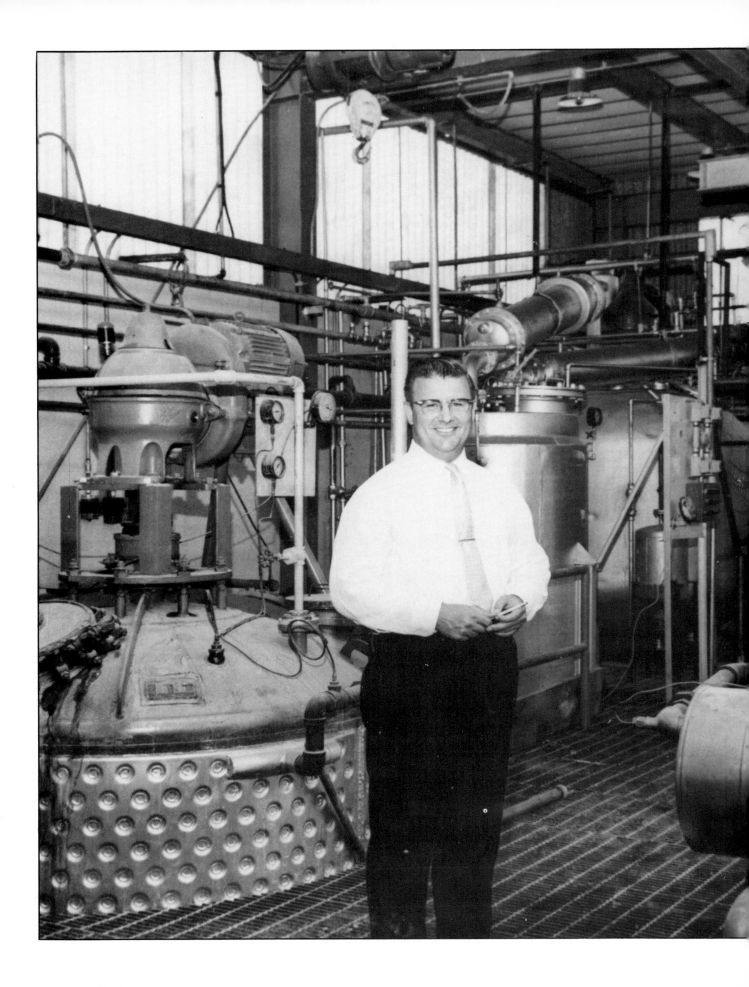

CHAPTER SIX

INTO THE PRESENT

1 9 5 5 - 1 9 9 0

In the last 35 years Lenawee has continued to grow and thrive. While a crude measure, the valuation of taxable property over the years does provide an indicator of how a society is doing. In the case of Lenawee, the valuation of taxable property grew from $241.7 million in 1961 to just over $1 billion by the late 1980s. This included some impressive inflationary jumps—especially in the 1970s—but the growth of real wealth was substantial nonetheless.

It was true, however, that Lenawee did not grow particularly fast during this period. From 1960 to 1970, for instance, the population rose only from 77,268 to 81,951. This amounted to an increase of about 5 percent, lower than during the Great Depression. By 1980, though, the population had risen to 89,948, almost a 10-percent increase. Compared to the growth of the previous period, this was not impressive, but it indicated a society capable not only of sustaining itself, but of growing. The fact that per capita income grew from $4,882 in 1973 to $9,523 in 1981 also indicated substantial growth.

The reason for growth during this period lay in Lenawee's remaining the manufacturing economy it had become by midcentury. By 1950, 40 percent of Lenawee employees had jobs in the manufacturing sector, amounting to 9,350 jobs. In 1969 Lenawee ranked as the 13th largest manufacturing county in the state with 14,100 workers in manufacturing. A dozen years later, in 1981, the manufacturing sector of the economy accounted for 48 percent of Lenawee workers' earnings— the eighth largest percentage in the state. The average in Michigan was about 40 percent, so Lenawee was markedly more industrial than most Michigan counties.

For many people who travel through Lenawee and know the county well, these figures seem at odds with Lenawee's reputation as a remarkably thriving and prosperous rural county. Everywhere one sees prosperous farms, and that is no illusion. In 1980, for instance, Lenawee ranked sixth in the state of Michigan in terms of dollars earned from marketing agricultural goods. Lenawee farmers earned $101 million that year alone. Throughout the postwar era, moreover,

Amos R. Anderson started several successful businesses beginning in 1946 with Anderson Laboratories in Adrian. In 1952 the firm moved to Weston, and this photo, taken in 1958, shows Anderson in front of equipment for a new patented chemical manufacturing process to make chewable aspirin. Courtesy, Anderson Development Company, Adrian

Lenawee farmers ranked in the top five in the state in the production of important crops like corn, winter wheat, and soybeans, and were near the top in the production of cattle and sheep.

In spite of these impressive figures, however, Lenawee was becoming less and less rural every year. The percentage of earnings derived from the agricultural sector tells the story of the declining importance of farming. In 1971 the percentage of earnings from agriculture in Lenawee amounted to 4.66 percent; by 1981 it was down to 2.75 percent. There were 37 counties in Michigan where farmers produced a greater percentage of overall earnings that year than Lenawee farmers did—even though it was true, at the same time, that only four or five counties actually produced more wealth from farming. The difference lay in the much greater amount of wealth produced by the manufacturing sector in Lenawee than in most other Michigan counties.

The development of the manufacturing sector after 1955 continued along the lines begun before World War II. The automobile and the refrigeration industries remained primary; Tecumseh Products, Blissfield Manufacturing, Addison Products, Brazeway, Bohn, and Sedco all continued as vital parts of the local economy. REVCO, unfortunately, chose to close completely in Lenawee in the mid-1960s in favor of Southern locales. Also, while both Brazeway and Tecumseh Products continued to grow and prosper, they did not grow in Lenawee. The county remained as the corporate headquarters for both companies and they continued to operate important plants here, but much of their new growth occurred elsewhere in the country.

It must be added immediately, though, that even if Tecumseh Products did grow elsewhere, the company also located one of its main non-compressor companies here in 1964. That company was Peerless Gear,

which manufactures transmissions and transaxles for lawn mowers and other small-motored products. The Peerless plant in Clinton became one of the largest plants in Lenawee, with 300 employees by 1976 and well over 500 by 1988.

Bohn Aluminum also did not grow much in Lenawee after 1955, but its Plant #13 continues to be of importance to the present day. Special mention should be made of the vast plant built by the federal government during the Second World War and operated by Bohn. In 1960 Bridgeport Brass, operator of the plant, suddenly indicated it would not continue operations in Adrian. The government decided to sell the plant, and

put out an invitation for bids. Much to the consternation of the local community, the high bid came from Strom Machinery of Hammond, Indiana, a well-known salvage firm. Strom's plan, it was feared, was to tear the plant down and sell it off as scrap. Harvey Aluminum, a West Coast manufacturer of aluminum equipment, had the second highest bid.

The Adrian community—led by Mayor Roy McPhail—appealed to the government to reject this bid. Senator Philip Hart and Congressman George Meader took up the cause of the plant with the General Services Administration, which was persuaded in December 1960 to reject initial bids. When

bids were opened a second time in February 1961, the salvage firm's bid was high again.

In March 1961, however, President Kennedy told the GSA to consider only those bids for the Adrian plant which came from companies planning to use the facility. When bids were opened for a third time, in April 1961, Harvey Aluminum was the only company that submitted a bid, and so it got the plant for $3.5 million. Harvey Aluminum went on to operate the plant throughout the 1960s. In 1972 Harvey became part of the Martin Marietta company, but it continued to operate in Adrian until the mid-1970s.

Once again, then, this wonderful facility lay idle for some time. Meanwhile,

In 1975 downtown Hudson was declared a National Historic District. This photo, from the early 1950s, looks east on Main Street and features the north side of W. Main. The 1894 Masonic Temple, second building from left, is a fine example of the French Second Empire style. East of that are three good examples of commercial Italianate buildings dating back to the 1860s and 1870s. Courtesy, Lenawee County Historical Museum

Norman Haft, the mayor of Adrian during much of the 1970s, got busy (along with the Chamber of Commerce and others) to find a new operator. In 1976 the largest industrial corporation in the world, General Motors, announced its intentions to take over the plant—to the delight of the entire Lenawee community.

In the other vital element in the industrial sector, the automobile parts industry, there was even more volatility. In Adrian, Gerity-Michigan was sold in 1956 to Hoover Ball and Bearing of Ann Arbor. In 1964 Hoover sold Gerity's 1940 plant on East Beecher to the Dura Corporation. Happily, Dura has continued to manufacture at this plant ever since. Another major employer in this field, Stubnitz-Greene, did

not last so long. It merged with Hoover Ball and Bearing in 1964, becoming the Stubnitz Spring Division of that company. Over 800 employees stayed busy at this company making automobile seat assemblies until the plant was closed in 1982. Another big employer in the automobile business, American Chain and Cable, did not shut down in Adrian, but its work force in the 1980s was a mere shadow of what it had once been, down from more than 1,000 employees to less than 200. At least it was still here, however, and it still employed a considerable number of people.

That could not be said of Hurd Lock. After the war Hurd went back to making locks for the auto industry, but in 1967 the plant was closed down entirely. Later, in

1985, the building itself was razed. Another significant auto parts manufacturer in the county, Clinton Engines, moved to Iowa in 1963.

On the positive side, however, almost all of the companies outside Adrian seemed to be fairly stable. This was certainly true of the firms in Hudson. M & S kept growing all through this period, and Metalloy also grew substantially. Since both firms employed up to 500 workers, their importance to the Hudson community was obvious. M & S was joined in the manufacture of screws by another firm, RIMA. This firm started up in 1955, grew until it needed a brand-new plant in 1978, and then grew some more. By 1988 RIMA had 160 employees. In the late 1980s yet another auto parts manufacturing firm was founded. This was KECY Products, a stamping and welding company, and a joint venture between Hudson's Donaldson Company and the Kitsuda Engineering Company of Japan. Kitsuda was the first Japanese firm to settle in Lenawee.

Meanwhile, Morenci Rubber Products remained the largest employer in Morenci.

Since 1969 the Adrian Mall has attracted shoppers with its fine stores, many special events, displays, and its feeling of energy, life, and fun. The fountain at the center of the mall has always been particularly attractive to children, as this photo from the mid-1980s shows. Courtesy, Adrian Mall Management

With its tall columns and massive pediment, the Bank of Lenawee building has always been considered one of the handsomest in the county. This view is taken from an old post-card photo of about 1910. Today the build-ing looks just the same as it did then. Courtesy, Lenawee County Histori-cal Museum

Parker Rust Proof also continued until 1989, when it shut its doors. After 60-some years in Lenawee, the loss of this firm was par-ticularly sad. In Clinton, the departure of Clinton Engines was compensated by the Budd Company's buying the facility and continuing to produce auto-related products. When Budd closed in the early 1980s (a very bad time for the industry nationwide), it took a few years for another company to take its place. In 1985, though, the Libby-Owens-Ford Company of Toledo took over the plant and added 200 workers to the Lenawee economy.

One more change was a plus for Tecumseh—though not for Adrian. This in-volved the old Schwarze Company, which had become Faraday in the 1940s. In 1961 the Tecumseh Industrial Development Agency

made an offer to build a new plant if Fara-day moved to Tecumseh. In 1962 it made the move, and it has been an important em-ployer there ever since.

The coming of General Motors to the county was another major development in the automobile sector of the Lenawee economy after 1955. In 1964 GM announced plans to build a new plant in Raisin Township near Tecumseh. Once the plant was operating at capacity, it employed 1,000 people and more. Together with the Air Force plant taken over in 1976, GM employed 1,500 people and had a combined payroll of $44 million. The presence of GM was partly responsible for Lenawee's growth in the 1970s.

Unfortunately, during a national cutback in production by GM, the Tecumseh plant was eliminated in 1987. The loss of the 1,000 jobs to the local economy was difficult to absorb, but the coming of a major new Japanese auto parts producer, Lenawee Stamping, reduced the harshness of the blow to some extent. Lenawee Stamping only began operations in 1989, but the promise of an eventual 300 to 400 jobs was heartening after the loss of GM-Tecumseh. There was the promise,

too, of an exciting new venture in the production of smaller engines for automobiles by an Australian firm, Orbital, in the plant vacated by GM-Tecumseh.

Lenawee had other types of industry as well. One was the furniture manufacturing business, and Kewaunee and Merillat were the two major companies in this field. In the 1980s Kewaunee joined the migration of companies to the South, closing its Adrian plant in 1984. The loss of Kewaunee, with its 300-plus jobs, came soon after the closing of Stubnitz-Hoover Ball and Bearing and the reduction of jobs at American Chain and Cable. For Adrian and the county, the loss of about 2,000 jobs at these three companies—plus the loss of another 1,000 jobs at GM-Tecumseh—made the 1980s a very difficult time.

The other major local furniture manufacturer, Merillat Industries, continued to grow in a steady fashion after the opening in 1954 of the new plant on West Beecher in Adrian. By the 1980s Merillat had 2,600 workers in nine plants around the country, although the Adrian plant remained at some 400 workers.

While the field of kitchen cabinets seemed as bright as ever as Merillat Industries entered the 1980s, the owners of the company, Orville and Ruth Merillat, were becoming more and more involved in an entirely different activity—philanthropy. Both of them already were very active in their church, and in 1985 they sold their company to Masco Industries of Detroit and became even more involved in charitable activities. Adrian College was a primary recipient in Lenawee County, with millions going into its Merillat Sport and Fitness Center, which opened in January 1990. However, the most remarkable recipient was a new creation called Lenawee Christian School. As it grew on the west side of Adrian in the later 1980s, the campus of this school, teaching preschool through 12th grade, demonstrated the remarkable commitment of the Merillats to their faith and its educational concerns.

For a county with only 90,000 people, it was extraordinary to have not only the massive Herrick Foundation and the very significant Sage Foundation, both of Tecumseh, but the Merillat Foundation as well. Lenawee had reason to be grateful that the old-time values of sharing and civic duty were alive and well in its community.

Another important business was chemical manufacturing. In Lenawee, much of this business was the work of a graduate of the old Clayton High School, Amos Anderson. Like the Merillats and the founders of Brazeway, Goldsmith and Hickman, Anderson started his business, Anderson Laboratories, in 1946. He founded it next to his father's

The Honorable Rex B Martin served as Lenawee Circuit Court judge from 1953 to 1982. There was never a more able or popular judge in Lenawee history. Few of his decisions were overruled by higher courts, and the public appreciated having this friendly, judicious man in a position of such importance. The county's new judicial building was named the Rex B Martin Judicial Building to honor him upon his retirement in 1982. This painting was created in 1985 by Thomas Thiery of Onsted. Courtesy, Lenawee County Circuit Court

After Zaragosa and Herminia Vargas moved to Lenawee County from Texas in 1948, they made sure their children stretched their minds and went as far as they could in school. This photo shows Olga Vargas, their daughter, when she became the first Hispanic homecoming queen in the history of Adrian High. Later, after graduating cum laude from Adrian College, Olga became a teacher in the language arts division at Springbrook Middle School, Adrian. Courtesy, Olga Vargas

FAR RIGHT: Sister Ann Joachim (1901-1981) was considered to be one of the most remarkable women from the Adrian Dominicans. She joined the order in 1928 and as a practicing attorney, served as legal counsel for the congregation throughout her long career. In 1936 she became the first nun in America to be admitted to practice law before the U.S. Supreme Court. Courtesy, Lenawee County Historical Museum

lumber business in Adrian. By the early 1950s Anderson had outgrown both this plant and a second one east of Adrian. Anderson's third plant was a former dairy company building in the village of Weston, between Adrian and Morenci.

In the 1950s Anderson began work in a new field of chemicals involving silicon. To attain the capital needed for this activity, Anderson approached Stauffer Chemical of New York to take over Anderson in 1958. Within a few years Anderson had so impressed Stauffer with the potential of silicon chemistry that the company decided to build a big new plant in Raisin Township. Anderson ran the plant until 1966 when he sold his interests. Stauffer continued to run this modern facility until it was acquired by Wacker Chemie A.G. of West Germany.

In 1966 Anderson began another firm, Anderson Development Co., which also became an innovative leader in the field of industrial chemistry. Unhappily, this company became involved for a serious environmental problem involving one of its products, curene. In 1979 the federal government declared curene a carcinogen, and some samples of the

chemical were discovered in Adrian outside the plant. This led to several years of arduous cleaning of the plant and the surrounding neighborhood (right down to removing topsoil from the schoolyards) to remove any traces of the chemical from the area. While this was going on, Anderson stopped producing curene while continuing to manufacture less contentious products. The company also kept on working on development of new products such as activated carbon. In 1988 Anderson sold Anderson Development to Mitsui Toatsu Chemicals of Japan while retaining an interest in an offshoot of the company, called Interamerican Zinc.

The chemical industry in Lenawee included other people besides Amos Anderson.

Another leader in the field was Dr. Lorene Patterson. Her firm was called Drug Research, Inc. Patterson, who founded it in 1949, continues at the helm to the present day. In the early 1960s Patterson was honored for her work in the production of cortisone. She has been best known, however, for finding safe and effective ways to use bromine as in the purification of swimming pools.

In the paper products business, another

prominent Lenawee industry, the earliest company in this field was Simplex Paper. Since 1919 Simplex has manufactured paperboard, first in Adrian and then also in a mill in Palmyra. With 200-plus employees, it has long been an important part of Lenawee's economy. In Tecumseh a much newer firm, Tecumseh Corrugated Box, got started in 1963. By the mid-1970s it already had 250 employees manufacturing corrugated and solid fiber boxes. Meanwhile, in Adrian, Uarco had a modern plant and over 100 workers turning out modern business forms such as those used with computers.

From Downtown Storefronts to Shopping Malls

With Lenawee's economy growing so substantially in the post-1955 period, it stands to reason that Lenawee's merchants would benefit. This proved to be the case, but it involved major changes in the way they attracted customers. Although Lenawee had a wealth of historic downtowns in its communities, they had been built long before the automobile. By the 1950s Lenawee's downtowns—especially Adrian's—experienced problems with congestion, lack of display space, parking, and the customer's increasing desire to shop from his or her car if possible.

In the 1960s new shopping centers began to emerge on routes leading into the various towns or downtowns. The first of these, the Adrian Plaza, opened just west of downtown on West Maumee in July 1961. Grant's and the A & P were its major tenants. It was followed in 1964 by the Southland Plaza Shopping Center on South Main in Adrian. The Tempo Department Store and a Kroger grocery store were this center's major tenants. Meanwhile, much of South Main from Beecher to Highway 223 a mile away was turning into an extended shopping district filled with car lots and smaller businesses.

The ultimate in these new commercial centers was an enclosed shopping center, and Adrian Mall addressed that need when it opened in 1969. On the outside it had no appeal architecturally, but acres of free parking spaces beckoned to the shopper in an appealing way. In the 1980s another major store, Elder-Beerman, would also build in the Adrian Mall to further add to the appeal of this shopping center.

The impact of these new commercial developments on the historic downtowns was of considerable interest. The downtowns

In 1955 Dr. John Dawson, right, president of Adrian College, and businessman Ray Herrick formed a partnership to improve, expand, and revitalize the school. Seen here in 1967 is the dedication ceremony for the new Herrick Tower erected at the east end of the campus mall. Courtesy, Shipman Library, Adrian College

contained many of Lenawee's most attractive and historic buildings, and many people had wonderful memories of "going downtown" to shop. What was going to happen to these areas if the department stores, variety stores, car agencies, and so on moved elsewhere? What would take their places?

Gradually, it became apparent that some businesses still found downtowns useful. First, some traditional firms like Kline's

Department Store in Adrian and Martin's Home Center in Tecumseh found ways to maintain customer traffic. Second, many businesses that had occupied the second and third floors of downtown buildings historically now moved down to the first floor. These were the lawyers, doctors, dentists, insurance agents, accountants, and other professional people. They saw their clients one at a time, and thus had no great need for a lot of

parking space. A third kind of business that began to appear involved consumer goods of a more specialized nature than the mass marketers sold. Tecumseh's downtown by the 1980s was an example of this with its design shops, antique malls, chocolate shops, and restaurants.

Finally, newer businesses like video and novelty stores were more apt to start up downtown than in the malls because of

lower rent. Altogether, it did seem as though the historic downtowns were going to endure after all.

New Residential Patterns

Changes in housing can affect a community socially, economically, and politically, and Lenawee saw some developments of this sort after 1955. Primarily, this involved new growth in the northern half of the county. First, the open space between Adrian and Tecumseh and between Tecumseh and Clinton began to fill up. Beginning in the 1970s, residential growth in the delightful Irish Hills was on an upward swing. As might be expected, the growth centered on new developments around the many lakes in Cambridge Township, including Dewey, Washington, and a new man-made lake, Loch Erin.

Much of this new growth came from retirees, or particularly from commuters. Some county residents would drive as far as Detroit or Flint for their work each day so that their families could live in the peace and quiet of rural Lenawee. In the 1980s this interest in living in Lenawee, while working elsewhere, began to extend into the northeast part of the county as well. Clinton, Tecumseh, and Macon Township began to feel pressure from the prosperous Washtenaw County just to the northeast. The Devil's Lake area in the Irish Hills also began to feel this pressure. Devil's Lake, of course, had been a popular summertime resort and cottage area since the late nineteenth century, but now property owners saw Devil's Lake as their year-round home, from which they commuted 60 miles or more to work.

Since these residents were in Lenawee for its peace and quiet, they tended to be unappreciative of the growth possibilities of large-scale industry or commerce in their area. The outstanding example of this attitude came in the mid-1970s when the major

As college officials planned for expansion of Adrian College in the 1960s, the new chapel, dedicated in 1964, was of special importance on the Methodist campus. As this photo from the mid-1960s shows, one way of demonstrating the significance of the chapel was by creating a pedestrian mall leading to the chapel at the west end of campus. Within the 1,000-seat chapel is a unique series of windows depicting the central doctrines and history of Christianity. Courtesy, Shipman Library, Adrian College

A production of My Fair Lady, *seen here in August 1977 at the Croswell revealed the Lenawee community's investment of time, energy and money in the old opera house. Courtesy, The Croswell Opera House and Fine Arts Association*

amusement park company, Cedar Point, announced plans to develop another amusement park in the heart of the Irish Hills on M-50. This led many people in Cambridge Township to join together to fight the project. In this effort they were completely successful.

This trend continued in the 1980s—especially in the latter half of the decade, when several new projects were proposed.

locate a low-level nuclear waste site. However these battles turned out, it was clear that the climate of opinion in Lenawee was opposed to large developments being established recklessly.

Government Expands Its Role

In addition to change and growth in municipal government in the period after 1935 (discussed in the last chapter), county government also began to take on new dimensions

The first was a coal-fired cogeneration plant proposed for the Wacker (originally Stauffer) Chemical plant location. Many residents of Raisin Township tried to stop this. In 1989 a similar battle was fought just north of Tecumseh to prevent a gravel-pit operation from being developed in and near residential areas. As the year came to a close, the biggest battle of all loomed in the offing. The state suggested that Riga Township, a prime agricultural area, might be a good place to

after World War II. By the 1950s the historic jail was so clearly inadequate in terms of space and facilities that it was condemned. A new jail was opened in 1953, and then a major addition was constructed in 1974.

Meanwhile, the business of the circuit court increased constantly. Rex B Martin served ably as circuit-court judge from 1953 to 1982, but by the late 1960s he was finding it increasingly difficult to handle all the business coming to his court. Thus, in 1977 a second circuit court judge was provided for Lenawee County. Also, the historic position of justice of the peace was phased out in 1968 in favor of two district courts.

By the 1960s the old courthouse, built in 1884, was bulging at the seams. One way of handling the problem was to encourage countywide agencies like the County Superintendent of Schools, the Road Commission, and the Extension Offices to establish offices

in the 1970s. The county used three years' worth of funds from that source to construct a new building for the law courts and their attendant offices. It was opened in 1979, and it was named the Rex B Martin Judicial Building in 1982. The county renovated its historic courthouse in the 1970s to serve as an office building for county departments and meeting place for the commissioners.

The county also saw its traditional func-

One of the necessary strengths of the Croswell Opera House has been the development of a cadre of talented and experienced players who have been able and willing to devote the time and energy to making plays and musicals work. This rehearsal shot is from the 1980 production of You Can't Take It With You. *Courtesy, The Croswell Opera House and Fine Arts Association*

elsewhere. Nevertheless, the old courthouse was still filled to capacity. Throughout the 1960s the county commissioners and the Adrian city commissioners worked on plans for a joint city-county building. Finally, though, the city despaired of the county's will to proceed, and in 1970 tore down its historic city hall in order to build a new one, which opened in 1972. The county's problems did not go away until an important new source of revenue, federal revenue sharing, appeared

tion of serving the aged and the needy increase in terms of responsibilities, staff, and numbers served. The nineteenth-century home for the aged was replaced in 1970 by the Lenawee Medical Care Facility building. The Social Services Department increased its capabilities to help the poor, and in the 1970s the county also took on the responsibility of helping the mentally ill as well. Also, the county's public health department added environmental health concerns to its sanitation and nursing tasks. In the 1970s Lenawee became one of the first counties in Michigan to bring all these agencies together into one building and one Human Services division.

Changes occurred even at the top, with the old Board of Supervisors (which tended to represent rural interests more than urban interests) giving way in the 1960s to a smaller Board of Commissioners whose members each represented thousands of people with urban concerns as well as a minority with strictly rural interests.

Municipal and village governments took much the same path as county government after 1955. Adrian, in particular, took on new responsibilities. In the 1970s a citywide bus system was developed, and a program was established to provide low-cost loans to homeowners of limited means so that they could improve their houses. Meanwhile, the city's Parks and Recreation Department evolved into the Community Services Agency. In addition to sponsoring athletic activities for men and women, the agency also provided a wide range of classes in an adult education program. In the early 1970s, moreover, it took over the now-closed Catholic Central High School and turned it into a splendid facility—renamed the Piotter Center after the late mayor of Adrian, "Duke" Piotter—for classes, meals, and activities for the aged.

The city's parks program took on new life during this period as well. Part of this resulted from the acquisition of a 370-acre farm north of Adrian, which the city named Heritage Park. Beyond this new park, the first sizable one in the city's history, the parks program benefited from the Harriet Kimball Fee Estate Trust. By 1970, after several court challenges to the will of Fee, member of an old Adrian family, the city was able to benefit from this estate, then worth several million dollars. By the mid-1980s the estate was worth $10 million and climbing. With the income from this estate the city was able to

hire a professional forester to manage the trees in this city—whose nickname, after all, was "the Maple City"—and was able to beautify all its parks throughout Adrian.

The Schools Reach Out

Reorganization of the 12 consolidated school systems continued into the 1960s. An indication of the importance of this development can be seen from the number of high-school graduates. In 1950 about 37 percent of residents over 25 years of age had graduated

from high school. By 1970 the percentage was up to 54 percent, and by 1980 it had grown to almost 68 percent. That represented an enormous investment in the education of all of Lenawee's youth. Clearly, though, there were still many who had not been reached.

Meanwhile, the 12 districts realized that for some students proper education necessitated that all 12 districts act together. Working with the County Superintendent of Schools, they began to reach out to the physically and mentally handicapped. As early as 1948 the schools collected money to pay for several teachers for homebound students and then for several speech teachers. In 1959 schooling for the handicapped went to a new level when the voters approved a permanent 0.5-mill charter tax for special education. Ten years later an even bigger 1.5-mill tax for special education was approved.

Meanwhile, an attractive campus for special education began to develop on Sutton Road in Raisin Township. Funded by a grant from Ray Herrick, it was called the Lenawee

The Adrian Carnegie Library, which always looked particularly attractive when garbed in ivy, provided the community with a wide variety of literature between 1909 and 1978. When the Lenawee County Historical Society took over the building and restored it in 1979, the ivy came down as it tends to hasten deterioration of bricks and mortar. The building has been on the National Register of Historic Places since 1976, and received the second largest National Register restoration grant ever given in Michigan. Courtesy, Lenawee County Historical Museum

Institute at first; later the name was changed to the Milton C. Porter Education Center to honor the retired County Superintendent of Schools. Students included the severely mentally impaired, the trainable mentally impaired, the deaf, the orthopedically handicapped, and the preschool physically handicapped.

In the mid-1960s the 12 systems began to work with the Intermediate School District (successor to the office of the County Superintendent of Schools) to form a countywide vocational educational center. The Lenawee Vo-Tech Center, on M-52 just north of Adrian, opened in the fall of 1970. Students from all 12 high schools in the county came for half-day sessions to take classes such as auto mechanics, farm-machinery mechanics, the building trades, data processing, horticulture, office skills, printing, child care, and other technical and commercial subjects.

In addition to growth and new departures in public education, the county also saw some ambitious private ventures in K-12 education. The first was the establishment of Adrian Catholic Central High School in 1954. Both Catholic parishes in Adrian, St. Mary's and St. Joseph's, joined together to form this school. The high school was built alongside St. Mary's Church on Erie Street. For 15 years—before it succumbed to the considerable financial burden such a private school places on its supporters—it provided a Catholic education through high school. The second major venture into private education, Lenawee Christian School, built an attractive educational complex in 1985 for its entire K-12 school of some 700 students. Declining enrollments, however, led to the closing of the high school portion of St. Joseph's Academy for Girls in 1975.

The period after 1955 led to important changes at both of the private colleges in Adrian. In the spring of 1949 Adrian College graduated its largest class ever with 75 graduates, and its enrollment during this time was over 500. After the outbreak of the Korean War in 1950, however, the school began to lose some of its male students because of the uncertainty of the draft. Also, the school's aging buildings made the college seem less desirable to many young students, male and female alike, who saw newer and nicer campuses springing up elsewhere. Enrollment dropped rapidly. By the spring of 1954 there were only 26 graduates.

When a young alumnus, Dr. John Dawson, took over as president in 1955, his problems included an aged campus, almost no endowment, a small enrollment, limited accreditation, and a struggling fund-raising effort. His assets included a good staff, loyal alumni, and a long history of good education. Soon Dawson added another important asset in the person of Ray Herrick, who took on the revival of the college as a personal challenge. By 1963 the school had built 17 new buildings thanks to his generosity, and the college was growing as it never had before. By 1958 enrollment was back to the late-1940s level of 500, and by 1963 enrollment had hit 1,000. Essentially, this was a century-old school with a brand new campus—only one of the original buildings, Downs Hall, was saved—and a young and growing faculty and administration.

During the 1970s, though, various problems and conditions sent enrollment plummeting from over 1,500 students to 750 students in a few years. In the 1980s the school put these problems behind it, and enrollment climbed back to about 1,200.

Meanwhile, Siena Heights College also went through some remarkable changes. In 1961 Mother Gerald Barry, who had charted the course of this college since the 1930s, died, and Vatican II was changing everything for Catholics—including education.

In 1964 Sister Mary Petronilla Francoeur, O.P. (Order of the Preacher), was appointed president by Mother Mary Genevieve

The River Raisin flows peacefully through Bach-mayer Park creating a lovely environment and recreation area for residents of Blissfield. Courtesy, Village of Blissfield

Displaying a collection of trinkets and treasures, Lucinda's Loot in Blissfield offers antiques shoppers an array of items from eras past. Courtesy, Lenawee Tomorrow

After a Saturday breakfast at one of Blissfield's cafes, these friendly youngsters await a day filled with fun in one of Lenawee's many parks. Courtesy, Lenawee Tomorrow

RIGHT: Excited young-sters await the commence-ment of Hudson's annual Christmas parade. Photo by Mark A. Rogers

BELOW: With abundant housing, a low cost of living, and a rural life-style, Tecumseh is truly a place for families. Photo by Linda Hewlett

The Hudson High band and drill team represent their school, playing spirited marching music and performing drill team exercises with un-flagging enthusiasm at the annual Hudson Christmas parade. Photo by Mark A. Rogers

Always prepared and ready to service the emergency needs of the community is the Tecumseh Fire Department. Courtesy, City of Tecumseh

ABOVE AND RIGHT:
Croswell Opera House
in downtown Adrian
originally opened in
1866, and is the third oldest continuously operat-
ing opera house in the
United States. The the-
ater continues to bring
the best in entertainment
to Lenawee County, as
witnessed here in this
scene from the musical,
Oklahoma. *Courtesy,
Lenawee Tomorrow*

FACING PAGE: This
turn-of-the-century Victorian home represents
the charm and elegance
found in Adrian's Histor-
ical District. *Courtesy,
Lenawee Tomorrow*

ABOVE: The Adrian Dominican Congregation was founded over 100 years ago. The Dominican Sisters aid people all over the world, focusing their missions on education and health care. Seen here is the Holy Rosary Chapel at the Motherhouse, world headquarters of the Dominican Sisters. Built around 1906, the impressive interior of the chapel displays intricate Gothic decor and architecture. Courtesy, Lenawee Tomorrow

RIGHT: The Lenawee County Courthouse is a striking architectural landmark in downtown Adrian. This Romanesque-style Victorian, built between 1884 and 1886, boasts classical columns, terra-cotta decorations and sculptures, and a frieze of colored tiles. Courtesy, Lenawee Tomorrow

A lightning-fast Indy car, owned by Douglas Shierson Racing, Inc. of Adrian, speeds passed spectators at the Michigan International Speedway in the Irish Hills. Courtesy, Lenawee Tomorrow, Photo by Dan R. Boyd

LEFT: Visitors wander through the Temperate House at Hidden Lake Gardens to examine the plethora of exotic plants, including cactus, camphor, tapioca, and vanilla. The gardens, which are located outside of Tipton in northern Lenawee county, comprise 670 acres of verdant flora surrounding Hidden Lake. Courtesy, Hidden Lake Gardens, Michigan State University

FACING PAGE: On any given fall day, anglers out for the afternoon bite will undoubtedly find beautiful surroundings and peaceful relaxation at W.B. Hayes State Park's Wamplers Lake. Photo by Sue Keyser

FOLLOWING PAGE: The winter snows leave a few shocks of corn standing, survivors of the fall plowing in rural Lenawee County. Photo by Haz Keyser

ABOVE: Flat and fertile, Lenawee County has some of the richest farmland in the United States and forms one of Michigan's leading agricultural regions. Photo by Haz Keyser

LEFT: In the rural countryside of cascading green hills and wide-open spaces, horse ranches are a common sight. Lenawee County's excellent stables are centers for standardbred horses that race in southern Michigan and northwest Ohio. Photo by Lad Strayer

The vivid colors of aerial vehicles are often seen in the skies above Lenawee County. Activities such as parachuting, hang gliding, and ballooning are popular with locals. Here a lazy hot air balloon drifts over the town of Morenci. Courtesy, Lenawee Tomorrow

RIGHT: In winter or summer, lovely waterways, like this river just north of Morenci, enhance the landscape across the county. Photo by Mark Rogers

Throngs of residents and visitors gather annually along the streets of downtown Clinton to enjoy the Fall Festival parade. Each autumn this event attracts more than 25,000 to this village of 2,500. Other highlights of the festival include arts, crafts, exhibitions, and comestibles. Courtesy, Village of Clinton

BELOW: Feeding time at this northern Lenawee County dairy farm is always "first come, first serve." Photo by Haz Keyser

Weber. Francoeur was the first president who was not simultaneously an officer of the Adrian congregation. By the time she resigned in 1969, Siena Heights had changed from a girls' school into a coeducational college. Moreover, the organization which had founded it, the Adrian Dominican Sisters, decided to establish an independent board for the college with the majority drawn from outside the congregation. The Adrian Dominicans would continue to support, but they would not control it. Essentially, what was happening was the evolution of Siena Heights College into a more secular liberal arts institution. Some confusion and uncertainty were only natural in the first decade of the new school, but by the 1980s Siena Heights had an enrollment well over 1,000, and its future seemed secure.

Nonprofit Concerns

In addition to what schools and governmental bodies could do in culture, education, health care, and religion, other institutions were also interested in these areas. At the forefront of these was the Croswell Opera House and Fine Arts Association. This organization was created in 1967 after plans were announced for the sale of the Croswell Opera House. This facility had a fine stage and a remarkable past going back to 1866, when it was first established by the future governor of Michigan, Charles Croswell. It had been turned into a moviehouse in 1921, but now it seemed as though it was finished. At this same time the wonderful Stair Auditorium in Morenci (dating back to 1908) and the Tecumseh Opera House (dating back to 1879) were both demolished.

However, the Croswell's fate would be different. In November 1967 a preservation group emerged to save the Croswell and turn it into a community theater. Charles Hickman, cofounder of Brazeway and in charge of the Adrian Foundation, was the person

most responsible, but others were also highly influential in this project. Catherine Smith helped in fund raising, and Carlo Heikkinen, Adrian Superintendent of Schools, committed the city's schools to use the building for concerts, lectures, and plays, and to pay a reasonable rent for this use. Knowing some group with the wherewithal wanted to use the theater made the project seem much more feasible.

By the spring of 1968 an initial $50,000 fund drive to fix up the old theater had been announced, and efforts were already in the works for a summer season of plays. That fall the Croswell got an inkling as to the community interest it could draw upon when 200 children showed up to audition for roles in *The Wizard of Oz*. In late 1969 a "Town Hall" series of lectures was opened in keeping with the Croswell's philosophy of providing live productions of all kinds.

In the spring of 1970 a professional theater man, Glen Crane, was brought in to manage the summer productions. It was clear by this time that there was a demand for quality summer musicals throughout Southeast Michigan and Northwest Ohio, and the Croswell began the process of becoming not just a good community theater but a major regional theater. Another excellent professional theater person, Robert Soller, joined the staff as set designer in 1974. He became manager in 1978, and although he gave up managing the business end of operations in the early 1980s, he has remained producer and set designer since then.

Since then the Croswell has had a solid corps of players—including Jerry Andrews, Milt Schoch, and Judy Vanzo—to rely upon. Financial supporters like the Adrian Rotary Club, the Stubnitz family, and the Adrian Foundation also have been important. In its first 20 years the Croswell raised over $1 million to renovate and expand the historic facilities. All told, the remarkable effort that went into the Croswell during this period indicated not merely the area's love of live

FACING PAGE: A shimmering reflection illuminates a Lenawee County family taking in the picturesque view at one of the many lakes in the Irish Hills area. Courtesy, Lenawee Tomorrow

theater and old buildings, but its sense of community pride and its ability to muster support for a worthy project.

The attraction of live theater also spread to Tecumseh, where in 1981 the Herrick Foundation financed the construction of the Tecumseh Civic Auditorium for live theater (provided by the Tecumseh Players and others), films, and lectures.

Another indication of a growing interest and commitment to local culture and education came with the emergence, beginning in the 1960s, of a number of local historical societies and museums. This interest began in the 1950s and early 1960s when it was realized that a number of important historic buildings and artifacts were being destroyed or thrown out with little or no appreciation for their historic value. A group of people, led by Don and Doris Frazier, began collecting historic objects for a museum, and in 1968 got the Lenawee County Historical Society to agree

to support such an endeavor. The Lenawee County Historical Museum opened its doors in 1972. In 1979 it moved to the former Adrian Public Library, both because the building was larger and because it wanted to save this landmark building, which is on the National Register of Historic Places. Other museums opened in Tecumseh in 1986 and in Hudson in 1989.

In addition to concern for the area's cultural values and traditions, interest also grew in Lenawee's social and personal health and well-being. This led to the emergence of a number of groups and organizations concerned with physical and mental health, drugs, domestic violence, and other social issues. A leading organization in this area was Call Someone Concerned. This nonprofit organization offered counseling in suicide prevention, drug use, alcohol, pregnancy, and other personal concerns. From its beginning in 1970 to the present, it has enjoyed wide public sup-

In the 1930s the YMCA helped to bring the successful Stubnitz-Greene Company to town. The head of the company, Maurice Stubnitz, thought a Y was beneficial to the people in his employ. Every day for years he came to the Y to swim laps. A retired Stubnitz is seen here in 1977 with his young friend, Alicia Camran and her mother, Mary Ann. Lenawee County presents a Maurice Stubnitz Humanitarian Award annually in honor of this amiable man. Courtesy, Lenawee County Young Men's Christian Association

port because of its leading role in helping people with serious personal problems.

The Lenawee YMCA also became more and more involved in helping people improve their physical fitness during this time. In the 1980s both Bixby and Herrick hospitals began developing extensive centers and programs to help people with physical, mental,

and drug-related problems. Other groups included Catholic Social Services, Hospice, the Red Cross, the Salvation Army, Family Counseling and Children's Services, Associated Charities, Pregnancy Counseling and Children's Services, HOPE Recreation, Goodwill LARC, Community Action Agency, and SER Jobs for Progress. Together, these organizations all contributed in reaching out to people needing help of different kinds or at different periods of their lives.

Continued Religious Vitality

The postwar era saw the emergence of new churches as well as the renovation of older churches. Certain denominations—the Adrian United Pentecostal Church, the Jehovah's Witnesses of Adrian, the Adullam Christian Fellowship Church, and the Bethel Baptist Church

of Adrian—were new to the area and achieved substantial success in developing congregations. Other new churches included the Calvary Baptist Church of Adrian, the New Apostolic Church of Morenci, the New Hope Tabernacle Church of Adrian, the Tecumseh Assembly of God, the Open Door Bible Church of Hudson, and Faith Temple of Adrian. Other churches, such as Bethany Assembly of God in Adrian, have grown phenomenally since their founding.

Other churches, such as the Church of the Nazarene, the Lutherans, and the Baptists, had been here for a much longer time, and they also grew significantly in numbers of churches and members. The Methodists, Presbyterians, Episcopalians, Friends, and other older denominations in the area also did well. To someone new to the area, the landscape—filled with churches both old and new—must have made them wonder if a new Age of Faith had burst upon the scene. There was something to that—church attendance across America did grow after World War II—but it also testified to the enduring traditional values that were still strong in Lenawee.

Perhaps there is no more appropriate way to close this account of the history of Lenawee than by pointing out how nineteenth-century values, interests, and institutions like the churches were still alive and seeking new ways of expressing themselves in contemporary Lenawee. Larger and more mechanized farms, shopping malls and strips, and industries in chemicals and plastics showed how Lenawee's age-old interests in agriculture, commerce, and manufacturing were keeping pace with modern times. In the same way the contemporary interests in better education, helping the less fortunate, and religion have their counterparts in Lenawee's pioneer and mid-nineteenth-century past. The county has changed, but in fundamental ways it has stayed very close to its age-old ways of thought and action.

In 1943 the Reverend Leonora Annabel (1890-1959) and an associate, Donna Liebler, were on their way to Kentucky when they came across a temporary housing project at Deerfield Park. Many families with children from the South had come for war work. The two women stayed and started the Bethany Assembly of God. The Reverend Annabel, depicted here in 1950, was the minister of the emerging church in Adrian until 1953. Courtesy, Bethany Assembly of God, Adrian

CHAPTER SEVEN

PARTNERS IN PROGRESS

Since the first white settlers began to arrive in Lenawee County in the 1820s, the history of the area has been marked by spurts of growth followed by periods of consolidation—with the constant productive influence of agriculture.

Lenawee County's roots in agriculture are deep and strong. Boasting some of the most fertile land and most industrious farmers, Lenawee was the leading agricultural county in the state of Michigan for many years. Lenawee hosts the oldest continuously operating county fair in the state, dating to the 1830s.

Industrial development has come in four primary waves. The first wave came with the arrival of railroads in the 1830s. Spurred by the aggressive promotion of the Comstocks and their allies, Lenawee had the first railroad west of New York, and through the 1880s prospered as a result.

The second wave came in the latter portion of the nineteenth century, when Lenawee became a leading producer of wire fencing. Claiming to be the nation's wire-fence capital, Lenawee used the railroad to ship its product nationwide.

With the twentieth century came the advent of the automobile. While Lenawee never became a producer of cars like Dearborn or Flint, it became home to a number of companies manufacturing parts for automobiles. Many of the leading employers in the county to the present day owe their prosperity to the automakers.

With the 1930s and the arrival of Tecumseh Products, Lenawee became a center for the manufacture of refrigeration and air-conditioning equipment and components. That industry continues to support many jobs in the county.

Throughout recent years there have been efforts to bring greater diversity to the county's industrial base in order to avoid total reliance on a single segment of the economy. The postwar era has seen the emergence of several chemical companies and the growth of the nation's largest kitchen and bathroom cabinetmaker.

Education has played an important role in the history of the county with private and public schools being established soon after the arrival of the first settlers. Adrian College and Siena Heights College have attracted bright students from all over Michigan and the Midwest, many of whom have chosen to remain and make their homes in Lenawee County, working for local companies.

Philanthropy has been an outstanding feature of Lenawee's development. Families that have made fortunes in Lenawee have shared their success with their neighbors by donating to the colleges, hospitals, public and private schools, parks, and charities—changing the face of the community.

Throughout the years Lenawee's economy has been sparked by people with spirit and big dreams, from the Comstocks of the early days to the Herricks and Merillats of more recent times. The stories of the organizations that have chosen to participate in this important literary and civic project—stories reflective of those dreams and spirit—appear on the pages that follow.

The Adrian Guards, established in 1842, were a military company who were last active in the Civil War. Portrayed here at a reunion around the turn of the century are several prominent men from Lenawee County who were members of the Guard. Courtesy, Lenawee County Historical Society

LENAWEE COUNTY CHAMBER OF COMMERCE

The Lenawee County Chamber of Commerce 1989-1990 Executive Committee. Seated, from left: Bruce Landis, secretary; Paul Ruesink, treasurer. Standing, from left: Garry Clift, past chairman; Michael Wade, chairman; Robert Krout, chairman-elect.

The Lenawee County Chamber of Commerce has been assisting local business and promoting economic development since 1916. Begun as the Adrian Area Chamber of Commerce, the organization served as a community center in its early years. Farm families coming to town for the day picnicked at lunch tables in the chamber offices before setting off to trade in the city's stores.

The chamber's primary mission has changed over the years to reflect the needs of the members and the community. Today the chamber is an action-oriented community-building organization dedicated to making Lenawee County a better place in which to live, work, and do business and a place in which everyone has an opportunity to share in economic growth.

Chamber accomplishments have included supporting Junior Achievement since 1956; helping rescue an abandoned Air Force plant from demolition in 1960-1961—

The professional staff of the Lenawee County Chamber of Commerce and Lenawee Tomorrow. Seated, from left: Ann Hughes, executive vice-president, chamber; David B. Munson, president, chamber and Lenawee Tomorrow. Standing, from left: Heather Liewert, clerical assistant, chamber; Carol Phipps, business manager, chamber; Jean Frey, administrative assistant, Lenawee Tomorrow; Sue Walker, vice-president, Lenawee Tomorrow.

that plant now houses the General Motors/Adrian-Inland Fisher Guide Plant and more than 1,000 employees; attraction of the Michigan International Speedway to the Irish Hills; serving as a focus for volunteerism; encouraging blood drives and disaster relief; supporting issues for the improvement of the community; promoting highways and water systems; and establishing the Maple Leaf Award of Lenawee to recognize outstanding individuals for lifetime volunteerism, leadership, and contributions to the community.

In May 1959 the chamber established the Greater Adrian Industrial Development Corporation. In 1974 the Economic Development Corporation of the County of Lenawee was created by the chamber to issue industrial revenue bonds for projects countywide.

Also in 1974, in keeping with the expanding role and mission of the chamber, the Greater Adrian Chamber of Commerce

became the Lenawee County Chamber of Commerce. During the mid-1980s the chamber successfully extended all of its services and programs countywide, and membership grew from 146 in 1984 to 425 in 1990.

Lenawee Tomorrow Economic Expansion Corporation was created by the chamber in 1985 to assume primary responsibility for economic development.

The chamber is a private, not-for-profit membership organization governed by a board of directors elected from the membership. The board annually adopts a written Program of Action, and it employs a professional staff to carry out its programs and policies.

The Lenawee County Chamber of Commerce's day-to-day activities are managed by Ann Hughes, executive vice-president and chief operating officer. According to Hughes, "chamber services include instructional seminars, programs focusing on business and community issues, the biennial Lenawee Expo trade show, issue-oriented lobbying activities, facilitating dialogue between Lenawee businesses and other county organizations, and special events designed to enable chamber members to develop and strengthen business relationships."

"While many chambers are thought of strictly as a lobbying group for business, we have a broader perspective because the members have allowed us to be a community advocate for many issues that go well beyond simple business promotion," says David Munson, chamber president.

LENAWEE TOMORROW ECONOMIC EXPANSION CORPORATION

Lenawee County was in the throes of a deep recession in 1983 and there were worries about the future. Several manufacturing plants had closed and unemployment had been in double digits for months. Something had to be done to bolster spirits and create cause for optimism.

A community project was created under the sponsorship of the Lenawee Intermediate School District, the Lenawee County Chamber of Commerce, and other community organizations. More than 150 leaders from the ranks of business and industry, education, government, and labor gathered at Lenawee Vocational-Technical Center for an intensive retreat aimed at taking stock and developing a plan for the future.

What emerged was a coalition that chose for its name Lenawee Tomorrow, Inc. Committees were formed to study the county's assets, needs, and possibilities. A report was prepared—but the only tangible results were a reaffirmation of confidence and some new connections forged among groups at the conference.

"It is fair to say that this conference widened the Lenawee County chamber's mission and increased its commitment to economic development," comments David Munson, who, two years later, as chamber president, revived the Lenawee Tomorrow name and vision following a consultant's study of the county's economic potential. Lenawee Tomorrow, Inc., was reborn as a new organization known as the Lenawee Tomorrow Economic Expansion Corporation under the sponsorship of the Lenawee County Chamber of Commerce.

Lenawee Tomorrow was given the challenge of coordinating the county's economic development efforts with the mission of creating jobs and inducing private investment, as well as maintaining existing employment.

On March 11, 1986, Lenawee Tomorrow was designated as a "Community Growth Alliance" by Michigan Governor James J. Blanchard. A Community Growth Alliance is a countywide coalition of public and private-sector representatives each with an interest in economic development. Members of the board of directors come from business and industry, elected officials, chambers of commerce and economic development organizations, utility companies, labor, and education.

The Lenawee Tomorrow 1990 Executive Committee and past chairmen. Seated, from left: Charles Gross, secretary; Robert Nystrom, chairman; Charles Vollers, chairman-elect. Standing, from left: Garry Clift, treasurer; James Toncre, past chairman; Merlyn Downing, past chairman; David B. Munson, president.

Under a contract with the state of Michigan, Lenawee Tomorrow is responsible for business development assistance, site selection services, financial packaging, and help for business with state and local permits and regulations. Lenawee Tomorrow also provides small business development services and assists firms interested in obtaining state and federal contracts. Lenawee Tomorrow is funded by the County of Lenawee, State of Michigan, Region II Private Industry Council, cities and villages, and the business community. "Lenawee Tomorrow offers single-source responsibility for packaging state and local business assistance programs," says David Munson.

Accomplishments attributable to Lenawee Tomorrow between 1985 and 1990 include creating 2,063 new industrial jobs; helping to retain 455 existing industrial jobs; assisting with 27 successful investment projects, 22 of which were with existing companies; and inducing more than $500 million in private investment.

The list of firms doing business in Lenawee County as a direct result of Lenawee Tomorrow's efforts is impressive: AMCO Manufacturing Corporation, Lenawee Stamping Corporation, Kecy Products, Inc., Adrian Fabricators, B&U Corporation (Jet Wheelblast), and Orbital Engine Manufacturing USA, Inc. Firms assisted with expansions include Anderson Development Co., Blissfield Manufacturing Corporation, Champion Morenci Engineered Rubber Products, and Wacker Silicones.

Lenawee Tomorrow also manages the county's Economic Development Corporation, which issues industrial revenue bonds.

GLEANER LIFE INSURANCE SOCIETY

Gleaner Life Insurance Society's Williamsburg-style headquarters is located on 106 acres at 5200 West U.S. 223. The bulk of the land is rented to local farmers.

The Gleaner Life Insurance Society takes pride in "being more than just an insurance company"; it is a fraternal benefit society offering both insurance and special benefits for its members.

The society was founded as the Ancient Order of Gleaners in 1894 in Caro, Michigan, by Grant Slocum. It was established to provide farmers with insurance, as commercial insurance companies would not accept them. The concept comes from the Biblical story of Ruth, and the term "gleaner" refers to the poor who would glean leftover grain from harvested fields.

Since its founding—it took its present name in 1932—the society's national headquarters has been located in Caro, Detroit, and Birmingham; it settled in Lenawee County in 1981.

"We wanted to remain in Michigan, and we wanted a quality place for our staff to live," says president Frank Dick of the decision to move to Lenawee County. "We looked at educational institutions and we saw fine public schools, private schools, and two colleges. We saw an excellent YMCA. We saw the opportunity to be adjacent to other cultural centers such as Ann Arbor, Jackson, and Toledo."

The Williamsburg-style headquarters is located at 5200 West U.S. 223, immediately west of the Adrian city limits, situated on 106 acres of land. The Gleaner Center building and surrounding grounds occupies only a small part of the acreage; the balance is rented out to farmers.

The society issues insurance certificates from Gleaner Center and administers the special benefits available to Gleaner members. One of these benefits is participation in its lodge system. To date 59 Gleaner lodges, called arbors, offer members both fellowship and the opportunity to perform volunteer work in the community where the arbors are located.

The arbors may also participate in national volunteer programs offered by the society— Gleaner offers two programs in cooperation with 4-H—as well as their own individual projects.

The 44,932 Gleaner members take pride in the financial strength of their society. In early 1989 Gleaner assets totaled more than $236 million; current premium income and other revenue total $71 million annually, with more than $652 million of insurance in force. The A.M. Best Company, an independent insurance analyst, rates the society an "A+ (superior)" insurer.

"Our membership is spread over 49 states, and many of these members are coming to Lenawee County to see their national headquarters," says Dick. They are coming to see the headquarters of an insurance organization, he says, "dedicated to serving the family as a unit, the foundation of the American way of life."

B&U CORP.

Not many firms can claim doubled sales since 1985, but that is the record of Adrian's Jet Wheelblast Equipment Division of B&U Corp. President Udo Kuehn believes this achievement results from a rededication in the firm since its purchase by Kuehn and Bernard B. Brown in 1985.

This Jet Wheelblast structural steel descaling machine is used for blasting steel plate and beams.

Jet Wheelblast Equipment and its sister division, Snedecker Machine Tool, located at 401 Miles Drive, are alike in serving industry, but quite different in the roles they play.

Ervin Industries created Jet Wheelblast Division in 1969 to manufacture metal-finishing equipment using jet wheelblast technology. This technology employs a high-speed impeller wheel to direct a stream of abrasive medium at the surface to be finished. Depending upon the medium used—sand-like steel pellets or plastic beads—and the velocity, the jet wheelblast device can strip sand and scale off heavy metal castings or gingerly remove paint from the surface of lightweight aircraft wing panels.

Ervin Industries built the Adrian plant in 1975, and there have been four expansions since. Also added to the plant was Snedecker Machine Tool, an existing Adrian company.

Brown and Kuehn created B&U Corp. in 1985 to purchase Jet Wheelblast and Snedecker. Brown serves as chairman, and Kuehn, the former plant manager, is president. According to Kuehn, they immediately set out to infuse the firm with new vigor by diversifying its products and expanding the sales force. New products developed by Kuehn and his engineering staff include plastic media equipment for paint stripping and plastic parts deflashing.

New in 1987 was the Blast Services Department, serving manufacturing firms in Lenawee and neighboring counties. Industrial metal parts are cleaned and deburred at the Wheelblast plant and returned ready to be shipped or installed. This department will be expanded to perform other surface-finishing services, Kuehn reports.

The jet wheelblast machine has been adapted for a variety of applications, including cleaning structural steel and foundry castings, peening metal products, etching steel mill rollers, defining castings and plastic parts, and, most recently, paint stripping of delicate surfaces.

Customers of Jet Wheelblast Equipment include auto and auto parts manufacturers, steel mills, steel fabricators, foundries, general metal manufacturing firms, and—with the paint stripping device—the United States Air Force. Kuehn hopes that certification of the paint stripping process will allow expansion into the civilian aircraft industry as well.

B&U's aggressive sales efforts have extended markets for Jet Wheelblast Equipment to the Far East, Europe, and Australia.

Snedecker Machine Tool Division does machine tool work for local industry, including tool and dies; designs and builds special machinery; and overhauls and remodels machinery. Most of Snedecker's customers are in southeastern Michigan, but some are as far away as Atlanta, Georgia.

"We've improved our capability by adding machines as well as sales and engineering staff," says Kuehn, adding that this part of B&U Corp.'s business is also in for growth and development.

B&U Corp. chairman Bernard B. Brown (left) and president Udo Kuehn look over plans after buying the Jet Wheelblast Division from Ervin Industries in 1985. Courtesy, The Daily Telegram—Roger Hart, photographer

B&U Corp. headquarters in Adrian houses Jet Wheelblast Equipment and Snedecker Machine Tool. Photo by Frederick G. Eaton

ANDERSON DEVELOPMENT CO.

Anderson's original plant and offices were located at 1425 East Michigan Street during 1969.

A view of the Mid-Bay production area at Anderson in 1969.

When Japanese chemical giant Mitsui Toatsu, Inc., purchased the Anderson Development Co. in Adrian in November 1988, it acquired a locally established and based firm with a reputation for innovation and success in the chemical business—especially in the area of specialty and performance polymers.

Anderson Development Co. was established in 1966, the third chemical plant launched in Lenawee County by Amos R. "Andy" Anderson. Anderson grew up in Lenawee County and graduated from Clayton High School and Adrian College. He earned a degree in chemistry, and during World War II he was involved with the Manhattan Project that developed the world's first atomic bomb.

Following the war he returned to Lenawee County and entered the chemical business, starting one company and launching two other plants for Stauffer Chemical Company. At first Anderson Development concentrated on research and development of products for other chemical firms. As time passed, however, Anderson chemists began developing new specialty chemicals for the corporation's own proprietary use. The research moved in the direction of urethanes, and then to catalysts, fire retardants, and curatives.

Today the firm continues its dual identity. Approximately one-half of the plant's output is products made under contract for other chemical companies, and one-half of its output is Anderson Development's own proprietary products, according to J. Paul Rupert, company president.

On the proprietary side, the firm develops, manufactures, and sells to the end-use market its own line of chemical products. Rupert says the company's products are mainly specialty and performance polymers, especially polyurethane for cast elastomer applications. Customer industries use these materials to make such products as ski boots, roller-skate wheels, assembly-line rollers, and hydrocyclones.

"We made the polymer that went into the wheels on the cars in Space Mountain at Walt Disney World," Rupert reports. The application illustrates some of the important characteristics of the polymers made from Anderson products.

"These polymers are characteristically very strong, durable, and impact resistant, and, depending upon how they are mixed, can be either very soft or very hard," Rupert explains. They are very useful as assembly-line rollers in industry, Rupert says, because they wear very little and can provide a measure of resiliency.

Other products, such as styrene-butadiene resins, are used in flooring material, carpet backing, shoe soles, and toner resins for copiers.

The other part of Anderson Development's business is custom manufacturing under contract for other companies. Rupert says these are typically large firms that contract with Anderson Development to make a product for them. Sometimes these firms need additional capacity for a product to be sold under their own name, and, in some cases, materials are made for products that are in the early stages of market development and to which the parent firm does not yet want to commit manufacturing capacity. "Our flexibility to produce another product in small batches quickly is important to our success," Rupert comments.

Products Anderson makes under such agreements go into laundry products, plastics, electronics, agriculture, and health care products.

In 1990 business was booming, with the Adrian plant working three shifts five days per week. The company employs 120 workers in Adrian and 15 at a facility in Gary, Indiana. In Adrian, 60 people are employed in production, with 20 people in construction and maintenance, and 40 people in professional management, technical, and administrative roles.

Adrian is the corporate headquarters, where sales, research, development, and administration are located, as well as the major manufacturing facility. Lab facilities at the plant are used both to evaluate the products being manufactured and to develop new products.

In November 1988 Mitsui Toatsu Chemicals, Inc., of Tokyo, Japan, purchased the stock of the company from Amos Anderson and other investors. Since the purchase the firm has been managed as a wholly owned subsidiary, with Rupert serving as president and chief executive officer. One of the first projects Mitsui Toatsu put into consideration for Adrian was a plant to make an acrylic resin for applications in industrial powder coatings systems.

Mitsui Toatsu is the fifth-largest chemical company in Japan, with sales of $3.5 billion per year serving markets in Japan, the Far East, Europe, and

North America. The firm is one of the 20 largest chemical companies in the world. Mitsui Toatsu is one of the Mitsui group of companies. Others include Toyota, Toshiba, Mitsui Bank, and Sapporo Beer.

"Mitsui purchased Anderson Development for the sake of establishing a resident U.S. operation," Rupert explains. "Now it has the capability of manufacturing in the United States, which it didn't have before. It will, in addition to existing operations, move in those manufacturing operations that it wants to do in this country for this market—products it now ships from Japan."

An aerial view of the Anderson Development facility around 1975.

Today Anderson's corporate offices are located at 1415 East Michigan Street.

RIMA MANUFACTURING COMPANY

R ima Manufacturing Company in Hudson is a leading supplier of precision contract machining services for the automotive, refrigeration, and communication markets.

"Rima was founded on the belief that good family values are good business values," says Ed Engle, Jr., president. "By striving to be both professional and family oriented, we've become a competent, competitive community of manufacturing people."

Ed Engle in 1955 in front of Rima's first home.

In 1955 Ed Engle and a partner left secure jobs to establish their own business. They set up shop in an old wooden shed that in a previous era had stabled the delivery wagons and horses of a local coal company. They named the new corporation by combining the first two letters in their wives' names, Rita and Marian, and began working 12-hour days with eight vintage screw machines that, according to Engle, "helped win the first World War."

Hard work and long days paid off. A year later Rima moved its headquarters to a concrete block building on Main Street. In 1962 Engle purchased his partner's interest.

The company grew. An addition was built in 1966, the same year that annual sales topped one million dollars. A full complement of secondary capability was developed, and Rima soon began machining aluminum die castings.

By 1979 Rima had outgrown its home. Team effort designed and constructed a new building on Munson Highway. The following year a subsidiary organization, Rima of Canada, was established in Kingsville, Ontario. In 1988 a facility for the sole purpose

Ed Engle (right), cofounder of Rima Manufacturing, was succeeded by his son, Ed Engle, Jr. (left), as company president.

of machining aluminum die-cast product was erected in Hudson.

Rima emphasizes people, quality, and technology.

In 35 years the Rima family has grown to be a work force of 200 people in the United States and Canada. Workers remain members of the Rima family for many years, and it's not unusual to find multigenerations of parents and children, as well as husband-and-wife teams in the organization. "We work together, solve problems together, and grow together," emphasizes Engle. "As a result, we trust and respect one another. We're family."

Rima's quality is achieved through the use of electronic measuring devices, statistical process control techniques, and carefully monitored and documented procedures. Together they assure consistent product quality. Concurrently, ongoing acquisition of the best machining technology creates a manufacturing capability that is both competitive and flexible.

Today Ed Engle continues as chairman of the board. Asked to compare his own and his father's role in the firm's development, Ed Engle, Jr., reflects, "As the entrepreneur, my father got us started, took risks, and ran on instinct. Our family orientation continued as I helped integrate professionalism and manufacturing to meet today's international market."

Nevertheless, Rima Manufacturing Company still retains its "family spirit." And solid belief in the Rima family remains a stepping stone into the future.

HARDWOODS OF MICHIGAN

Persons who cut and removed a nice walnut tree 30 years ago from the Service family's farm near Clinton probably had no idea that they were changing history, but they did. Young Richard Service, who had previously thought of trees as only providers of shade and objects of beauty, heard his father discuss the dollar value of the stolen tree, and realized that trees can offer assets beyond shade and beauty.

When a sawmill became available in 1972, 27-year-old Richard Service bought it and went into business as Tri-County Logging. The seed planted by the tree thieves had borne fruit.

The sawmill found adequate stock of hardwood trees in the area at first, but Service expanded the operation aggressively. Today trees come from as far as the Mackinac Bridge.

A major expansion of the business and a name change came in 1983, when lumber drying began. Before that Tri-County Logging had sold green lumber to its customers. By drying lumber, the newly named Hardwoods of Michigan added value to its product and volume for sales.

Service first built a pre-dryer structure in Clinton and transported his wood to drying kilns in Monroe leased from La-Z-Boy. Once established as a supplier of dried lumber, Service installed kilns in Clinton. The kilns have since been expanded.

The company was restructured in 1988 into three divisions. The sawmill division, still known as Tri-County Logging, employs 45 people with sales of $5 million. This division buys hardwood trees from forests in Michigan and other states, then saws the trees into lumber. Hardwoods of Michigan employs 100 people in the lumber-drying and marketing division with sales of $23 million to customers worldwide. The veneer division has four employees and sales of $1.5 million.

Sales are primarily to lumber wholesalers who in turn sell the hardwood to furniture makers, cabinetmakers, and hobbyists. International sales go to Japan, Great Britain, Australia, and other countries.

Hardwoods of Michigan is consistently ranked among the fastest growing companies in Michigan, a fact Service attributes to his organization's modern facilities, mechanization, and an insistence upon quality. Hardwoods of Michigan employs modern band saws in its mill and uses an abrasive planing process that Service says is superior to conventional blade planing.

Service is chairman of the board of Hardwoods of Michigan; Jeff Hardcastle is president; and Robert Vogel and Edward Evans are vice-presidents.

Hardwoods of Michigan, on the south side of Clinton, began as a modest sawmill but has grown to become one of the major hardwood lumber producers in the country.

GURDJIAN & ASSOCIATES, INC.

Gurdjian & Associates' qualified staff provides protection and accumulation products through well-trained representatives, including their own associates and the Kemner-Iott Agency, which helps with property and casualty coverage.

Richard A. Gurdjian credits teamwork and association with Guarantee Mutual Life Insurance Company for the success achieved by Gurdjian & Associates over the past two decades.

Although Gurdjian has been in the insurance business since 1970, when he opened an office in his home, it was June 1973 when he moved downtown. On July 6, 1982, Gurdjian & Associates grew into its

and employee benefits planning. "We service the agents, who are really self-employed, and they service the policyowner," Gurdjian says.

Service begins with Guarantee Mutual Life Company, an "A+"-rated life insurance company founded in 1901 that provides life, disability, and group insurance.

"The representative accomplishes his objective of selling and servicing products by

fourth downtown location, 309 North Winter Street.

The firm has 18 associates located in southeastern Michigan and northwestern Ohio. Three additional employees complete Gurdjian & Associates.

"The mission of the agency," according to Gurdjian, "is to serve our communities by providing protection and accumulation products sold by well-trained representatives to clients."

Products offered to individuals by the agency include life insurance, disability and earnings replacement insurance, annuities, and hospitalization. Property and casualty insurance is offered through an affiliation with the Kemner-Iott Agency.

Services provided by Gurdjian & Associates include individual and family insurance-based financial planning, estate planning, retirement planning, business protection and continuation planning,

working with the philosophy of doing for his client that which he would want done for him if he were the client. Our representatives always strive to be more professional by becoming continuously more educated through industry courses, company courses, and attainment of such designations as CLU and ChFC," Gurdjian says.

"Each of us at Gurdjian & Associates pledges to serve our clients as we ourselves would want to be served. Honesty, integrity, and the confidentiality of our clients' trusted information remain our cornerstones," Gurdjian states.

Like most modern industries, the field of insurance is an ever-changing one—with the exception of the reason why this market exists. "Some things don't change," says Gurdjian. "The reason life insurance is sold has to do with love of remaining family members—that hasn't changed. The way to sell has—computers, changes in tax laws—there have been many changes in products offered. We study constantly to keep up with changes."

Richard A. Gurdjian began his career in 1970 with Guarantee Mutual Life Company. Today this association extends to the 18 representatives affiliated with Gurdjian & Associates.

INLAND FISHER GUIDE DIVISION OF GENERAL MOTORS

The Inland Fisher Guide/Adrian plant was built during World War II by the federal government to produce aluminum components for military aircraft. At that time the plant was operated by Bohn Aluminum, some of its employees being German prisoners of war. As part of Germany's reparation to the United States following the war, Bohn Aluminum received one of the world's largest German forging presses.

After the war different aluminum companies took turns running the plant. It became known as the "white elephant" of Michigan's industrial facilities. No one wanted it or knew what to do with it.

In 1961 Bridgeport Brass, which owned the complex, decided to cease operations, leaving 800 employees jobless. This decision left Adrian's employment picture very bleak.

National attention was brought to this community when competitive bids for the property were made by a salvage company and Harvey Aluminum. The salvage company's higher bid would lead to the sale of existing machinery and the dismantling of the plant. Harvey Aluminum's lower bid would allow continuing operation of the facility and provide employment.

Adrian civic leaders and businessmen mounted an intensive campaign to persuade the federal government to intervene and accept Harvey Aluminum's lower bid to preserve employment. Following a press conference on March 17, 1961, President John F. Kennedy pledged that Adrian's employment future would not suffer further. Harvey Aluminum gained control of the facility, employing more than 400 people.

In 1969, through stock acquisition, Martin-Marietta owned and operated the plant until it was sold to Chevrolet five years later. Due to the Arab oil embargo, GM let the plant

sit idle until operations began in April 1977.

During the past 12 years the Adrian plant has undergone three name changes that include Chevrolet Adrian (1977 to 1984), Chevrolet-Pontiac-Canada or C-P-C Adrian (1984 to 1986), Inland Division(1986 to mid-1989), and Inland Fisher Guide/Adrian Plant (mid-1989 to the present).

Today IFG Adrian is the home of 1,050 hourly and salaried employees, with an estimated payroll of $42 million per year, and taxes of $1.4 million per year. The plant actively sponsors and supports many community activities, including the United Way Drive, Associated Charities, American Red Cross Blood Drive, Care and Share Food

campaign, Junior Achievement, and Boy Scouts and Explorers. The plant contributed $128,000 to the 1989 United Way Campaign, or 20 percent of the total campaign goal.

The Inland Fisher Guide plant is projected to set a sales record of more than $200 million for 1989. The plant purchases approximately 28 million pounds of plastic annually to manufacture the various products made at this facility.

The Inland Fisher Guide Division of General Motors, Adrian's largest factory and the second largest in Lenawee County, has 1,050 employees on its payroll and actively sponsors many community activities.

BRAZEWAY, INC.

Innovation has been the hallmark at Brazeway, Inc., since 1946, when it was founded by two entrepreneurs to produce aluminum products. Together with a corporate commitment to excellence and communication, that spirit of innovation has led to growth and success for the Adrian firm, according to Stephen L. Hickman, president.

Hickman is the son of Charles E. Hickman, who joined with Allen L. Goldsmith to launch the firm. The company's first products were made from purchased aluminum tubing and sheet. The tubing was brazed (the metal-soldering process the firm is named after) to the sheet for the refrigeration industry.

The company purchased its first 500-ton aluminum extrusion press in late 1948. The tube-form business grew, and more presses were purchased to meet demand.

Hickman and Goldsmith recognized the potential for aluminum tubing in components for refrigeration and air-conditioning products, but there was a problem. The copper used in compressors can't be welded or soldered to aluminum. Attempts to join aluminum tubing to the copper tube coming out of the compressor had always failed.

In 1946 Hickman and Goldsmith devised and patented a way of manufacturing a coupling to connect copper tubing to aluminum tubing. The invention's impact has been revolutionary. The copper-to-aluminum transition tube quickly became a backbone of Brazeway's business, with millions produced each year in a variety of sizes and configurations.

With the resulting growth in the use of aluminum evaporators in refrigeration, Brazeway grew and prospered. More extrusion presses were added to produce a wide range of aluminum products.

Until 1965 all of Brazeway's products went to the refrigeration industry. That year the company was instrumental in pioneering the use of aluminum tubing for air-conditioning applications.

Today Brazeway's products include aluminum tubing and a wide variety of tube forms, accumulators, refrigerator and dehumidifier evaporators and condensers, aluminum hairpins, and copper-to-aluminum transition joints.

With the growth of the business has come continued growth in Brazeway's facilities. From a handful of employees who joined Goldsmith and Hickman in 1946, the firm has grown to build and operate a manufacturing plant and a technical center in Adrian, Michigan; a plant in Shelbyville, Indiana; a plant in Tillsonburg, Ontario, Canada; and a plant that opened in 1988 in Hopkinsville, Kentucky. Company headquarters is in Adrian.

Allen Goldsmith died in 1964, and Charles Hickman died in 1978. After the elder Hickman's death, the firm was directed by his sons; it is now owned and operated by Stephen Hickman.

Brazeway employs 350 men and women: 290 production workers and 60 salaried employees. Annual sales total $45 million to

Brazeway's current products: evaporators, condensors, accumulators, transition tubes, and various formed tubes.

Left to right: Peter Hogan, visitor; David Maxwell, executive vice-president; Stephen Hickman, chief executive officer; Lai Berg, visitor; and Tom Hummel, vice-president/marketing, in front of Brazeway's Technical Center, which was dedicated October 16, 1984.

$50 million, including foreign sales.

Brazeway is involved in a joint venture in Japan to manufacture and sell extruded tubing in Asia. In April 1989 the company signed an agreement for a joint manufacturing and sales venture in England.

The plant in Indiana is an extrusion facility, while the plants in Kentucky and Ontario manufacture products primarily for the appliance industry. Brazeway's plant in Adrian produces parts primarily for the automotive industry.

Customers include the major appliance manufacturers, who use Brazeway evaporators and other components in refrigerators and freezers; air-conditioning manufacturers; and the auto industry. Automotive customers include several Japanese firms producing vehicles in this country.

In Brazeway's highly competitive business, innovation is of vital importance. Recognizing this, the company opened a technical center in the headquarters complex in Adrian in 1984.

Named for Charles Hickman and Allen Goldsmith, the center has been responsible for a number of important developments in improved manufacturing techniques and metal alloys. The center divides its work between finding solutions for customers and creating new products and methods for Brazeway's manufacturing needs.

Among the most important lines of research at the technical center is eliminating joints between aluminum tubing components. "Each time there's a joint, there's a potential leak," Hickman explains. The effort has been successful, and a number or products have been brought onto the market employing sophisticated extruding techniques that have reduced the number of joints in the pressurized heat-transfer systems Brazeway's customers manufacture.

As a corporation Brazeway has encouraged involvement in community activities. The Hickman family has established a record of philanthropy in the community, and Brazeway employees have been key figures in a variety of activities ranging from the United Way to the Adrian Board of Education.

"The community has been very good to us as a company," Hickman comments. "We like Adrian and Lenawee County and hope to make them better to give our people and their neighbors a better environment to live in."

Hickman is enthusiastic about his coworkers at Brazeway, Inc. "We have extremely talented and competent people moving the company forward," he says, adding that the firm makes every effort to help employees to reach their potential. "We have a commitment to train and upgrade our employees to meet the requirements of today and the requirements of the future.

"There's been a continuing theme to our business from start to finish," Hickman says. "Identify customer need and then find ways to meet the need."

Brazeway's first manufacturing plant on Maumee Street in Adrian. The walls of this building are still in use today, but it has been surrounded by numerous plant additions since this 1948 photo.

CITIZENS GAS FUEL COMPANY

Citizens Gas Fuel Company enjoys a level of success and confidence elusive for most of its 133 years. Once a supplier of coal gas for Adrian streetlights, Citizens Gas currently furnishes natural gas for residential, commercial, and industrial purposes.

Founded in 1856, the Adrian Gas Light Company served 98 customers. Homes of Adrian's 3,000 residents were heated by wood or coal. There were no factories, and the local economy depended upon the railroad and agriculture. Gas was made from coal in a

This 1912 photo shows construction work on the old gas plant on Race Street.

plant located behind Citizens' present Winter Street facility.

The company grew slowly, increasing the number of customers as gas lighting moved from the street into homes. Over the next 60 years the firm changed ownership and names several times, becoming Citizens Gas Fuel Company in 1923. Growth was slow dur-

ing periods of financial struggle—especially during the Great Depression.

The company was purchased in 1939 by R.E. Burger and George Shaw, and three years later the war effort brought natural gas pipelines north from the Texas and Louisiana gas fields. Panhandle Eastern Pipeline Company reached Adrian in 1942. An aggressive sales effort extended clean and safe natural gas into homes for heating, and gas finally could compete successfully with electricity.

In 1951 the man who was a central figure in Citizens' modern era, Robert Mikesell, purchased the firm, and under his leadership the company rode the national boom of the 1950s to become a successful modern utility.

Citizens Gas Fuel Company today provides gas service to 10,400 residential, 950 commercial, and 29 industrial customers, selling approximately 3 billion cubic feet of gas each year. The close-knit staff of 50 employees "not only know one another," says president Robert I. Nystrom, "but in a real sense we are a family who share each other's happiness and sorrows, successes and failures."

Citizens is again adjusting to the times. Deregulation means new challenges in purchasing and selling natural gas, with protected territories a thing of the past and increased industrial customer demand for custom services. Under current management the company has met this challenge, and increased its customer base and gas sendout. The firm also sells and services home appliances and services furnaces.

Citizens Gas, a civic-oriented organization, offers its Blue Flame Room cost free to community groups for projects and meetings. In 1988 it was used 108 times.

Citizens Gas Fuel Company is active in promoting Lenawee County economic development. The firm recently optioned an 80-acre parcel on Beecher Street west of Adrian for development as an industrial site to attract new industry, as well as new customers.

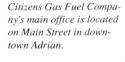

Citizens Gas Fuel Company's main office is located on Main Street in downtown Adrian.

INTERAMERICAN ZINC, INC.

Interamerican Zinc, Inc., is the fourth Lenawee County enterprise started by Amos R. "Andy" Anderson, and the only one he still owns. The company began as an international joint venture to extract zinc from contaminated metal dross with galvanizing units. A patented process separates pure zinc from iron and removes other contaminants.

Andy Anderson moved to Lenawee County when he was six years old. He graduated from Clayton High School and then from Adrian College, with a degree in chemistry.

After earning master's degrees in chemistry and chemical engineering, he started working in Louisville, Kentucky, before entering the service during World War II. Anderson was discharged and assigned as a civilian to the Manhattan Project, the secret program that developed the first atomic bomb.

After the war he went to work for Parker Rustproofing Co. in Detroit. Six months later he moved to Adrian and established Anderson Laboratories. In 1947 the firm built a chemical plant in Weston to produce organometallic products.

When Stauffer Chemical Co. bought his business in 1952, Anderson went to work for the giant firm. He founded and directed construction of a plant in Texas (Texas Alkyls), and in 1964 built the silicones plant on Sutton Road for Stauffer. The Weston plant is now owned by AKZO Chemical Co. and the Sutton Road plant by Wacker Chemie GmBH.

Anderson then left Stauffer and in 1966 started the Anderson Development Co. in

Adrian. That firm was purchased in 1988 by Mitsui Toatsu Chemical Co.

The Interamerican Zinc joint venture linked Anderson Development Co. with a Spanish company, Real Companion Asturian de Minos (RCA). When Anderson Development was sold, Anderson purchased the firm's interest in the joint venture. Today Anderson and the Spanish firm are principal owners of Interamerican Zinc.

Zinc is used to rustproof steel by galvanizing. Leftover zinc is contaminated with iron. Interamerican Zinc separates the zinc from slabs of iron dross and returns pure zinc to the steel mill for another use.

About 70 percent of the zinc used in this country is imported, Anderson reports. The zinc that Anderson's company returns to the steel producers displaces imported zinc.

Almost all new car bodies are galvanized, and other uses for the rustproofed steel include offshore oil drilling rigs and other structural steel.

Interamerican Zinc was the first plant in North America to use the patented technology. The process was so successful that Interamerican Zinc is now the nation's largest producer of secondary zinc. There is no waste, because all by-products can be sold.

Reminded that enterprises he started have created a great many jobs, Anderson says, "I have been fortunate to have been working in an era when there was a lot going on, and I've been fortunate to have worked with some good people."

Charging a 3,000-pound block of continuous galvanizing zinc dross into the electric furnace for melting. Shown in this picture are the electric melting furnace, agitator, reactor, and process control panel.

BELOW LEFT: Pouring the molten dross from the electric melting furnace into the reactor. The zinc is recovered from the dross and purified in the reactor. The agitator used to separate and purify the zinc is shown in its retracted position on the right.

BELOW: Purified zinc recovered from zinc dross that is ready to be used for galvanizing. Clockwise from top: a 2,200-pound unit of zinc slabs, a 4,000-pound zinc block, a 2,400-pound zinc block, and a 2,700-pound zinc block.

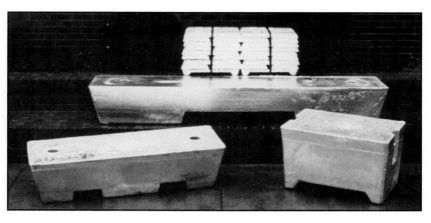

LENAWEE INDUSTRIAL MACHINE, INC.

The management team of the company (from left): Mike Cunningham, vice-president; Wendell Lapham, chief executive officer; and Rich Collom, president.

The quality of life in Lenawee County, rather than proximity to markets, is the reason Lenawee Industrial Machine, Inc., is located in Adrian, according to Mike Cunningham, vice-president. "For our type of business, we should be located near a metropolitan airport or the city," Cunningham says. "But we chose Lenawee County because it is the kind of place where we want to live."

Lenawee Industrial Machine, Inc., rebuilds machine tools, as well as builds special machine tools, and sells used and rebuilt machines. Its customers include auto manufacturers and other industries that use machine tools to make steel parts.

Wendell Lapham established Lenawee Industrial Center in 1971 as a machine sales company. Lapham grew up in Detroit, but as a boy he visited his parents' cottage in the Irish Hills. He attended Onsted High School, and since he was familiar with Lenawee, it seemed a good place to start his business.

He was joined in 1977 by Cunningham and Rich Collom. They had been working for Production & Equipment Company in Detroit, and had decided they wanted to move their families away from the crime and crowds of the city to a smaller community. They brought knowledge of the tool-rebuilding business. Lenawee Industrial Center became Lenawee Industrial Machine (LIM) and began its rebuilding operations. Lapham is chief executive officer, Collom is president and chief operating officer, and Cunningham is vice-president/sales and purchasing.

The backbone of LIM's business is rebuilding used machine tools. Typically a machine is torn down and cleaned, worn parts

are replaced, electronics are replaced and often upgraded, and the machine is calibrated to precise tolerances. Cunningham says a machine tool often is a better quality piece of equipment after an LIM rebuild than when first manufactured.

LIM also designs tools to order. Working from a part or part print, LIM's process engineers conceptualize and design the machine and tooling needed to produce the part.

Lenawee Industrial Machine has two plant buildings on Nelson Street in Adrian and a warehouse in Deerfield. The firm has customers throughout the United States and overseas, in such countries as Brazil, Mexico, and Singapore.

There are 30 employees, seven in the office and 23 skilled workers. LIM operates its own apprentice program to train skilled workers and serves as the on-the-job training site for Jackson Community College's rebuilding course.

LIM installed state-of-the-art gauging equipment, because as manufacturing techniques for finished products are refined to closer tolerances, so must the machines that make the parts that go into those products.

Lapham did $40,000 in sales in 1971. Eighteen years later, Cunningham says, Lenawee Industrial Machine, Inc., had sales 100 times higher.

The quality of life in the Lenawee County area helped to determine the location of Lenawee Industrial Machine, Inc., in Adrian.

UNITED SAVINGS BANK

The lobby was decorated with flower baskets from well-wishers. Bank officers checked their watches. A small line of customers stood expectantly outside. When the doors opened at 9 a.m. on April 15, 1933, James Marks strode up to a teller window, made a deposit, and began a new era in Lenawee County banking as United Savings Bank opened for business.

Since then USB has grown from a single banking office to eight county-wide locations, including a new main office building that opened in 1980. Reflecting the steady growth of Lenawee County, bank assets have increased consistently since 1933, making USB one of the largest financial institutions in the area today.

Over the years, despite the many changes in the banking industry, United Savings Bank has relied upon its local roots and the human touch of its people to remain responsive to the special needs of all customers. David S. Hickman, president of United Savings Bank, attributes this business perspective to Merlyn H. Downing, chairman and chief executive officer. "He is the foundation of our bank," says Hickman. "He's a customer-oriented, street-smart individual whose greatest asset is his flexibility. Merlyn continually amazes me with his reception to change while still treating customers as well today as he did when he began at USB in 1946."

Spanning the history of United Savings Bank, 1976 stands out as a banner year. It was then that USB opened its Trust Department after being granted full trust powers from the state of Michigan. Since then USB has been assisting clients in planning for the continued

Merlyn H. Downing, chairman and chief executive officer of United Savings Bank and United Bancorp, Inc., began his career with the bank in 1946 after his graduation from Britton High School.

protection of their families through diversified long and short-term trust services. The department is currently the only full-service, locally owned trust department in Lenawee County.

The year 1986 saw the formation of United Bancorp, Inc., a bank holding company with United Savings Bank as its subsidiary. Such progress has opened the door to many new options necessary to meet the ever-changing demands of the financial services industry.

United Savings Bank has committed itself to being a financially sound community bank dedicated to serving Lenawee County. Its mission statement says it all: "To be a responsible, independent financial institution that renders high-quality service to customers through the efforts of fairly treated employees, maintaining a visible profile within the communities we serve. We will maximize our sustainable earnings while maintaining adequate capital, liquidity, and safety standards for the protection of our depositors and shareholders."

United Savings Bank's main office, located at 205 East Chicago Boulevard in Tecumseh. USB operates seven other Lenawee County banking locations in Tecumseh, Adrian, Britton, and Clinton.

ADRIAN PUBLIC SCHOOLS

V ery soon after Adrian was established by Addison Comstock and other pioneers, a school was started. The first classes were held in 1828 in the home of Dr. C.N. Ormsby. Thus began the oldest continuous institution in Adrian other than the community itself.

School was private in the early days, and as the settlement grew, four independent district schools were established. In 1846-1847 the state chartered the Adrian Seminary, later known as Adrian Academy, which served as a high school. The school had no public tax support and struggled financially.

By 1849 it was apparent that the four district schools should be consolidated as a tax-supported public school district. A union school was forged from the four, thanks to civic leaders such as Dr. John Cadman, W.M. Comstock, R.H. Whitney, and William L. Greenly.

Adrian's modern high school was built in the late 1950s, replacing a nineteenth-century structure.

dents were quickly distributed among several nearby churches and homes that were rented to be temporary schools. The new Central School, built to house 1,000 students, was ready for occupancy by 1869, on the present site of Drager Middle School.

By the turn of the century school buildings were aging and filled to capacity, and the first of two major building programs was launched. Between 1902 and 1908 a new high school was built near the Central School; Jefferson School was rebuilt on Center Street; and additions were built on the East Branch and South Branch school buildings.

In 1915 the junior high concept was adopted, with grades seven, eight, and nine designated as junior high and grades 10, 11, and 12 as high school. Junior high classes were housed in the old Central School building.

By 1917 the school system's enrollment

A cornerstone was laid in the fall of 1850 for a union school building between Maumee and Church streets, nearly across from what is now the Drager Middle School. The three-story building with space for 312 students was completed for fall classes in 1852.

The community was growing fast, and between 1857 and 1861 four new schools were built. The high school graduated its first class in 1857.

The community responded quickly when the Union School building burned in 1866. The fire occurred just days before the fall term was to have begun, and its 500 stu-

had reached 1,972 students. Another major building program took place during the 1920s, when Lincoln, McKinley, and Garfield elementary schools were built.

Construction continued through the 1950s, adding Alexander and Michener schools and the new high school building. Later, Comstock School was built to replace the 1857-vintage McKinley Primary, and Prairie School was built to accommodate children from the "airport subdivision."

It was also during the 1950s that consolidation of small districts into larger districts accelerated. The Adrian district absorbed many smaller districts, giving its present

reach into Adrian, Raisin, Palmyra, and Madison townships.

During the 1970s the new Springbrook Middle School was built, and the Drager Middle School took its present shape with the complete remodeling of the structure. The 1980s saw no new construction, but a major renovation program put new roofs on several buildings, replaced several boilers, and weatherized school buildings.

But bricks and mortar alone do not tell the story of education. It is a human endeavor in which the adult generation attempts to impart to its children the knowledge, values, and skills needed to perpetuate the community.

Thus it has been in Adrian. There were only seven homes in the frontier town when the first school was convened. At each stage in the development of the modern school system the community supported whatever changes would be needed to make the schools excel, agreeing to be taxed for each of the building projects and responding in times of crisis.

The scope of the education offered has grown as well. In the earliest days the three "R"s of reading, writing, and 'rithmetic were taught. The classics of Greek and Latin were offered in the higher grades early on, and debate continued through much of the nineteenth century whether they should be continued.

The Adrian public schools of today offer programs and classes that would have dazzled teachers of the bygone era. Starting with developmental kindergarten, the elementary schools provide a standard curriculum through fifth grade. Middle schools expand the programming with shop, home economics, and science labs for the sixth, seventh, and eighth grades, and the high school offers a full program for college-bound students and those training for occupations.

The Adrian schools work closely with the Lenawee Intermediate School District to provide special programming for learning disabled and handicapped students, and students who want vocational training attend the LISD's Vo-Tech campus.

During the 1980s, under the direction of superintendent James Leary, renewed emphasis has been placed on curriculum and on staff development, with the result that Adrian students have shown steady improvement on standardized achievement tests.

Federal programs in the schools strive to ensure a quality education for students from disadvantaged homes, and during the 1980s an anti-drug-abuse program developed in the Adrian schools that won a presidential citation has become a model for other school districts. An alternative education program helps dropouts to complete their education.

Community involvement is emphasized with the use of many volunteers in the Adrian Public Schools, as well.

"Our program has been carefully designed to provide programs for all needs, interests, and desires," Leary comments. "Our program is goal driven and pupil oriented," he adds. "The focus is on kids."

One of Adrian's newest elementary schools is Alexander Elementary School, located near the high school and Springbrook Middle School.

BALES TRUCKING

A 1920s era photograph of (from left) Bales Trucking founder W.W. Bales, grandson Virgil, and an unidentified hired hand.

Bales Trucking has been a family affair in Lenawee County for more than 70 years. It was founded around 1917, when W.W. Bales moved to Lenawee County from Toledo. He started the business with a team of horses in Madison Center. Today his greatgrandson, Merrill Bales, gets the job done with approximately 45 pieces of equipment on a five-acre parcel of land on West Maple Avenue in Adrian. The move from Madison Center to West Maple took place in 1956.

Using horses and slip scrapers, W.W. Bales worked on such early buildings as the National Guard Armory on West Maumee Street and the Masonic Temple on East Maumee Street. Some of the recent Bales Trucking projects include the Lenawee County Courthouse building on North Main Street; most of the construction at Adrian College, including work on the Orville and Ruth Merillat Sport and Fitness Center; sewers and parking lots for the Lenawee Christian School on U.S. Route 223; the Gleaner Life Insurance Society national headquarters on U.S. Route 223; the Lenawee County Road Commission garage on Treat Highway; the Tecumseh Credit Union and Merillat Industries' corporate offices on U.S. Route 223; and the plant facility on West Beecher Street. In addition, the company built quite a few streets in Loch Erin, a development near Tipton. The firm has grown from revenues of $320,000 in 1958 to more than $3 million in 1989.

Bales Trucking handles such diverse tasks as excavating, grading, asphalt paving, underground utility site preparation, and demolition. Bales Trucking is involved in some facet of the building work in 80 percent of the construction done in Adrian.

Bales' fleet of 20 trucks ranges from pickups to trucks with more than a 50-ton capacity. Bales' trucks haul approximately 1,000 tons of materials per day, including sand, gravel, stone, and crushed limestone. The company owns between 20 and 25 pieces of excavating and grading equipment.

Bales is "most proud of our service to the customer—to be able to do the complete site job from digging the footings to putting in the asphalt. And we try to service the small as well as the large. We do residential as well as commercial."

Other Bales family members contributing to the success of Bales Trucking include Merrill Bales' father, Virgil, who was at the helm between the tenure of W.W. Bales and Merrill. Virgil currently serves as vicepresident of the company. Also involved are Merrill's son, Howard, who is the fourth generation to become involved in the company; Tim, another of Virgil's sons; Judy, who is Merrill's wife and secretary/treasurer of the company; and Olga, Virgil's wife.

After 70 years the Bales family is still actively involved in the business. Shown here are (from left) Tim, Virgil, Merrill, Olga, and Howard Bales.

FRY MECHANICAL, INC.

H. Nelson Fry launched the Monroe Plumbing and Heating Co. in 1941. He later opened a branch in Adrian. His son Vernon purchased the Adrian branch in 1975, renaming it Fry Mechanical, Inc. The Monroe firm was sold in 1982.

In construction, the mechanical contractor installs plumbing, heating, ventilating, and air-conditioning equipment.

In 1975 Fry Mechanical did business in Lenawee County only, on projects of $500,000 or less in mechanical work—such as Springbrook School, Friendship Village, Maple Village, and the Rex B Martin Judicial Building. Fry says, "Our job was to carry out the instructions of other design engineers. Our purpose was to satisfy the functionality and comfort needs of the building, with cost being a key factor."

Fourteen years later the process was more complex. Energy efficiency and environmental concerns had become considerations, and the mechanical contractor was expected to help design the mechanical systems.

"The technological explosion in the industry has greatly increased the demand on all, from the designer to the installing mechanic," Fry explains. "Our criterion is no longer simply the initial capitalization; now we must consider the life-cycle cost of the installation. We now spend much more time in education and training than we did 15 years ago."

In 1984 Fry created a consulting division, F.M. Engineering, Inc. "It's a think tank that designs and markets consulting services," Fry says.

Fry has worked closely for years with Adrian architect David Siler and general contractor Krieghoff Lenawee. In 1989 they co-constructed such projects as the Lenawee County Human Services Building and the Merillat Sport and Fitness

Center at Adrian College.

Joining Vernon Fry as vice-presidents are his sons, Todd D. Fry and Rodney E. Fry. After college both went through extensive apprenticeships in mechanical work. Todd is responsible for marketing, and Rodney, with a degree in microtechnology, is in charge of microtechnology-based controls and energy management systems.

In 15 years the firm grew from five employees to 35. The office has been computerized, and the service area has grown to a range of 100 miles. The consulting firm ranged even farther into Ohio and Indiana. Fry Mechanical, Inc., has tackled projects as big as $2 million in mechanical work.

Two unique projects that gave Fry great pleasure were the difficult but exciting renovations of the Bank of Lenawee building and the old Adrian fire station.

Fry credits most of his success to his staff. He says, "I can't say enough about the people we employ. I'll put our people up against anybody in the world."

In 1989 Fry Mechanical was involved in the construction of the Lenawee County Human Services Building.

One of Vernon Fry's favorite projects was the modernization of the historic old Adrian fire barn to serve as a professional office building. The 1840s building is owned by David Siler and Associates.

STEVENSON LUMBER, INC.

One of the oldest firms in Adrian, Stevenson Lumber, Inc., was founded in 1873 as A. Stevenson & Sons. The business remained in the family until 1984, when eight employees of the firm, a family in their own right after working together for more than 10 years, bought the company.

The purchasers of Stevenson Lumber in 1984 were Daniel N. DeLine, Dale A. Couts, Jr., Daniel L. Giroux, Calvin R. DeLine, Frederick A. Tiede, J.A. Frear, William H. Devonshire, and F. Denver Hedge. Frear and Devonshire both retired in 1988, with the other six remaining as partners.

In July 1989 employees of Stevenson Lumber took a moment from a busy summer day to pose for this picture. "We give service we'd want to receive," says F. Denver Hedge, vice-president.

Stevenson Lumber, Inc., one of the oldest businesses in Adrian, was owned by the Stevenson family from 1873 until 1984, when company employees purchased the business.

When Archimedes Stevenson founded A. Stevenson & Sons, as the business originally was named, the products differed considerably from those sold today. It was primarily a coal business in those days, and the lumber business was seasonal. Lumber was a mainstay in the summer months. When the weather became cold the coal business took over, and coal was delivered to customers with a wagon and a team of horses.

Today Stevenson Lumber, Inc., sells lumber, plywood, doors, windows, roofing, cement products, roof trusses, mill work, paneling, hardware, hand and power tools, paints, insulation, ceiling tiles, nails, plumbing and electrical supplies, and bathroom vanities and cabinets. Customers range from builders to retail buyers.

"I think we strive to provide the quality and service the company has become known for in its 100-plus years," says F. Denver Hedge, vice-president and chief executive officer of Stevenson Lumber. "We look at each sale and each customer as an important part of our business."

Family members involved in Stevenson Lumber after Archimedes Stevenson were Frank Stevenson, followed by William H. Stevenson, a well-known Adrian resident who died in 1965. His daughter, Mrs. Kenneth A. (Mary) Wassink, was the fourth-generation Stevenson to become involved in the store, and her husband worked for the company for 42 years.

"When the fourth generation of the Stevenson family, the Wassinks, were ready to sell the business, they had two daughters living in different parts of the country," says Hedge.

"We put our heads together and believed we could make a workable arrangement that would be agreeable to everyone. When a business has gone on 100 years, I'm sure the family hoped it could go on in some form. We—as employees—had worked together for more than 10 years. We weren't strangers to one another. The youngest purchaser had 10 years of seniority."

Hedge has been with Stevenson Lumber, Inc., for 25 years, starting as an accounts receivable clerk and attended Adrian College while he worked his way up to chief executive officer of the company.

MEYERS INDUSTRIES

Tecumseh's Meyers Industries uses manufacturing techniques practiced by aviation pioneer Allen Meyers to produce a popular line of welded-hull aluminum boats and canoes.

Meyers launched Meyers Aircraft in the late 1930s to produce airplanes of his own design. His plant on the north edge of Tecumseh adjoining Al Meyers Field was important in the development of aluminum aircraft and the legendary Meyers all-aluminum trainer biplanes, used to teach thousands of World War II pilots how to fly. Although they have been out of production for many years, Meyers planes are still flown by airplane enthusiasts who value their speed and quality.

In 1952 the company began producing aluminum boats, and in the mid-1960s the name was changed to Meyers Industries. Al Meyers died in 1976; a year later his firm was purchased by Alan E. Beatty.

A CPA, Beatty had gained experience in the recreation industry as a group vice-president with Victor Recreation Products Group of Victor Comptometer Corp. in Des Plaines, Illinois. Since purchasing Meyers Industries, Beatty has continued in the tradition established by Al Meyers of building welded-seam hulls for his recreational boats, rather than the standard industry practice of riveting seams. Indeed, for many years Meyers boats were the only welded-hull recreational aluminum boats in the water.

Soon after purchasing Meyers Industries, Beatty bought the Sportspal Canoe Company of Johnstown, Pennsylvania, and moved the operation to a facility in Blissfield, where it operates as a division of Meyers Industries. Sportspal canoes also feature welded-hull construction and are noted among sports enthusiasts for their strength and lightness.

Al Meyers earned his reputation as a supplier of airplanes to the military, and the company he founded continues as a defense contractor. While Meyers boats and Sportspal canoes are the foundation of the business,

Meyers Industries also manufactures jeep and truck cabs for the military.

Today Meyers Industries employs 50 people, with 10 working at Sportspal in Blissfield. The firm expects annual sales of approximately 2,000 aluminum boats in a variety of models ranging from 12 to 16 feet, 2,000 aluminum canoes, and "all the fiberglass boats we can make," Beatty says.

Meyers boats are delivered by company-owned trucks to dealers nationwide, with primary distribution areas in the Midwest and East.

Beatty is president of Meyers Industries, and his son, Lorne, is vice-president. Bruce Hardcastle, Beatty's son-in-law, is plant manager.

Meyers aluminum boats have been made in Tecumseh for 40 years. These fishermen are fishing on Evans Lake in a Meyers 14-foot Laker model.

Sportspal canoes are lightweight and the safest canoes made because of their foam interior and outside sponsons. This young couple is canoeing on the River Raisin.

BANK OF LENAWEE

B ank of Lenawee has enjoyed a long and eventful history of service to the Land of Lenawee.

Established late in 1869, with capital stock of $50,000, its doors first opened on January 13, 1870, near the present headquarters in downtown Adrian. The founders named it Lenawee County Savings Bank, and this title adorned its facilities for the next 86 years.

In 1872 the new bank moved to the Masonic Temple at the corner of West Maumee and Winter streets.

Ground-breaking ceremonies for a handsome new building at 135 East Maumee Street, next to the Croswell Opera House, were held on May 15, 1906. The *Adrian Daily Telegram* described it at that time as "brick construction with a Bedford Stone trim. The front has two Ionic fluted columns, 25 feet high and 35 inches in diameter." The bank celebrated the grand opening of this structure on June 26, 1907.

Four mergers have occurred during the bank's history. The first was consummated on August 2, 1915, when Waldby & Clay's Bank joined LCSB.

After operating in two separate buildings for the next three years, the bank began construction of a new headquarters at the Four Corners—Main at East Maumee Street. In late 1919 the relocation was completed. This building, which was substantially enlarged some 45 years later, served as the bank's main office until 1987.

Allan F. Brittain, president of Bank of Lenawee, began his career at the bank in 1963 in bookkeeping and has worked his way up through the ranks.

The Bank of Lenawee proved one can go home again when it moved back to 135 East Maumee, after extensive reconstruction and remodeling of the building. The Grecian architecture structure was first occupied by the bank in 1907.

The National Bank of Adrian was acquired in mid-1942. This merger brought total assets to the $4-million mark, including $200,000 in capital stock.

LCSB's first branch was opened in 1953 at Main and Front streets. Called the Courthouse Office, this facility initially served driveup customers at one window. Seven years later the structure was expanded to four driveups and a walkup window. In 1967 an inside lobby was added. In 1980 these facilities were razed, and a new two-story building was constructed there. An automatic teller machine nicknamed "Lenny Wallbank" also was installed.

With the acquisition of First State Savings Bank of Morenci in 1956, the bank came to another community. Lenawee County Savings Bank then became Bank of Lenawee County. This office was substantially expanded in 1982.

The third Adrian office, called Westside, was opened in a new building at the intersection of Sand Creek Highway and West Maumee Street in 1972.

Shareholders approved a minor name change by eliminating the word "County" in 1986.

The year 1987 was perhaps the single most momentous period in the bank's history. Culminating years of planning, reconstruction, and new construction, the headquarters and downtown Adrian customer service areas moved back "home" to 135 East Maumee Street.

Shortly after the bank moved to the Four

Corners in 1919, the classic 1907 building was purchased by businessmen who moved their company's offices to the structure. They sold it to Walper Furniture which subsequently constructed a major addition and installed showroom windows across the front. The latter caused considerable damage to the facing brick, stonework, and tall columns.

The painstaking efforts of stonemasons, bricklayers, carpenters, and other tradesmen restored the former bank building's exterior and interior elegance. Extensive remodeling of the Walper addition also highlighted the project. In addition, a new entranceway and three-story addition at the north side was constructed.

Outside, the space between the bank and the Adrian Public Library was uplifted with planter boxes, opaque globe lamp poles, and a combination of inlaid brick and concrete for this walkway, which was named Library Lane. On the west side, the project included major improvements for the newly named Croswell Court walkway.

In 1988, on a parcel of land adjacent to the bank and library, an attractive minipark was constructed by the City of Adrian. Called Library Square and dedicated to the memory of the bank's 11th president, Edward P. Fisher, this land was contributed by the bank.

The outcome of the move home has been good in many ways, according to Allan F. Brittain, who is the bank's 12th president. "It's a piece of us; it's part of our heritage. It helps provide strength and stability—a foundation that is very important. And it isn't just this building. It's all of our people. Because we are concerned about the needs of each customer, we are proud of our role as a

community bank where friends, relatives, and neighbors provide products and services to friends, relatives, and neighbors.

"We have a strong community orientation. We are willing partners in contributing to worthy factors affecting the growth of this area and its economic base. Many of our employees are civic oriented," says Brittain, who has been active in most major community organizations and boards during his 27-year career at the bank.

"I feel privileged to be the person who's here to link the history of the bank to its future and pass it along. And I'm only a piece of it. Our board of directors also is a very important part of the big picture. They deserve a large measure of our success," Brittain emphasizes.

The bank was srengthened on July 1, 1987, when the former Hudson State Savings Bank was acquired. The two Hudson offices each became a Hudson Banking Center of Bank of Lenawee. Similarly, local identities were restored at Waldron and Morenci when each of these offices became a Banking Center.

In late-1989, as Bank of Lenawee approached its 120th anniversary, total assets had risen to $142.5 million, including capital accounts of $10.726 million.

A three-story modern addition highlights the north-side entrance of the bank. A cul-de-sac provides easy access to an automatic teller machine.

The elegance of tradition and simplicity of modern design are combined in Bank of Lenawee's reconstructed facility. Marble columns, period furniture, and original teller windows tastefully highlight the interior.

WABJ/Q-95 RADIO

The WABJ/Q-95 studios stand on a historic spot in downtown Adrian. This building's site was once the location of the law office of Thomas Cooley, a legal and political giant in nineteenth-century Michigan. The plaque on the right denotes the historical significance of the site.

Greg Vaughn (left) and Al Campbell are program directors for WABJ and Q-95. Vaughn directs programming at WABJ, while Campbell manages operations for Q-95.

WABJ was Lenawee County's first commercial radio station when it went on the air in 1946, and in 1990, together with its sister station Q-95 FM, is an important communications force in Lenawee County.

WABJ was launched in 1946 by two amateur radio enthusiasts. Gail D. Greiner of Detroit and Alden Cooper of Toledo, Ohio, had become acquainted in conversation on their two-way amateur radios. When they later met in person, they agreed to start a station in Adrian, since there was no station in the Maple City.

The first broadcast by the new 250-watt station was to have been an Armistice Day ceremony on November 11, 1946, but a glitch delayed sign-on until November 13.

The station had a community orientation from the start, featuring local performers and personalities. At first the station operated during daytime only. The studio and transmitter were at Treat Street and U.S. Route 223.

One year after that station went on the air it was purchased by one of Adrian's most prominent citizens, industrialist James Gerity, for $62,000. Soon after purchasing WABJ, Gerity secured FCC permission to begin broadcasting 24 hours per day, and the station has been full time ever since. An ABC network affiliation was secured, and WABJ became a full-service information and entertainment station.

By 1958 the station had outgrown the original studio facility and moved to the former Commercial Savings Bank building on South Main Street in downtown Adrian. In 1972 Gerity secured a license for a new FM station in Adrian. Named WQTE, the station is at 95.3 on the dial and broadcasts in stereo. The stations moved to 121 West Maumee Street in 1960.

Upon Gerity's death in 1973, the Adrian stations were purchased from his family by a group of investors, most of whom were local. They operated the station until 1985, when Central Broadcasting Corp. of Richmond, Indiana, purchased them.

In December 1988 the stations were acquired by Mid-American Radio Group, Inc., of Martinsville, Indiana. This 30-year-old company is owned by David Keister. Keister is a native of Hillsdale, Michigan, where his family once owned WCSR. Mid-American owns 11 stations in six cities.

WABJ-AM offers an adult-contemporary format, with an emphasis on local news, sports, and information. The stations offer the only full-time news and sports staff to provide complete coverage for Lenawee County. The signal covers all of Lenawee County. WQTE, known as Q-95, offers a modern country-music format and is the only full-time music station in the county.

BETHANY ASSEMBLY OF GOD

The Bethany Assembly of God had its humble beginnings 47 years ago, when two young women from northern Michigan came to Lenawee and saw the need for children of the Deerfield Park wartime housing project to have spiritual life. The Reverend Leonora B. Annabel of Petoskey founded the church in 1943 with a Sunday School for the housing project. She was assisted by Donna Liebler of Grass Lake.

The church and Sunday School moved several times in the coming months, even meeting outdoors and in cars, but finally, in 1947, a large house on Mulzer Street became home to what was to be known as Bethany Chapel. Growing pains led the group of worshipers to purchase a small church building on the corner of Park Street and Michigan Avenue in 1950.

In 1951 two people who would be instrumental in the phenomenal growth of the church moved to Adrian. They were Reverend and Mrs. Arthur Clay. Within three years the congregation had outgrown the Park Street church and built a church at Airport Road and West Beecher streets, moving in on September 9, 1956. In 1971, 50 acres at East U.S. Route 223 and Treat Highway were purchased for a new building, which housed the exceptionally large Sunday School classes that make up the church's special area of ministry. Pastor Clay never saw the church building he envisioned. He died in 1972 and youth minister William Leach became pastor.

Ground breaking for the new building was in July 1975, and church facilities were ready for occupation on March 12, 1978. Encompassed in the 63,000-square-foot building is a 1,500-seating-capacity sanctuary, a gymnasium, a balcony area, kitchen with fellowship hall, offices, nursery facilities, and 35 classrooms.

Reverend Leach continued as pastor for 17 years, leaving in July 1988. Mrs. Audrey Clay was interim pastor until her son, youth pastor Richard Clay, was voted in as senior pastor, occupying the position his father once held. At present Bethany Assembly provides a wide variety of programs and activities for all ages, from birth to senior citizen. Working with Pastor Clay are the children's pastor, youth pastor, 50-plus pastor, and the minister of music, who provide leadership for these specialized activities.

Today the church has a fleet of 10 buses that transports children to services on Sundays and Wednesdays. "We're willing to bring children who don't have that availability," says the Reverend Richard Clay. "We are youth oriented and Sunday School oriented."

The transition from that small room in a housing project years ago to Bethany Assembly of God's facility today has not always been easy. "It's just been miracle after miracle," Mrs. Audrey Clay says of the money that has been raised when needed. Timely donations and the hard work of the congregation have made it all come together.

According to Pastor Clay: "We want it to be clearly seen that this is a ministry that God has had his hands upon. My goal is that people hear the message of God and Jesus Christ."

The Reverend Leonora B. Annabel (left) and Donna Liebler.

FROM LEFT TO RIGHT:

The Reverend William F. Leach.

The Reverend Arthur Clay.

The Reverend Richard Clay.

ADRIAN STEEL CO.

Adrian Steel Co. has come a long way in 37 years, from a small structural steel jobber to ranking in the top 100 publicly traded manufacturers in Michigan and third in earnings as a percentage of sales.

Adrian Steel makes modular steel service van interior racks and cabinets—a market the company helped create in the 1960s. Before discovering its niche, the firm produced a succession of products that provided employment and profitability, but not the springboard to growth afforded by the van-interiors line.

Adrian Steel was founded in 1953 by Robert "Bob" Westfall at 421 College Avenue, employing four people. They bought and sold structural steel beams and trusses, with some fabricating. Two years later the company moved to 235 West Maple Avenue, making racks for

cement blocks for a block manufacturer.

In May 1957 the firm moved to its present location, 906 James Street, and began to take on the character of today's company. The building was 14,000 square feet, and products were block racks and galvanized pans, and cabinets for air-conditioning units built by Acme in Jackson. The firm also made parts for Addison Products, Blissfield Manufacturing, and Primore Products.

In 1958 the organization began welding automotive seat frames for nearby Stubnitz & Greene Co. For three years this was the firm's principal work, employing 70 people. But in 1961 "Stubby's" took the work in house. The next two years were a struggle, as Adrian Steel had a plant and people, but not much work.

Refusing to be daunted, Bob Westfall issued a stock offering to raise the capital to

"The A-Team," employees of Adrian Steel's home plant, proudly posed for this group photo in 1989. That year employees became members of a profit-sharing plan funded by company stock.

ROBERT BARTON WESTFALL (1919-1980)

To understand the success of Adrian Steel Co., one must appreciate the spirit, determination, leadership, and work ethic of founder Robert Barton Westfall.

Westfall's success came despite—or perhaps evolved from—facing adversity throughout his life. He was born in 1919 in Hamtramck, Michigan. His father abandoned the family when Westfall was two years old. His mother moved Westfall and his sister to Ann Arbor in 1924.

There Westfall's mother worked 14-hour days in a laundry six days per week, and the children worked, too, to make ends meet. At age 10 Westfall started as a caddie and worked other jobs. His sister sewed.

They lived in a tiny second-floor apartment near Michigan Stadium—a location perhaps affecting the future. Showing leadership at an early age, Westfall was class president from eighth grade at Tappan Junior High School through 12th grade at Ann Arbor High School.

Demonstrating a remarkable talent for athletics, Westfall starred in football, basketball, track, and baseball at Ann Arbor High. Engaging in sports at all was remarkable, due to severe asthma that affected him from age nine throughout his life. His determination to succeed—and determination to play football at the University of Michigan—made him refuse to allow his medical condition to hold him back.

Westfall enrolled at the University of Michigan in 1938. His accomplishments as a spinning fullback for the Wolverines are legendary. Just five feet six inches tall and weighing only 165 pounds, Westfall was Michigan's starting fullback from 1939 to 1941, playing in the same backfield as Tom Harmon. He was team captain in 1941 and a unanimous selection to Grantland Rice's All-American team. He was captain of the East team in the 1942 East-West Shrine game.

Westfall enlisted in the Army Air Corps after Pearl Harbor was bombed, convincing a doctor to falsify his medical report. He was honorably discharged 18 months later because of his asthma.

Westfall married in February 1942, and his wife had a baby that November. In 1944 Westfall signed with the Detroit Lions and played four years. In 1945 he was named All-Pro fullback.

In 1948 Westfall ended his football-playing days and moved to Adrian, entering the salvage business. He did not give up football, though. He coached Adrian's Big Reds semi-pro team for three years, compiling a record of 20-4-3. In 1950 the team was unbeaten, untied, and unscored upon. He did some high school coaching as well.

In 1953 Westfall established Adrian Steel Co. Working at first with a handful of people in a small building, he managed to build a strong and successful organization.

Applying the same determination, spirit, leadership, and work ethic that had guided him through a difficult childhood and a heroic athletic career, he created a company that, like him, became an acknowledged leader.

THE RECORD

1939-1941	*Starting fullback and defensive halfback for all 24 games at University of Michigan.*
1940	*Second in nation in rushing only to teammate and Heisman trophy winner Tom Harmon.*
1941	*Captain, U of M football team. All-American fullback, first team.*
1939-1941	*Rushed for 1,864 yards on 428 carries (4.36 yards per carry), a Michigan fullback rushing record for 30 years.*
1942	*Captain, East team, East-West Shrine Game. Rushed for 103 yards, breaking Bronko Nagurski's 1930 record.*
1942	*Fullback, College All-Star Chicago Tribune Football Game and Philadelphia Enquirer Charity Football Game.*
1945	*Chosen All-Pro fullback with the Detroit Lions.*
1979	*Selected as one of the 25 all-time great U of M football players by U of M officials.*
1982	*Posthumously inducted into U of M Hall of Honor, Crisler Arena.*
1986	*Posthumously inducted into State of Michigan Sports Hall of Fame, Cobo Hall, Detroit.*
1987	*Posthumously inducted into the National Football Foundation's College Football Hall of Fame, Waldorf Astoria Hotel.*
1988	*Posthumously enshrined in the National Football Foundation's College Football Hall of Fame, King's Island.*

*Adrian Steel produces
modular steel service van
interiors designed for all
major van models and
specially selected for customers' particular needs.*

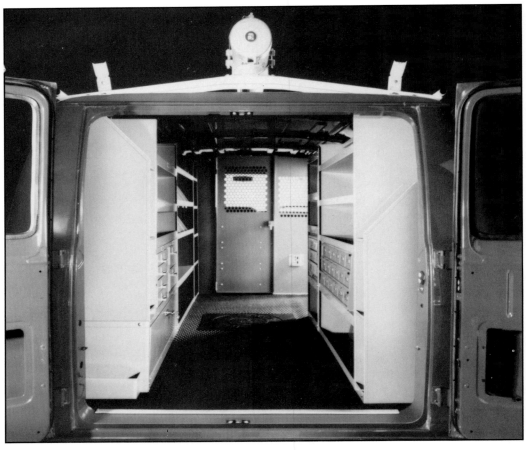

*Adrian Steel produces
modular steel service van
interiors designed for all
major van models and
specially selected for customers' particular needs.*

*Robert Barton Westfall,
founder of Adrian Steel, in
1941.*

produce a rooftop air-conditioning unit and a
fan-coil-type room heater/air-conditioning
unit. Workers made post-office carts,
material-handling racks, refuse dumpsters,

and steel tanks.

The breakthrough came in 1963. Company president Harley Westfall, Bob's son,
recalls that in that year a firm in Ohio sub-
contracted out some sheet-metal work for
bins and storage units to carry tools and components in newly introduced Ford Econoline
vans purchased by Consumers Power Co.

Over the next five years Adrian Steel
shifted production to van interiors. Chief
engineer Mac Ambrose designed the original
modular cabinets, bins, and drawer units.
Harold Bournes directed manufacturing; Carl
Tavierne did the accounting; and Bob Westfall did much of the selling in those days,
although Westfall's health had begun to fail
after a heart attack in 1961.

Expansion followed the success of the
van interiors. In 1970 a facility was established in Warren, Ohio, to do factory installation of interior units in full-size Chevrolet
vans. Three other subsidiaries have followed.

Today Adrian Steel Co. has 103,500
square feet of plant space in Adrian with
approximately 100 employees. Another 40
employees work in the firm's subsidiaries.

RIVERBEND TIMBER FRAMING, INC.

The roots of Riverbend Timber Framing, Inc., of Blissfield trace to the banks of the River Raisin, where in 1979 Frank Baker built a barn the old-fashioned way. From this modest start at 4141 Iffland Road, Riverbend has become the largest custom timber-framing business in the nation. Its distinctive homes and commercial buildings have been featured in such publications as *The New York Times,* the *Chicago Tribune, Better Homes and Gardens,* and *Fine Homebuilding.*

Unlike conventional stick-built structures, held up by lots of two-by-fours concealed within the walls, timber-frame buildings are supported by massive wooden posts, beams, and braces. These timbers are exposed to the interior and connected not with nails and screws, but the same types of mortise and tenon joinery found in fine furniture.

Timber framing has been in use for thousands of years but was virtually forgotten in the rush to build quick, cheap housing. Fortunately a few individuals understood the value of fine construction. About 15 years ago these individuals researched centuries-old timber-frame houses, barns, and churches to see what held the structures together all these years.

A leader of this timber-frame revival was Stewart Elliott, and when Baker was ready to build his barn, he invited Elliott to lead the effort. Joining them were Baker's former college classmate Sandy Bennett; Bennett's brother, John; and Art Hassen—all key players at Riverbend today.

Satisfaction from building that barn convinced Baker he had found his niche, and on November 7, 1979, he officially established Riverbend Timber Framing as a sole propri-

etorship. The barn served as the shop, and in the spring of the following year Baker and his wife, Brenda, assembled the crew to build the first Riverbend project—the Baker's home.

Growth came quickly, though not always easily. In January 1981 Riverbend was incorporated, with Baker and Bennett as the stockholders. They built six structures that year, and in March 1982 they moved to larger quarters at 415 East Adrian Street.

Three years and 60 frames later, Riverbend moved to the former Goble Lumber Company, west of Blissfield, where two long lumber sheds were converted to shops. In 1988 Riverbend's office was enlarged and remodeled, and a third shop was added at the former Kohler Building near Riga.

Riverbend's Timber Framing, Inc.'s, sales have increased an average of 30 percent per year to more than $4 million in 1989. Baker and Bennett attribute Riverbend's growth to a cooperative team effort. "It is the employees, families, friends, and suppliers of Riverbend that have made this company a success," Baker says. "We appreciate all of them and are confident that through their efforts, Riverbend will continue to prosper."

The "original cast" of Riverbend Timber Framing takes a break beneath the nearly completed frame of their first Riverbend home in May 1980.

By 1989 Riverbend had completed more than 500 timber-frame structures, and the staff had grown to 50 employees, most of whom are pictured here.

ADRIAN COLLEGE

Adrian College, a private college of liberal arts and sciences founded in 1859, traces its roots to a theological institute established by the Wesleyan Methodist denomination at Leoni, Michigan, 14 years earlier in 1845. The theological institute united with the Leoni Seminary, a Methodist Protestant institution, in 1855 to establish Michigan Union College.

Differences with the community forced a decision to relocate or close the school in 1859. Dr. Asa Mahan, pastor of the Plymouth Congregational Church in Adrian, was encouraged by Adrian residents at about the same time to establish a college in Adrian. An experienced educator, Mahan served as the first president of Oberlin College and as an officer of Lane Theological Seminary in Cincinnati, Ohio.

Michigan Union College accepted Mahan's invitation to help in establishing the new college at Adrian. On March 28, 1859, Adrian College was chartered by the state legislature as a degree-granting institution. Mahan was its first president. In 1916 a Methodist Protestant college in West Lafayette, Ohio, consolidated with Adrian College.

Today Adrian has an enrollment of more than 1,200 students from 15 states and 10 countries. About 75 percent of the faculty have a Ph.D. or the highest degree in their field. In 1989 *U.S. News and World Report* named Adrian College one of the 10 best regional liberal arts colleges in America.

Adrian offers a personal approach to college education, according to Dr. Stanley Caine, president of Adrian College. The institution offers 34 academic majors and more than 60 programs of study. Adrian is well known for its programs in business, accounting, pre-medicine, pre-dentistry, biology, chemistry, psychology, and teacher education,

David S. Hickman (left), chairman of the Adrian College Board of Trustees, welcomes Dr. Stanley P. Caine to campus after Caine's appointment as president.

Caine says. Adrian graduates have had a job-placement percentage of more than 90 percent for the past decade.

While the college is 131 years old, all but a few of its buildings were constructed in the past 31 years. For almost a century the Adrian campus consisted of several brick buildings fronting Madison Street. In the mid-1950s, largely as a result of benefactor Ray W. Herrick, Adrian recommitted itself to the future through construction and development. Today the campus sits on a 100-acre site in a west-side residential section of the city. New to the campus is the Merillat Sport and Fitness Center.

"Adrian College is grateful to the many people in this county who, over the more than 130 years of the college's history, have helped it pursue its important mission," says Caine. The campus and the community have been enriched by a tradition of sharing resources and developing cooperative programs. The college, the city, and the county are very closely linked. Generations of local students have attended Adrian College. Local corporations, foundations, and individuals have played a vital role in sustaining and strengthening the college.

An architect's rendering depicts the new Merillat Sport and Fitness Center.

LIBBEY-OWENS-FORD

The Libbey-Owens-Ford plant on Tecumseh-Clinton Road near Clinton opened in 1984 to produce value-added glass products primarily for the auto market. The plant opened as a new division of the corporation and helped to create a new market by performing tasks that had previously been done by automakers in their own factories.

The plant was good news for the Clinton area, as LOF moved into a facility that had been vacated three years earlier by the Budd Co. Budd built the plant to produce disc brake rotors, and the plant was closed in the depths of the recession that began in the 1980s. Most of the workers hired by LOF are Lenawee County residents, and some are former employees of the Budd Co.

The 510 employees of the LOF plant install mounting hardware and frames to auto glass panels shipped from other LOF plants. The parts made at the Clinton plant go into a variety of General Motors cars and trucks, including Chevrolet and GMC pickup trucks, Buick LeSabre and Oldsmobile Delta 88, Pontiac Grand Prix, and Buick Regal and Reatta models, as well as Jeep Cherokees. The output of models using glass from the plant in the 1989 model year totals more than one million vehicles. "We have a lot of product through here for this size of plant," says LOF's Mike Moore.

Before the Clinton plant opened, workers in the auto plants would have installed the frames and hardware before they could put the windows into the cars. By having the hardware already mounted when the part comes out of the shipping crate, the assembly workers can mount the part directly in the auto. Also made in the plant are auto glass products for the aftermarket, such as for glass replacement and sunroofs.

The Clinton plant made auto glass history recently when it pioneered the first-ever encapsulated automotive part—a flipper window for Jeeps. The part has a plastic urethane seal around the outside with a window that opens from the inside.

Libbey-Owens-Ford was started in the late nineteenth century by Toledoan Edward Drummond Libbey. LOF established an early, close relationship with the emerging auto industry and has been a major supplier of auto glass ever since.

Libbey was a major figure in the life of Toledo, having started the Toledo Art Museum and having supported many other civic and philanthropic causes. LOF executives continue to serve their community through service on hospital and charitable boards. Clinton plant personnel are also actively involved in Lenawee County community activities, according to LOF's Roger Bortel.

In 1987 Libbey-Owens-Ford was acquired by Pilkington, Limited, of England, the world's largest glassmaker. Two years later Nippon Sheet Glass acquired a 20 percent share of LOF, making it a truly international company.

The Libbey-Owens-Ford plant in Clinton was opened in 1984.

COMFORT ENTERPRISES, INC.

Lenawee County was a magnet to settlers from the East in 1840 when Aaron Comfort moved his family from Bucks County, Pennsylvania, to Raisin Township. Comfort bought land at Russell Road and Green Highway and began farming.

Nineteen years later Comfort's son Elwood built a home of his own by digging clay near his homestead on Rogers Highway and burning bricks for the house. That project finished, he was encouraged to go into the brick business. Many of Tecumseh's impressive historic homes and public buildings are made of Comfort brick.

sustain brick and tile manufacturing well into the twentieth century. By the 1950s, however, clay was also brought in from other sources.

Tile was the backbone of the Comfort operation, but bricks were made until 1942. The last project supplied with bricks from the yard was the power-plant addition at the Hayden Mill in Tecumseh, built when Henry Ford converted the mill for war production.

As the readily available clay in the Comfort holdings was played out in the 1950s, a new plant was built to use previously unserviceable clay. This extended the life of the tile yard into the modern era, when the industry began to change to plastic pipe. The Comforts began making plastic pipe in 1971. Both plastic and clay pipe were sold until 1975, when the changeover to plastic was complete.

The business continued to evolve, however, and in 1985 the Comfort yard switched entirely to sale of products manufactured elsewhere. Today Comfort Enterprises supplies the agriculture industry with drain tile and related products and supplies the construction industry with a variety of

Comfort's brick and tile yard showed 100 years of development in the mid-1960s. Kilns for firing tile are in the foreground, and settling ponds in the background. The operation dates back to 1859.

The business he launched in 1859 is still in the family and still supplying building materials, although Comfort's stock in trade has changed over the years. The first change took place soon after Elwood Comfort got started, when he began making clay drain tiles. Comfort tiles have been draining farms throughout Michigan and surrounding states ever since.

Comfort had the good fortune to establish his business on ground that contained ancient lake-deposit clay, says Gordon Comfort, the fifth and current Comfort to lead the company. The clay was undisturbed by prehistoric glaciers and was plentiful enough to

water-management products, including pipe, hydrants, pumps, and, most recently, swimming pools.

Operation of the company passed in the last century from founder Elwood Comfort to his son William. In 1984 Elwood's son Albert Aaron Comfort took over, continuing until his death in 1934. Albert's son Ralph then assumed ownership and has continued his association to the present. Ralph's son Gordon Albert Comfort now heads Comfort Enterprises, Inc., joined by his wife, Marjorie.

Ralph Comfort was born in and still occupies the house Elwood built to start it all.

SOCIETY BANK

Society Bank is the new name of one of Lenawee County's oldest businesses—the familiar Commercial Savings Bank. The bank assumed its new name in January 1990, after Trustcorp Bank and Society Corporation of Cleveland merged.

The firm's local history traces to a bank established by Langford G. Berry and William H. Stone in 1849. In 1888 the bank's owners—Major Seymour Howell, Edwin L. Baker, and William B. Thompson—seized an opportunity created by a change in state law, enabling one bank to conduct both commercial banking and personal savings and mortgage services. The institution was reborn as The Commercial Savings Bank, with initial capital of $75,000 contributed by 33 stockholders.

The new bank was successful from the start. After one year assets were $392,986. In five years assets topped $500,000. In 1894 the bank moved to 6 South Main Street (now 110 South Main).

In 1915 the institution expanded and remodeled its building, and by 1920 the bank's assets had grown to nearly $1.7 million. The Depression hit the community hard, but in 1933 Commercial Savings was the first Adrian bank allowed to reopen on an unrestricted basis after the statewide bank holiday.

The following decades saw remarkable growth. By 1969 assets had grown to more than $35 million, and by 1988 assets stood at $180 million. Growth had come through expansion of services and acquisition. The bank aggressively marketed a full range of business and personal banking services. Acquisition began in 1956 with the purchase of Addison State Bank. Later acquisitions included the Exchange Bank of Clayton and Blissfield's Jipson-Carter State Bank.

In 1958 the bank moved into a larger space at 117 East Maumee and seven years later expanded into the building to the west. In 1966 the bank's first branch opened in Adrian, at Southland Plaza. Branches have been added since at the north edge of Adrian, on West Maumee, and in Tecumseh.

In 1969, upon the retirement of president Russell McAfee, John "Jack" L. Germond was named president. In 1976 Com-

The original bank building in 1888.

mercial Savings Bank reorganized into a bank holding company called Commercial Bankshares Corp., with the former shareholders of the bank becoming owners of the new corporation.

In 1987 Commercial Bankshares, Inc., was merged into Trustcorp, Inc., and Commercial Savings Bank and The Jipson-Carter State Bank were consolidated as Trustcorp Bank, Lenawee, the first Michigan affiliates of Toledo's leading bank. Soon after the merger, Trustcorp's Toledo bank ran into difficulties with loans made for that city's riverfront development and sought a merger with another institution that could bolster its capital. Society Corporation of Cleveland and Trustcorp, Inc., merged in 1989, leading to the new name and new signs in Lenawee County.

John "Jack" L. Germond has served as president and chief executive officer of Society Bank since 1969.

SOUTHEASTERN MICHIGAN RURAL ELECTRIC COOPERATIVE, INC.

An underground cable is plowed in on U.S. 223.

Much of rural Lenawee County was without electric service in May 1937, when Lee Bettis and Bill Thompson called a meeting of people from Lenawee and Ohio to propose they take advantage of President Franklin Delano Roosevelt's new Rural Electrification Administration and establish an REA cooperative.

The Southeastern Michigan Rural Electric Cooperative, Inc., was the result of their idea. Bettis and Thompson were joined on the incorporating board by Henry Silberhorn, Elmer H. Green, Worthy W. Sell, W.S. Kaufman, Clifton C. Nye, and Leon F. Stautz.

Money was the key ingredient needed to get the proposition off the ground, and that was what Roosevelt's REA program made possible. The new cooperative borrowed the money needed—at a low interest rate—to create a skeleton distribution system from the REA, and soon the rural residents in the area served were able to begin enjoying the modern convenience of electricity.

The cooperative now serves 3,900 customers in Lenawee County and the Ohio counties of Fulton and Williams. Service extends from as far north as Woodstock Township in Lenawee County to south within two miles of Archbold, Ohio. The biggest single user of power is the Lenawee Intermediate School District, but other major users are Ten Pin Alley in Raisin Township and several large dairy farms, according to Don Grimes, the cooperative's manager since 1980. Grimes says that the area with the heaviest population and greatest power demand is in the Adrian-Tecumseh corridor of Raisin Township. During the growing season the co-op also sees increased demand from time to time when farmers irrigate their fields.

The co-op generated its own power for years, with the plant located at the co-op's headquarters on East Maumee in Adrian. But in 1946 the organization sold its generators and began buying power from Consumers Power Co. Later, in 1969, there was a partial switch to Detroit Edison as a dual electricity supplier. Since the mid-1980s, however, power supply for Michigan members has been purchased from the City of Lansing, Consumers Power Co., and Toledo Edison via firm power contracts. The Buckeye Power Co. supplies Ohio customers, which include the surrounding areas of Wauseon and Fayette.

The Southeastern Michigan Rural Electric Cooperative's offices and plant operation are located on the original site where the co-op began in 1937, but it occupies a building that was erected in 1978 to replace the outdated original structure. Two substations manage the distribution of power to the cooperative's far-flung service area.

While the co-op has been a dependable supplier of electricity to its members over the years, its financial situation has left room for improvement. In recent years operating and financial practices have been sharpened to put it on "a sound financial footing," according to Grimes.

An example of the co-op's forward-

A meter service technician sets up a meter for testing.

thinking approach is its pole-replacement program. Aging poles are a problem for many REAs, because systems all across the country were built at about the same time, and the original poles have reached their 50-year life expectancy at about the same time. SEMREA workers inspect poles regularly on a rotating basis, and those needing replacement are taken care of each year. Funds for replacing poles are included in the annual budget. Timely pole replacement helps to guard against service interruptions, Grimes explains.

The cooperative bids to be the electrical energy supplier to businesses and industries that locate within the SEMREA service area. The cooperative became regulated in 1965 for territorial integrity protection but larger firms may purchase electricity from the supplier of their choice—not just the local electric company. As a result, SEMREA must compete for business against Consumers Power, Detroit Edison, and any other supplier that might decide to try for the business. The co-op has the capacity to be able to accommodate more industry, Grimes says, and he hopes boosting revenues in the years to come by securing several large-consumption customers.

At the end of the 1980s an ambitious five-year capital improvement program was begun, with the goal of upgrading the

system's capacity to handle peak expected loads in areas of growth.

Grimes set about to instill sound business practices that would place the cooperative on a solid footing with its principal creditor, the REA, and ensure successful operations in the years to come. The task was complicated by government changes that resulted in a tightening of financial requirements imposed by the REA, but the cooperative has been able to rise to the challenge and meet those requirements.

The cooperative's fleet of vehicles includes two bucket trucks, a digger derrick for installing new poles, a service truck, a dump truck, an underground plow for installing underground service, as well as chipper trailers for use with tree-trimming maintenance.

As a cooperative, Southeast Michigan Rural Electric Cooperative, Inc., is governed by its members, who elect the board of directors that hires a manager and sets policy. Members of the board of directors are elected at an annual meeting usually held in the Adrian area. Under the bylaws of the cooperative, three directors are drawn from each of the three districts. The north district is the area of Lenawee County that lies north of Beecher Highway/Deerfield Road; the southwest district lies south of Beecher and west of M-52; and the southeast district is east of M-52 and south of Deerfield Road.

Board members are Roger Wolf, president; Norm Bless, vice-president; Gene Winzeler, secretary; David Feldkamp, treasurer; and Arlie Pickles, Alice Pliska, Wendell Young, David Keller, and Harold Gentz.

Jerry Bates is operations supervisor and Bob Willet is member services director. In the office there are three full-time and one part-time employees, and seven workers handle outside duties.

The Southeastern Michigan Rural Electric Cooperative headquarters is located at 1610 East Maumee Street in Adrian.

A lineman works on a transmission line.

MICHIGAN BUILDING SPECIALTIES

In 1960 John Brielmaier, Sr., opened shop here at Center and Erie streets.

I f tenacity and hard work are the keys to success, then John Brielmaier, Sr., was working on a sure thing from the moment he launched Michigan Building Specialties.

A native of Detroit, Brielmaier moved to Adrian in 1951 at the age of 29. He had been a flight engineer in World War II and married Margaret Rogan in 1946. The couple moved to Adrian when he took a job in engineering and sales with Oro Manufacturing Co.

Brielmaier left Oro in 1957 and launched Michigan Building Specialties from the basement of the family home at 699 Budlong Street. He sold windows and doors to contractors in lower Michigan, taking his business to the customer.

Brielmaier traveled the east side of the state one week, then covered the west side the following week, recalls his son Jim. "He had to keep going," Jim says fondly. "There were seven kids."

By 1960 John Brielmaier was ready to get off the road and set up shop in Adrian. He opened at Center and Erie streets, and hired two part-time installers. From this location Michigan Building Specialties installed windows and doors locally. The hard work continued, and the business grew. In 1963 Brielmaier built a new 7,200-square-foot shop at 1001 West Beecher Street. With the added space he was able to successfully expand into the aluminum siding business.

The first Michigan Building Specialties aluminum siding job was in 1965, on South Scott Street, and still looks great. By 1971 Brielmaier employed six people full time, and by 1979 the payroll had increased to nine.

Aluminum siding sold well until the mid-1970s, when vinyl siding came onto the

market and quickly took over. Vinyl's durability, colorfastness, and appearance made it the siding of choice. Michigan Building Specialties was on top of the trend, and by 1979 its siding work was almost completely in vinyl.

In 1978 Jim Brielmaier purchased the business from his father. The middle child of John and Margaret Brielmaier's seven, Jim was the only one to remain involved with the family business.

John and Margaret moved to Florida and shortly thereafter found themselves starting a small commercial fishing business. After two commercial fishing boats and 10 years of business, they finally decided to retire.

Jim, meanwhile, set about to expand the business further. By 1990 Michigan Building Specialties had grown into one of the area's largest, full-time remodeling firms. By employing more than 19 well-trained personnel, it offers a complete package of interior and exterior design work. It is the proud recipient of more than 17 national awards and has had some of its work published in national trade magazines.

So as one can see, what started as a young man's dream more than 30 years ago has survived and grown into a company the Brielmaier family is very proud of.

After 30 years of growth and expansion, Michigan Building Specialties has become a leader in professional remodeling.

KAPNICK AND COMPANY, INC.

Kapnick and Company has enjoyed a healthy growth rate under the leadership of Douglas L. Kapnick, son of founder and chairman of the board Elmer L. Kapnick.

In 1946 Elmer Kapnick founded a one-man, one-room insurance agency on the top floor of the old Bank of Lenawee Building on the Four Corners in downtown Adrian. Today Kapnick and Company, Inc., is a multimillion-dollar agency employing 60 people in a 20,000-square-foot building that was built in 1986.

"In the beginning I was on my own; it was just me," says chairman Elmer Kapnick. "Right away I hired part-time help so I could work outside of the office a half-day."

The years since have held three changes in location and an emphasis on goal setting and goal achieving, Kapnick says.

From the Four Corners the agency moved to North Winter Street, where it remained until 1971, when a building was constructed at 1390 West Maumee Street. In 1986 the company built its present headquarters at 1801 West Maumee.

As the firm grew and moved to larger buildings, its areas of service grew as well, and Kapnick's son, Doug, who today is president of the organization, joined his father. Doug Kapnick is an active community worker, having served on the school board as a member and as president, along with service to the YMCA, chamber of commerce, and GAIDC. The staff is also active in the community.

Whereas the early days of Kapnick and Company were confined to property and casualty insurance, the agency greeted the 1970s with expanded marketing plans. In the early 1970s the firm wrote programs for import auto dealers and gained a reputation for providing coverage to auto dealerships throughout Michigan. The Kapnicks expanded to other areas, putting together programs for screw machine shop businesses.

In the 1970s and 1980s the company became known throughout Michigan, Indiana, and Ohio for specialty market programs. It began providing risk and management services to such diverse markets as railroads, golf courses, grain elevators, flour milling, and metalworking. "We provide clients with fast, accurate, professional service," says president Doug Kapnick.

"We're in Adrian because we want to be in Adrian, but we can't do all the business we want to do in Lenawee County," according to Elmer. Fifty percent of Kapnick and Company, Inc.'s, business is done outside the county. Other offices are in Chelsea, Michigan, and Findlay, Ohio.

In addition to hiring Lenawee County residents and people returning from college, "We have hired people from Detroit, Chicago, and Boston," Doug says. "We brought them to Adrian and showed them the community and the life-style. Because of the kind of community it is, we were able to convince them to move to Lenawee."

He emphasizes there is "real opportunity for small businesses to thrive and prosper in a small town. Business is thriving, and we're looking at expansion in the near future."

Pictured is the staff, which includes customer-service, claims, accounting, data-processing, and underwriting departments.

SIENA HEIGHTS COLLEGE

Sacred Heart Hall was the first of the buildings erected by the Dominican Sisters for Siena Heights College in 1922. Today the structure serves as the school's administration building.

S iena Heights College was established in 1919 by the Adrian Dominican Sisters and has been adapting to meet the community's needs ever since. The Dominicans had operated St. Joseph's Academy, a boarding school for girls, for several years. There was no Catholic college of arts and sciences in the area, so Mother Camilla Madden opened the college.

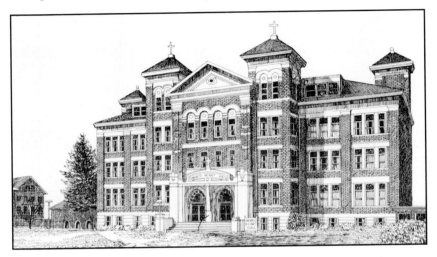

Siena Heights College is well known for its performing arts. The Charles Verheyden Performing Arts Center houses Francoeur Theatre and the smaller Lab Theater.

Sacred Heart Hall, the first college building, was completed in 1922. Benincasa Hall and Archangelus Hall, a dining hall and residence, were completed in 1938. The following year the college was renamed in honor of St. Catherine of Siena, a fifteenth-century Italian Dominican who dedicated her life to a quest for truth and social responsibility.

Through its formative years the college was guided by Mother Mary Camilla Madden and Mother Mary Augustine Walsh. In 1933 Mother Mary Gerald Barry became the first

official president. Under her leadership many new educational concepts were introduced.

Sister Benedicta Marie Ledwidge became president in 1957. Programs were expanded to include coeducational graduate work in secondary and elementary education, administration, and guidance.

Sister Mary Petronilla Francoeur presided during a period of change and reevaluation. Taking the reins in 1965, she established a lay advisory board composed of prominent citizens of Michigan and Ohio. Members were later invited to join the religious members of the governing board. Studies were also carried out leading to the decision to make the college coeducational.

Sister Mary Petronilla's tenure was cut short by an automobile accident, and in 1970 Richard Reaume served as interim president. Dr. Hugh Thompson was named president in 1971, and under his stewardship the college experienced its most rapid growth in programming, facilities, and enrollment. He was followed in 1978 by Dr. Louis C. Vaccaro, who continued Thompson's aggressive expansion of the college's programs and reach.

Siena Heights has three off-campus baccalaureate programs, one in Southfield, one with Lake Michigan College in Benton Harbor, and one in Monroe, Michigan. The programs offer night and weekend classes especially geared to working people who wish to pursue a bachelor's degree. More than 1,000 students have gained their degrees in Southfield. "We've been very successful in meeting the needs of working adults," comments John Bennett, Dean of the College and Provost.

The Adrian campus has 775 full-time and nearly 450 part-time students. Many of the Adrian students are older than traditional college students, and many are commuters.

Currently Siena Heights College is headed by Sister Cathleen Real and offers a broad-based liberal arts curriculum. The college is especially noted for its art and business departments, and offers graduate courses in education. A source of great pride on campus is the success of the school's athletic teams. The college continually seeks to offer quality educational programs in response to social changes.

PRIMORE, INC.

Primore, Inc., emerged from the engineering and entrepreneurial efforts of Gorton Price and Stan Morse. The firm is in the business of designing and selling refrigeration shutoff valves and manufacturing, designing, and selling refrigeration relief valves.

Gorton Price and Morse founded Primor Products, a sales and engineering firm, after World War II. In 1949 they established Primus Company in Addison. The firm, now known as Addison Products Company, is owned and operated by Cliff Knight.

Primus Company manufactured air conditioners and related refrigeration products such as soda-pop dispenser machines for gas stations (the old lift-top cabinets with slides for the bottles). The firm was sold in 1952 to Knight and a group of investors who worked for Tecumseh Products.

Primor Products moved to Adrian in 1953 to make central air-conditioning systems. They built a plant on the south side of Beecher Street just west of Adrian, producing complete air-conditioning units. Shutoff valves were later added to the company's line of products.

In 1956 Borg-Warner Corp. bought out Primor's air-conditioner business, but Price and Morse retained the product design and sales organization.

Primore Sales, Inc., was then established, with shutoff valves the main product. The valves were made in Attleboro, Massachusetts, by Automatic Machine Products Co., with Primore providing the engineering and sales on an exclusive basis.

Sedco, Inc. (Sales, Engineering, and Development Co.), was established in 1958 to develop and sell new product ideas. The firm soon started to manufacture refrigeration products such as egg coolers, marine refrigerators, dehumidifiers, and vacuum pumps. Within three years Sedco became a wholly owned subsidiary of Primore.

In the mid-1960s Sedco began to manufacture a new Primore-developed product—a pressure-relief valve for air-conditioning systems. The device has been adapted for use by automotive and commercial air-conditioning compressor manufacturers.

Over the years Primore has worked closely with and done business with other refrigeration industry firms in Lenawee County such as Tecumseh Products, Blissfield Manufacturing, and Brazeway, and the executives of the companies have been close friends.

The firm is now owned by Robert Price, who started in the business in 1950 after graduating from Michigan State University as an engineer. Price began as a designer, later taking turns at sales and, in recent years, management of the firm.

The company maintains its close relationship with Automatic Machine Products and still engineers and sells the shutoff valves manufactured in the Massachusetts plant.

Sedco manufactures and sells relief valves for most major compressor manufacturers and is a principal supplier for automotive air-conditioning compressors. Among the firm's major customers are Ford Motor Company and Chrysler Motors.

Long-term associates of Primore, Inc., include Price, who serves as president and treasurer; Dick Hutt, vice-president/sales and engineering; Tom Barto, comptroller and secretary; and Ed Kuhn, chief engineer.

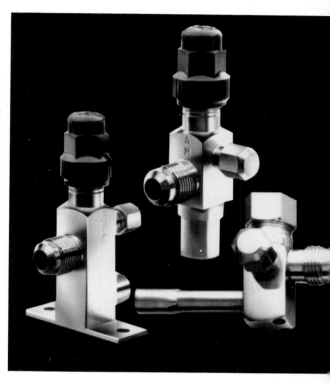

Primore refrigeration and air-conditioning shut-off valves.

Sedco pressure relief valves.

CONSUMERS POWER CO.

RIGHT: W.A. Foote, founder of Consumers Power Co. Photo circa 1917

Consumers Power Co. has had Lenawee County connections from its earliest days. Company founder W.A. Foote was a native of Adrian, attended Adrian schools, and tested his first generator in Adrian.

Foote's first business venture was a flour mill in Adrian. That business was not particularly successful, so Foote decided to parlay his fascination with electricity into a business.

Americans had been experimenting with electricity for years, but in the 1880s the first practical applications of electricity were found. In cities nationwide, small water-powered generators were installed—often alongside the waterwheels in existing factories—to produce electricity for streetlight.

Foote started an electric company in Jackson, then started and bought into companies in Kalamazoo, Grand Rapids, Albion, and Battle Creek. At the turn of the century, with his younger brother J.B. and George Stecker, self-taught engineers, the entrepreneur W.A. Foote was the first in the world to conceive and build high-voltage electric transmission lines to carry power from a central large hydrogenerator to several communities. Foote's innovation coincided with the development of electric rail transit companies in southern Michigan.

Foote was also the first to combine many small electric companies into a multicity system. His creation, first called Commonwealth Power Company and, starting in 1910 Consumers Power, is thus a pioneer not only in Michigan, but in the world.

Foote died in 1915, but his firm continued to grow and innovate. Consumers Power and the industrial and commercial development of Michigan have been inseparable since Foote's day. Today Consumers Power is the

BELOW: J.B. Foote was the founding engineer of Consumers Power Co. Photo circa 1917

biggest utility in Michigan and one of the biggest in the country, providing electric service to more than half the area of Lower Michigan and natural gas to communities from Kalamazoo to Bay City and Lake St. Clair.

Consumers sells both gas and electricity in much of Lenawee County. The Adrian service center employs 90 people and serves customers in Lenawee and Monroe counties. The Adrian center is part of the Jackson district, which serves 118,000 electric customers and 59,000 gas customers.

Today Consumers Power Co. serves nearly 6 million of the state's 9 million residents, and serves all or part of 67 of the 68 counties in Lower Michigan.

Consumers Power Co. has from its earliest days promoted new business and economic development. The firm supports the effort to have U.S. Route 223 improved through Lenawee County, and in 1989 upgraded its transmission facilities in Tecumseh, increasing electrical capacity in anticipation of continued development in that area.

LUNDY'S HEATING AND PLUMBING

Dave Lundy had already had a fascinating career before he first came to Adrian in 1964. He'd helped build three of the engineering marvels of the modern age: the Mackinac Bridge near his Sault Ste. Marie home, the Soo Locks, and the Radio Ionospheric Probe at Arecibo, Puerto Rico, a 1,000-foot radio dish that probes deepest space for signs of extraterrestrial life. Those experiences taught the importance of excellence and training—lessons he applies today to his plumbing and heating business.

Lundy's travels in construction took him from Puerto Rico to New York State, where he worked on a road project. After joining the Stauffer Chemical Co. in Cortland, New York, the firm punched his ticket for Lenawee County, where he ended up sinking his roots.

He came to Lenawee in 1964 to build Stauffer's silicones plant on Sutton Road, now Wacker Silicones. "I was the first one on the job," he recalls. When the job was done, Stauffer moved him to Alabama, Delaware, and Louisiana. He wound up in an office in New York City. But he liked Lenawee County. He quit the company and moved back to Adrian.

Lundy worked sales at Baldwin's Hardware in Tecumseh. Later joining Sears, he was hardware department manager when Sears opened at Adrian Mall. He left Sears for a traveling sales job with D&C Plumbing and earned his plumbing license.

In 1975 Lundy bought Eisch Plumbing and Heating in Adrian. He has been in the business ever since. Lundy's Heating and Plumbing's emphasis is on residential heating and air-conditioning sales and installation. The firm serves all of Lenawee County with 1,418 employees.

It is a competitive industry. "In 1975 there were 38 companies in Lenawee County in the business. I'm now the third oldest in the county under continuous ownership," Lundy says.

Lundy's belief in training and certification is being tested. "Training and certification are getting to be difficult because the heating and air-conditioning equipment is becoming so complex," he comments. "Once, if a fellow was mechanically inclined and had a case of tools, he could be a technician. That's not so any more. I spend nearly $3,000 each year for training for each technician."

Lundy served from 1983 to 1989 on the Adrian City Commission, and from 1984 to 1989 on the state board of the Air Conditioning Contractors of America.

His interest in engineering has not waned. In 1989 he dug up the backyard of his home to install a grid of copper tubes five feet below ground for a ground source heat pump. Lundy is a regional representative for the system, and he wanted to try it out. Lundy expects another fossil fuel price shock, and believes the technology is an economical solution.

David Lundy has adopted Adrian as his home and has been in the plumbing and heating business since 1975. Lundy has served on the Adrian City Commission and has been an active member of trade associations.

BLISSFIELD MANUFACTURING CO.

The original Blissfield Manufacturing plant was a mere fraction of today's modern, 245,000-square-foot facility when this photo was taken in the 1950s. Much of this building was destroyed by fire in 1959. Today the company operates two other plants in Indiana.

Technicians at Blissfield Manufacturing designed a refrigeration unit for this Meadowridge Dairy milk truck back in the 1950s. The dairy served customers in Tecumseh.

Orville W. Farver has a talent for turning disaster into opportunity. Blissfield Manufacturing Co. stands as a testament to that talent.

He founded the business in January 1946. Farver had been plant superintendent at Tecumseh Products for 10 years, but he left the company after declining to get into an internal power struggle with another production executive. Farver and his former boss Ray Herrick parted on good terms, and Herrick asked Farver to take over assembly of a compressor model with the company Farver later established.

While his plant was under construction in Blissfield, Farver began production in Adrian, in the building on Maumee Street by the River Raisin that is known as the Fireside Building. Farver drove daily from Tecumseh, bringing with him five compressors to be built into refrigeration HiSides. Products were added to the company's catalog, and after one year the move was made to Blissfield.

O.W. Farver was joined in the business early on by his son, O. Herbert Farver. "Herb"

Farver assumed the title of president in 1978. O.W. Farver is now chairman of the board.

Other Lenawee County refrigeration companies specialized with various types of products, but Blissfield Manufacturing developed a more diverse line of products. The firm developed steel and aluminum condensers; copper/aluminum coils; oil coolers for off-road, automotive, and agricultural applications; complete hermetic refrigeration systems; and steel tubing and contract manufacturing services. "If you think of heat transfer products, we've made them," Pat Farver says.

Blissfield Manufacturing Co. established an early relationship with vending machine manufacturers, producing systems and steel condensers for bottle vending machines. Over the years, reports Farver, O.W.'s grandson and the firm's vice-president/sales and public relations, Blissfield Manufacturing has made products for every pop vending machine company in the country.

"I think a lot of the company's success has been our flexibility over the years, to be able to take advantage when opportunities arose," Pat Farver comments. "We were very open to look at them—we were very open to look at almost anything. We are customer driven. If a customer wants a new product or service, we'll look at it and see if there is a way we can fill their need."

Blissfield Manufacturing's close relationship with Tecumseh Products continues, with the Blissfield plant still producing compressors and other units for "The Products."

The Blissfield factory and general office facility now contains 245,000 square feet. Two subsidiaries have been established in Indiana:

Jay Products Co. in Portland, and Berne Tube Products in Berne. Each plant produces a different line of the company's products, and the two subsidiaries add 150,000 square feet of manufacturing capacity.

Through the years the firm has been guided by two principles set down by O.W. Farver: "We must be a step ahead in our thinking, never once believing we have reached perfection in anything," and "The most important principle is to treat everyone—customer, supplier, and competitor—with fairness and honesty."

The attitudes and the reputation those principles produced for the company proved to be quite important when disaster struck November 1, 1959. A fire damaged a large portion of the Blissfield plant, creating a $1.5-million loss and destroying the plant's entire inventory. "We never missed an order," Herb Farver recalls with evident pride.

"The workers figured they were out of a job when they saw the fire," he remembers, "but dad put out the word they were to come to work with shovels, and we began immediately to get things back together.

"Because of the relationship we had with our customers and suppliers, our suppliers all broke into their production lines and restocked us, and we never missed a shipment," he adds. "In 10 days we were back in production.

"I had a man call me from California," Herb Farver remembers. "I never heard of him before or since, but he said 'I heard about your fire. I have a new automatic charging board [a metering device] for you; it's not even out of the crate yet. If you want I'll just

ship it to you, and when you're done with it ship it back.'" Farver said he didn't take the man up on the offer, "but it was just the thought" that was gratifying.

Workers salvaged what could be saved, and rebuilding began at once. A year after the fire the company hosted an open house in its newly restored plant.

Pat Farver credits much of the firm's success to its emphasis on quality and people. "We pride ourselves on longevity, loyalty, quality, and creativity," he comments. "And we like to feel our people are our greatest asset."

Blissfield Manufacturing is very much a family business. Not only do three generations of Farvers direct the company, but there are many families represented among the workers. "There are a lot of two- and three-generation families working here," Pat Farver reports with pride.

An expansion took place in Blissfield in 1989, when a manufacturing operation was brought in from one of the Indiana plants. As for the future, Blissfield Manufacturing Co. plans further diversification, with greater emphasis on new markets for existing products and services as well as new products for existing markets. "If you want the best quality on time at a fair price, we do it," he says.

Three generations of Farvers direct Blissfield Manufacturing Co.: founder O.W. Farver, right, is board chairman; his son, Herb, left, is president; and Herb's son, Pat, center, is vice-president/sales and public relations.

Workers at Blissfield Manufacturing assemble refrigeration units along a conveyor line in this photo dating from the 1950s. Many Blissfield employees represent families that have been with the company for two and three generations.

MERILLAT INDUSTRIES, INC.

Orville and Ruth Merillat, partners in marriage and business.

Merrillat Industries, Inc., has grown in 44 years from a small cabinet shop on Springbrook Avenue in Adrian to become the nation's largest cabinetmaker, with 11 plants and nearly 3,000 employees.

The company is the creation of Orville and Ruth Merillat, who have succeeded in transforming a dream into a life of success and philanthropy.

Orville Merillat was born in 1916 on a farm near Wauseon, Ohio, one of 13 children. He left school in the ninth grade to help support the family during the Depression, and at the age of 19 got a job with a Morenci contractor as a carpenter. He enjoyed working with wood and learned all types of woodworking, including building kitchen cabinets.

He married Ruth Meller before shipping off to the South Pacific as a Coast Guard ship's carpenter in World War II. Ruth worked during the war years at the Air Force bomber plant in Adrian.

After the war the couple took their savings of $8,250 and built the cabinet shop on Springbrook, opening September 2, 1946, as Merillat Woodworking Company with a payroll of three—including themselves. Their family had become three as well, with the arrival of son Richard.

The business got off to a good start. There was plenty of new home-building in the postwar years and plenty of demand for cabinets. The shop soon specialized in kitchen cabinets, and two Toledo home building firms began using them. By 1953 the company had grown to the point more space was needed, and a new plant was built on Beecher Street at the west edge of Adrian.

The new 15,000-square-foot plant was six times the size of the original building. It employed an idea Merillat had been nurturing for a long time—a modular kitchen cabinet factory.

The plant opened in 1954 with 17

Merillat Woodworking Company made a modest start in 1946 in this building on Springbrook Avenue in Adrian.

employees. They built as many as 14 kitchens each day, using Merillat's modular concept. In 1956 Kitchen Distributors of America, in Chicago, approached Merillat and became the company's first distributor. The following year Michigan Kitchen Distributors of Marshall, Michigan, signed on, and the firm took off.

Innovations such as the self-closing hinge, aluminum drawer guides, and high-pressure laminates kept Merillat ahead of the industry. A mechanized assembly line helped meet demand. In 1963 the company's net worth reached one million dollars, and a year later the plant was expanded to 76,000 square feet. In 1965 the plant was increased to 135,000 square feet. The following year Merillat Woodworking Company had 210

Today Merillat Industries' Adrian plant sprawls on Beecher Street. First built in 1953 with 15,000 square feet of space, the plant now encloses 400,000 square feet. Merillat Industries now operates 11 plants nationwide.

employees making 1,500 cabinets per day, supplying 46 distributors in 12 states.

Growth since has been rapid and steady. Today Merillat Industries, Inc., renamed in 1971, operates 11 plants in seven states. Distribution is nationwide, and since 1985 the company has been ranked as the number-one producer of kitchen and bath cabinets in the country. Merillat employs nearly 3,000 people nationwide, and operates a fleet of trucks—which are cleaned before they start any trip.

In 1985 the company merged with Masco Corporation, with Orville Merillat remaining as chairman and Richard Merillat as president.

John Thurman, vice-president/finance and treasurer, believes the company's success is the result of Orville and Ruth's commitment to their people, products, plants, and customers. "We operate today with principles set down by Orville and Ruth," Thurman says, "principles of fair dealing with employees and customers. Orville said, 'Excel in what you undertake; there's room above second best.' We still believe that.

"Orville has been an innovator not only in products but also in the way he has dealt with his employees," Thurman observes.

In 1976, when the company built its first plant outside Adrian, Orville decided to put workers on salary rather than hourly wages. "We count on these people to do an awful lot, we ought to trust them," Thurman recalls him saying.

The salaried concept is in place at nearly all Merillat plants, and Thurman says the results have been that productivity is far higher than industry averages and absenteeism is lower.

In 1957 Orville Merillat instituted an incentive plan that rewards productivity with more pay. That system is employed at every Merillat Industries plant. The resulting productivity allows Merillat Industries to pay more and yet sell its products at competitive prices.

Until 1982 the company was run from offices in the Adrian plant. By that year corporate growth had outstripped that space, and a modern new corporate office was built on U.S. 223 west of Adrian. That building was expanded and more than tripled in 1987. The corporate office complex now houses nearly 200 people.

Orville and Ruth Merillat are devout members of the United Brethren Church and have used the fruits of their success in many ways to help further the work of the church. Their contributions have helped to build the Trenton Hills United Brethren Church in Adrian, as well as the Trenton Hills School and its successor, Lenawee Christian School. Their contributions have helped to build the Christian Family Center complex adjoining the school, and they have also generously benefacted Huntington College in Indiana, a United Brethren-affiliated college. Adrian College dedicated the Ruth and Orville Merillat Sport and Fitness Center on campus in January 1990.

Thurman believes that the same principles of hard work, honesty, and Christian concern the Merillats have applied in their personal lives have been central to the success of Merillat Industries.

Merillat Industries' Heather Cathedral line of kitchen cabinets.

FIRST FEDERAL SAVINGS OF LENAWEE

First Federal Savings and Loan of Lenawee was founded in 1889 under new Michigan banking laws by 12 prominent Adrian citizens, who called their venture the Adrian Building and Loan Association. Founding board members were D.M. Baker, W.H. Barrett, F.H. Knapp, W.B. Thompson, T.J. Goodsell, G.W. Ayers, H.B. Waldby, W.F. Matthes, A.J. Kaiser, E.L. Baker, Charles H. Lords, and L. Ladd.

"The objects of the association are to promote thrift by providing a convenient and safe method for people to save and invest money and to provide for the sound and economical financing of homes," declared the original bylaws of the association.

"Those objects are as true today as they were 100 years ago," says William H. Glencorse, chairman, president, and chief executive officer.

The new business opened in the Wheeler Block at the southeast corner of Maumee and Winter streets, and over the next few years moved to several rented office spaces before arriving at 121 West Maumee in 1926. By 1928 the building and loan could claim "1,500 homes financed in Adrian" on its semiannual financial statement.

In 1933 Roy McPhail became president, guiding the organization through difficult Depression days. Three years later the Adrian Building and Loan received a federal charter, changing its name to Adrian Federal Savings and Loan.

The postwar era saw a lot of home building in Lenawee County and a lot of growth for Adrian Federal. Harold H. Sherman was elected president in 1950, with McPhail becoming chairman of the board—a post he held until 1966. Expansion followed, and in 1953 a branch office was opened at 138 West Chicago Avenue in Tecumseh. Six years later the Adrian office moved to its present location at 202 North Main Street.

Sherman resigned as president in 1966 after the institution's longest presidential tenure, and Allan C. Graybiel was named executive vice-president. He was elected president the following year, and directed a major expansion of the scope of the association's business.

The name was changed to First Federal Savings and Loan Association of Lenawee County in 1969, foreshadowing the opening of a branch in Blissfield in 1971, Temperance and Clinton branches in 1976, Brooklyn in 1978, and Morenci in 1981. The main office in Adrian was expanded in 1976, with work on both the lower and upper levels to accommodate a bigger accounting department, and making way for the association's own mainframe computer for in-house data processing. The loan-servicing department was expanded as well.

After directing the successful transformation of the association into a county-wide financial institution, Graybiel retired as president in 1981, becoming chairman of the board. He was succeeded as president by Glencorse, on whom fell the task of sustaining member confidence and stimulating growth through the difficult 1980s.

This decade was a period of deregulation of the savings and loan industry. With

deregulation scores of savings and loans nationwide got into trouble by making speculative loans and by offering excessive interest rates. Newspapers began to carry scare stories about the crumbling savings and loan industry.

These problems did not exist for First Federal. Its management had continued doing the same sort of business that had brought the institution's historic success—home mortgages supported by member savings deposits. There was no need for panic in Lenawee County, but the depositors had to be convinced of this. That is what Glencorse and his associates succeeded in doing, with gratifying results for the community.

In 1988 *The Detroit News* ranked First Federal the strongest thrift institution in Michigan. A national independent financial rating agency named First Federal the third-strongest savings and loan in the country among associations of comparable size.

The success has been done the old-

fashioned way. Glencorse reports that in 1988 nearly $30 million in new loans were closed, a 10.1-percent increase from the previous year, and "significantly, 94.8 percent of our gross loan portfolio of $143 million in 1988 is for relatively low-risk one-to-four family residential mortgages."

First Federal's market area includes the southeastern Michigan counties of Lenawee, Jackson, Monroe, Hillsdale, and Washtenaw; northwestern Ohio; and northeastern Indiana, with a total population exceeding 3 million.

The strategic placement of branch offices has proven important. The Temperance office is involved with the rapid residential development along the Interstate 75 corridor in Monroe County, and the Clinton and Tecumseh offices are servicing the needs of people moving out to Lenawee County from Ann Arbor. The Brooklyn branch has been busy with people moving into the Irish Hills resort area.

On June 6, 1988, First Federal was converted from a mutual association to a public corporation, becoming First Federal Savings of Lenawee. A total of 1.5 million shares of common stock was sold at eight dollars per share, resulting in an $11.3-million increase in the net worth of the association.

On August 30, 1989, First Federal celebrated its 100th anniversary with a gala banquet at Adrian College. As the community congratulated the association for its success, perhaps the most significant statement appeared on the program: "During our first 100 years First Federal Savings of Lenawee has helped nearly 30,000 families realize the American dream of owning their own home."

CITY OF ADRIAN

The City of Adrian dates to 1825, when Addison J. Comstock purchased 640 acres from the government to start a town. He was joined by his father, Darius, and in the years that followed a thriving community emerged.

Early development was guided by Addison Comstock. His name is attached to most of the "firsts" from those early days, including the first plat of the city, which he did in 1828. That is also the year his wife named the town Adrian, after the Roman emperor Hadrian. Addison Comstock built the first gristmill and sawmill, meeting the basic needs of the new community.

A township government was established in 1827 with Comstock as clerk. Adrian was not chartered as a city until 1853—with Addison Comstock the first mayor. Before that, most civil activities were handled on a volunteer basis. A volunteer fire company was established in 1841, and one of the first acts of the new city government in 1853 was the commissioning of a fire station. In 1987 the fire department moved into its new facility across from city hall.

Minutes of early city council meetings show concerns were streetlights (installed in the 1880s), sidewalks (which were made of

Adrian mayor James Berryman's five-year tenure has seen growth and prosperity in the Maple City, with new businesses and a state correctional institution credited to Berryman's efforts.

wood), and loose livestock. Adrian was a rail center, and the city council voted to limit trains to six miles per hour along Railroad Street.

The main purpose of city government has been to provide services such as water and sewer, and to provide for public protection. In 1883 the city signed a contract for installation of 13 miles of water lines and 120 fire hydrants.

Only the rich had running water in those early days. Folks in working class neighborhoods carried buckets to communal water spigots.

At first the water for the system came from wells, but as demand increased, water was taken from Wolf Creek near the location of today's Bixby Hospital (it had been determined in the 1870s that Wolf Creek water was purer than River Raisin water). The central pumping station and reservoir were on Merrick Street, where the buildings still stand.

Adrian was the second city in the country to try chlorinating water in 1885-1887, but that was abandoned. Adrian was still a pioneer in 1912 when the chlorination of water became a regular practice. Cases of typhoid in the area dropped by one-half soon after. The dreaded disease was finally eliminated from the city seven years later with pasteurization of milk.

A water-filtration plant was built in the 1890s at Riverside Park. The water system grew with the city. In 1943 a dam across Wolf Creek created Lake Adrian, assuring a dependable water supply. In 1945 the water plant on Wolf Creek Highway went on line, and it was enlarged in 1956 and 1957.

The first sewer was installed by the city in the mid-1860s. It was brick arch and ran down Pearl Street to drain swampy land into the River Raisin. In later years the system branched to the east and north, following natural ravines and ditches.

With running water there came a need for sewers that could carry a greater volume of fluid, so the old brick arch sewers were replaced by tile lines. Many of the eight-inch sewer lines installed at the end of the last century are still in use.

In those early days the same sewer line carried storm water and sewage. A major

The City of Adrian's oldest building was replaced by its newest in 1987 when firefighters moved into this new facility across from City Hall on Main Street.

sewer project in 1978 finally completed the separation of storm and water sewers so all sewage went to the treatment plant built in 1925 on North Winter Street and upgraded in 1978.

In the early days the streets were mud and wood—sidewalks were built and maintained to get people up out of the muck. By 1900 the city had started a brick-paving program. Curbs and gutters were installed in the 1920s. Wood sidewalks were replaced by concrete starting around the turn of the century, amid the same controversy that arises today when a tax is proposed for city construction. During the Depression WPA crews built Terrace and University streets and developed Island Park.

As for the seat of city government, it had no permanent home until 1885, when a grand city hall was built at the south end of downtown. In 1970 it was razed and replaced with today's modern building.

The city library was begun in 1868 in Central School. When city hall was completed, the library moved to a first-floor room there, and remained until 1909, when a Carnegie grant made construction of a library building next door possible. That building served until 1978, when the city library moved to the former JCPenney store downtown, and the old building became the county historical museum.

Parks have been part of the cityscape since the early days. In recent years the city has used funds willed by Harriet Kimball Fee for park development, providing Adrian with many beautiful park facilities.

In 1990 the city government had 14 public parks with approximately 500 acres; 31 sworn police officers; 22 fire-department personnel; 162 full-time employees, including police and fire, utilities, public works, parks and recreation, and administration; 44 miles of local streets, 22 miles of major streets, and 17 miles of state trunk lines; a senior-citizen center in the old Catholic Central school building on Erie Street; a major park north of the city on a former farm, including ball diamonds, an authentic one-room school, a farmhouse and barn, and facilities for a variety of entertaining and educational activities; and Oakwood Cemetery, acquired by the city during the Depression.

Since 1957 the city has been governed by a mayor; six city commissioners, elected at large on a nonpartisan ballot; and a city administrator.

In the works is another park project, a greenbelt along the former railroad right-of-way through the city that eventually will link Riverside and Island parks.

WACKER SILICONES CORPORATION

The Wacker Silicones complex occupies two sites on Sutton Road in Raisin Township. Manufacturing operations are conducted in the plant in the foreground, while marketing, research and development, and administration are in the complex at right center.

Wacker Silicones Corporation, on Sutton Road in Raisin Township, is an innovative firm manufacturing raw materials for the auto industry and for consumer products, such as car polish and cosmetics.

The Wacker plant was built in 1964 by Stauffer Chemical Company and was started for Stauffer by Andy Anderson, who had already made a mark in Lenawee with the Anderson Chemical Company in Weston, which, by 1964, had been purchased by Stauffer.

The new silicones plant struggled against stiff competition and did not begin to realize its full potential until 1975.

In 1969 Stauffer formed a joint venture with a West German firm, Wacker-Chemie GmbH, which acquired a one-third interest in the plant. The name changed to SWS Silicones, and Wacker began sharing technology and insight into applications and markets that helped make SWS a prominent supplier of silicone rubber to the automotive industry. By 1975 Wacker had increased its share of ownership to 49 percent.

Since then SWS has enjoyed steady growth and penetration into new markets. Noteworthy was the invention of products that helped reduce air pollution by making the conversion to unleaded gasoline possible. Products developed for other industries, such as the tire industry, permitted a change from solvent to water-based systems, reducing emissions of pollutants into the atmosphere by millions of gallons.

In 1985 Stauffer Chemical Company was purchased by Chesebrough-Pond's Inc. Soon after, Wacker

Products made from Wacker Silicones' compounds run a wide range from sealants and caulks to gaskets, spark-plug wires, and drive-axle joint boots. Versatile silicones can be liquids or rubber, pliable or rigid.

increased its share of ownership of the facility to 50 percent and, in 1987, became the sole owner. The company was then renamed Wacker Silicones Corporation.

The firm employed 470 people in 1989, 50 more than the year before. Guenther Lengnick is the president. Most employees work on Sutton Road in manufacturing, research, sales and marketing, and administration. Sales offices are located in Adrian, Atlanta, Chicago, Los Angeles, and in Edison, New Jersey.

Silicones are synthetic polymers with many applications. About half of Wacker Silicones' output consists of rubber-like products useful for automobile ignition systems, for the aircraft and aerospace industries, and for radiator hoses and seals. Silicones remain stable when hot and flexible when cold. They are insulators, yet can be altered to be conductors.

The remainder of the company's output consists of liquid polymers for applications such as car polishes—with Rain Dance polish being an example—where they serve as a detergent-resistant ingredient.

Silicones are also used in caulks and sealants, gaskets, and in resinous forms for high-temperature paints and masonry water repellents. They are physiologically inert and harmless to the environment.

New products are the name of the game. "Our researchers have developed products that represent as much as 80 percent of our sales," Lengnick reports. "We are not a 'me too' company. We live by our wits and innovations."

AKZO CHEMICALS INC.

Akzo Chemicals' plant in Weston in southern Lenawee County manufactures and markets ethyl silicates, primarily used as binders in investment casting molds to make high-precision metal components, along with transition metal catalysts used in the production of plastics and synthetic rubbers.

The Weston plant was established in 1952 by Amos "Andy" Anderson, whose Anderson Laboratories had outgrown facilities in Adrian. In Weston, Anderson found two buildings that had been used by Page Dairy Company. Anderson established Anderson Chemical Sales Co. to purchase and operate the Weston facility. In 1954 the name was changed to Anderson Chemical Company.

Anderson was a pioneer in the development of organometallic compounds, and between 1955 and 1958 the demand for these compounds mushroomed. To keep up with the demand, Anderson Chemical Company merged with Stauffer Chemical Co. in 1958. Construction began immediately on five new buildings. In 1965 Stauffer completed the acquisition, and in 1984 a new ethyl silicate plant was dedicated. Ethyl silicates are now the plant's principal product.

In March 1985 Stauffer Chemical was acquired by Chesebrough-Pond's, Inc., a worldwide manufacturer and marketer of consumer products. Chesebrough-Pond's was in turn purchased in 1987 by Unilever Corp. Six months later, in late 1987, Unilever sold Stauffer's specialty chemical division, including the Weston plant, to Akzo. Headquartered in the Netherlands, Akzo is a major international chemicals corporation with operations in more than 50 countries at more than 250 locations.

The ethyl silicates produced at Weston are used in the production of castings for a variety of industrial and consumer applications. The biggest user of these products is the aircraft industry, for jet-engine castings. One notable item cast using ethyl silicate from Weston was the *Three Fighting Men* sculpture at the Vietnam Memorial in Washington, D.C.

Ethyl silicates also act as binders in zinc-rich coatings used for corrosion protection of structural steel in highways and bridges, building construction, shipbuilding, and offshore drilling rigs.

An ethyl silicate reactor was installed at the Akzo Chemicals plant in 1984.

The transition metal catalysts produced at Weston include various titanium and vanadium compounds used in the manufacture of polyethylene, polypropylene, and various synthetic rubbers. The plastic and rubber products produced by these catalysts are then used in such common consumer products as sandwich bags, car bumpers, and automotive tires.

The plant survived one close brush with closing. "In 1986 Chesebrough-Pond's announced plans to close the plant," recalls plant manager Chet Bartkavage. "But through the efforts of the Steelworkers Union Local 15295 and salaried personnel, as well as several other local, county, and state officials, we were able to come to terms under which the plant was able to stay open."

Bartkavage says the plant works closely with the Fairfield Township Fire Department on emergency preparedness and response time.

Prospects for the future seem bright, Bartkavage reports, as Akzo is continually looking for new products to be produced at Weston. It is not as if the plant lacked for work in 1989. Bartkavage says, "We produce more than 21 million pounds per year of assorted industrial chemicals."

The Akzo Chemicals Inc. plant in Weston. Headquartered in the Netherlands, Akzo is a major international chemicals corporation with operations in more than 50 countries and 350 locations.

METALLOY CORPORATION

Metalloy Corporation, headquartered in Hudson, is a firm specializing in aluminum castings that has been successful in large measure because it pursues a diversified approach to its specialty.

Metalloy was established in 1945 by Richard "Dick" Berlin. During World War II he had been employed as a metallurgist at WrightPatterson Aeronautical. By war's end, he had advanced to manager of the 200-person department. His department tested the castings used in making airplane engines, so Berlin was familiar with aluminum-casting technology. After the war he returned home to start a business himself.

Soon after, Berlin's father, Nelson, quit his job as a foundry superintendent to join the fledgling business. A lifelong foundryman, "Nellie" brought know-how and experience to the firm. The need for capital led them to take on Charles Gibbons, a metallurgist who had worked for Dick during the war, as a partner.

They set up shop in Pittsford, in Hillsdale County, in an old schoolhouse next to the family home. They bought some used molding machines and built their own melting furnaces. It was a family affair—every member, including Dick's wife, Hazel, spent the day making castings. Their products were sold to industrial customers in the area. If a customer came to them with a part or even an idea, they would help him make a drawing and then produce the part. Many times the parts were delivered personally by Dick in his 1941 Ford.

They soon gained a reputation for being able to solve tough casting problems and, as a result, outgrew their location. In 1947 a new 5,000-square-foot facility was built in nearby Hudson.

It was in the mid-1950s that Metalloy's first big break came. After months of trying, the firm landed some orders with Detroit Diesel Allison Division of General Motors. Over the next 20 years Detroit Diesel was in the forefront of converting heavy iron castings into lighter aluminum castings. Detroit Diesel enjoyed dramatic growth, and Metalloy grew with it.

In 1960 Metalloy needed more space, and it purchased the old Hardie Manufacturing building in downtown Hudson.

The year 1971 was auspicious for Metalloy. That year the company broke into the die-casting business by buying the assets of the Hudson Die Cast Company.

At the same time the Berlins consolidated all outside machining operations in house, creating yet another new business. These moves greatly diversified the company, making it one of the first full-service casting sources in the country. "We are the only aluminum foundry of any size in the country to have all three processes—sand casting, permanent mold casting, and die casting—in one company," explains Dave Berlin, Dick's son, who today serves as president of Metalloy Corporation.

At first the machine shop was combined with the die cast plant in Hudson, but by 1981 both

The Hudson foundry in 1947 (right) and, 40 years later, in 1987 (above).

operations had grown so much that the old Hudson Ford dealership was purchased and converted into a machine shop. Since then there have been three additions.

Dave Berlin says most foundries do not machine their own castings. "Having this shop has given us a competitive advantage," he says.

As the 1970s drew to a close, Metalloy's major product line was still diesel-engine parts, which were sold to several customers including Ford Motor Company Truck Division. As the price of oil skyrocketed, Ford decided to substitute aluminum castings for iron in automotive engines, much as the diesel industry had done years before. Because of the high volumes required, Metalloy built a new, highly automated plant in Tupelo, Mississippi, in 1978. This plant helped the company become Ford's top supplier of aluminum castings.

The excellent reputation for quality earned by the Tupelo facility brought more and more work from Ford and other customers for Metalloy's Hudson locations, and by 1986 more than $4 million had been spent modernizing the Hudson facilities. In 1985 a new die-cast facility was built in Fremont, Indiana, and the size was doubled four years later. In 1986 the original die-cast plant in Hudson was completely modernized, including robotic operation of all casting machines.

Metalloy currently op-

erates five plants in three states comprising 350,000 square feet of manufacturing space. Ford Motor Company is the largest single customer, but a much larger customer base has been established than in past years, including many Japanese firms. All facilities are highly automated with robots and computers. The original Rima Manufacturing plant in Hudson was purchased and converted into a comprehensive engineering and research department.

Dick Berlin is chairman of the board, with Dave Berlin, president; Phil Long, vice-president/operations; Bob Cavanaugh, vice-president/ finance; and Mark Moulin, vice-president/marketing.

The firm employs a total of 500 people, with 350 in Lenawee County. Local area customers include Tecumseh Products and Aget Fan.

The future? "My father was schooled in aircraft quality and technology and applied it to mass-produced parts," says Dave Berlin. "That same philosophy, along with our diversified approach to aluminum castings, should serve us well in the future."

Proof of Metalloy Corporation's quality are the four prized Q-1 awards from Ford that hang in the headquarters building.

LEFT: Sand molds are filled with 1,500-degree molten aluminum.

ABOVE: Automotive intake manifold castings are machined on a transfer line.

Computerized equipment is used to measure castings.

TECUMSEH PRODUCTS COMPANY

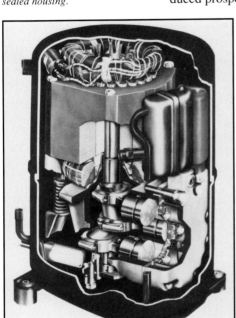

Tecumseh Products' hermetic self-contained motor compressor units made residential air conditioners feasible. In the cutaway, the electric motor is at the top while the compressor is at the bottom, all within a sealed housing.

People in Tecumseh recognized an opportunity in 1934 when industrialist Ray W. Herrick expressed interest in an abandoned fence plant in town. Townspeople scrambled to clean up the property and make it useable for Herrick's company, which had outgrown facilities in Hillsdale.

Thus began a relationship that has produced prosperity for the city and success beyond Herrick's dreams. Herrick started Hillsdale Machine and Tool Co. in 1930. It began as a conventional machine shop, but Herrick recognized a market for affordable mechanical refrigeration. People were tired of using iceboxes, and Herrick reckoned that refrigerators would soon be in demand.

There resulted development of a belt-driven compressor and condensing unit. Hillsdale Machine and Tool Co. soon became the genesis of the nation's largest independent compressor manufacturer.

Herrick arrived in Tecumseh with his compressor design and the ambition to make it a success, despite the Depression. He found a willing work force and soon put people to work at the new Tecumseh Products Company.

The business grew. In 1941 the plant was converted for war production and manufactured artillery shells and rockets, earning decorations from the War Department many times. War's end saw an explosion of a different kind—a family housing explosion. Americans discovered the suburbs, and returning veterans used cheap government loans to build homes for their brides and babies. Each needed a refrigerator, and Tecumseh Products boomed. The company became and continues to be Lenawee County's biggest employer, with some 2,000 workers on the payroll.

The boom accelerated in the 1950s when Tecumseh Products engineers designed smaller and more efficient compressors, the self-contained hermetic units that made home window air conditioners practical, creating another new market.

In 1955 the firm began to diversify, buying two organizations making small engines, Lauson Engine Co. and Power Products Co. In 1989 Tecumseh Products Company was the second-largest maker of small engines in the country, with its 3.5 million two- and four-stroke engines commanding 42 percent of the domestic market.

In the 1960s another new market emerged—automotive air conditioning—spurring more growth. In 1964 the firm purchased the Peerless Machine Tool Company and opened its Peerless Gear Division plant in Clinton, making differentials, transaxles, and transmissions for lawn tractors.

Subsequent acquisitions have made Tecumseh Products a multinational corporation, listed in the *Fortune* 500 with wholly owned subsidiaries in Brazil, France, Italy, and West Germany.

Ray Herrick died in 1973. His son Kenneth became chairman of the board in 1970 and continues in that position. Todd W. Herrick, Kenneth's son, became president in 1984. He has directed the firm's international expansion.

Tecumseh Products Company looks forward to opportunities in Eastern Europe, with negotiations having begun even before the dust of the crumbling Berlin Wall had settled.

Tecumseh Products' forerunner, Hillsdale Tool and Machine, advertised this HP-14 compressor for use in refrigerators. Ray W. Herrick had found the product that would lead to his fortune.

HIDDEN LAKE GARDENS

Hidden Lake Gardens, nestled in the Irish Hills, is one of the area's most pleasant surprises. Nature lovers visit this scenic 670 acres near Tipton year round.

The idea for the gardens began in 1926, when Harry A. Fee, a prominent Adrian businessman interested in scenic land formations, bought the land and supervised its development. Fee had been interested in starting a nursery business. However, the Depression made him loathe to increased competition, so he took the plantings intended for his nursery and created a landscape picture instead. In 1945 he donated his labor of love to Michigan State College.

From the beautiful lake to unusual geological formations, numerous plant collections, five miles of marked hiking trails, a plant conservatory, picnic area, and visitor center, its caretakers strive to maintain and improve the gardens for the education and pleasure of the viewing public.

The 55,000 annual visitors to the site find manicured grounds and natural forest growth. Flowers, trees, and shrubs are marked. Hikers and picnickers will see raccoons, squirrels, pheasant, deer, rabbits, and ducks.

The visitor center offers an exhibit concourse with subjects as varied as geology and plant propagation and succession. Meeting rooms are available to any organization wishing to use them. There are also a reference library and gift shop.

The visitor center building was a gift from the Herrick family of Tecumseh in 1966. In 1972 the family donated a plant conservatory, enabling avid gardeners and winterweary people a view of summer, no matter what the month.

Behind the scenes at Hidden Lake Gar-

Harry Fee arranged for this 65-ton rock to be a memorial at the park entrance in September 1949. The boulder was moved 28 miles from the Russell Leffingwell farm near Hudson. Courtesy, Michigan State University

dens is the campus park and planning division of Michigan State University, which took responsibility from MSU's Horticulture Department in 1962.

At the helm day to day is Jack C. Wolf, who joined the staff in 1956. Wolf cites Dr. Fred W. Freeman, director from 1955 to 1986, as "the most significant person to the progress of Hidden Lake Gardens. He really instituted the whole process of neatness and organization into Hidden Lake Gardens."

Another 30-year-plus employee, Richard Luck, the botanical technician in charge of greenhouse conservatory, joined the staff in 1957.

Wolf calls the three men "a tribute to the continuity of Hidden Lake Gardens" and says there are several 10- to 17-year employees at the gardens.

Despite the generosity of both the Fee Foundation, which provides maintenance and operation money, and the Herrick family donations, the gardens terminated plant research in the late 1970s. Looking to future goals, Wolf says, "We are looking to reinstate plant research, to upgrade and increase plant collections, and to improve education programs to the public."

Meanwhile, visitors from as near as Ohio and as far away as Australia continue to enjoy the beauty of Hidden Lake Gardens.

LEFT: The visitor center building, a gift of the Herrick family, was opened in 1966 and offers informative exhibits, an auditorium, meeting rooms, a reference library, and a gift shop.

BELOW: The plant conservatory includes a tropical dome, arid dome, and greenhouse ornamentals. Plants featured are bamboo, banana, cactus, camphor, cocoa, coffee, fig, palm, sisal, sugar cane, tapioca, and vanilla.

LENAWEE CHRISTIAN SCHOOL AND CHRISTIAN FAMILY CENTRE

With completion of the Lenawee Christian School and the Christian Family Centre, Orville and Ruth Merillat have realized their dream of an interdenominational school and a recreation center that would be active in fostering Christian and traditional family values. Both the LCS and the CFC are under the guidance of the Christian Family Foundation.

The Lenawee Christian School traces its origins to 1976, when a meeting at the Trenton Hills United Brethren Church led to the decision to build a Christian school. Orville and Ruth Merillat offered to make a building possible and assured operating funds for the first year of operation.

In 1977 school started in the church with 17 students in kindergarten through third grade, two teachers, and an administrator. "The main goal was to provide academically, socially, and physically, a quality education for the children," recalls Dorothy Arnold, one of the founding board members. "They wanted to add the fourth dimension of a Christian approach."

She recalls that Orville Merillat said from the first that the school was not to be in competition with the public schools, but was to be in addition to them.

Following Merillat's suggestion, teachers were state certified and experienced. The curriculum was state approved, and conduct was based on general Christian principles.

A grade was added each year after the school opened, and by 1984 classes extended through the eighth grade. "We were bursting at the seams," recalls Paul Palpant, elementary school principal, who joined the staff from the Hudson public schools in 1982. Ground was broken in spring of 1984 for an addition for the school, and in the fall the addition was occupied.

Soon after that a survey was commissioned to learn the potential for a Christian high school. The results were encouraging, and in February 1985 the board decided to go ahead with plans for a high school. Modular classrooms were used, along with church facilities, to make the space during the 1985-1986 school year.

From the beginning the school had been operated by the Trenton Hills United Brethren Church. In 1985 a new governing structure

was created, with an 11-member board to operate the Lenawee Christian School. Four members are from the church, four are parents of students, and three represent the Christian Family Foundation.

At that time John DeLine was hired as high school principal, and eight teachers came on board. In two months a curriculum was assembled, and classes began in the fall.

At the same time the property at Wolf Creek Highway and U.S. Route 223 was being looked at with an eye to construct a new school building. Things happened fast. The property was acquired and ground was broken by October 1985 for a 110,000-square-foot, fully equipped school. A year later grades six through 12 moved from Maple Avenue to the new school building. The elementary wing was not yet completed; there was no gym, no library, and no music room, but there was no complaining. "We were happy to move, because we were in desperate straits on Maple Avenue with 425 students," DeLine recalls.

Eight more teachers had been hired, totaling to 16. The remainder of the new

The auditorium in the Christian Family Centre is used for concerts, films, and programs consistent with the Christian mission of the institution. The auditorium seats between 650 and 700 people.

as Christian schools in Michigan and Ohio.

"It's what goes on in this school that's important to us," comments DeLine. "We want to meet the needs of the families that are concerned about a Christian education."

No sooner was work complete at the Lenawee Christian School than ground was broken next door for the new Christian Family Centre. Built by the Christian Family Foundation, the center opened November 1, 1988, and quickly attracted more than 4,500 members with its recreational facilities.

school building was finished by March 1987, and the elementary grades moved then. Completion of the building from ground breaking to moving day was 16 months. Dedication ceremonies were held April 26, 1987, and later in the spring the first graduating class, with 10 students, received their diplomas.

Today the school has an enrollment of approximately 700 students, and operates with 35 teachers. The school is accredited by the state, the Association of Christian Schools International, the University of Michigan, and has become the first unit school in the state of Michigan to gain accreditation from the North Central Association.

The curriculum is a traditional college preparatory program, and teachers are "really encouraged to integrate biblical truths throughout the curriculum, not just to isolate the biblical teaching into one little cubicle," DeLine says.

The school maintains good relations with public schools and the Lenawee Intermediate School District. Its athletic teams compete against public schools in the area as well

The center includes a gymnasium, bowling alley, swimming pool, racquet ball courts, a dining area, an auditorium, fully equipped health club, and private meeting rooms. The auditorium features live and film Christian entertainment and programs. Smoking and alcoholic beverages are not permitted.

"The guiding principle of the center's founders is to provide a biblically centered quality of life through the promotion of pro-family activities in a Christ-centered atmosphere," says Christian Family Foundation's executive director, James A. McClellan, Jr. Among the center's offerings that pleases its director, Ed Gore, is what he calls one of the finest Christian video libraries available. The foundation's endowment helps to keep membership fees low at the 95,000-square-foot facility.

The center is very much the realization of the vision of Orville and Ruth Merillat, Gore says. "It was their intent to provide a multipurpose Christian facility. One would be hard-pressed to find a more comprehensive facility."

TLC COMMUNITY CREDIT UNION

Opened in 1987, the Adrian office is the center of all credit union operations.

The Tecumseh Products Credit Union was begun in 1956 by the company and its union for Products workers. The first day 56 members deposited $258. Services offered were savings accounts, loans, and life insurance. Nearly all deposits were by payroll deduction.

By 1961 the credit union had grown to 1,200 members and assets of $480,000. The credit union paid the then-generous interest of 4 percent on funds on account for one year. A share was counted for each five dollars on deposit.

As a working people's institution the credit union has always kept long hours, opening early for third-shift workers and staying open late for second shift. "We've always adjusted very well to the community's needs, adjusting to their schedule," says general manager Wayne Zettel.

Business continued as usual, with a menu of savings plans such as Christmas club, vacation club, and conventional savings accounts until 1975, when checking accounts became available to members. Another major change came in 1985, when the credit union began to offer mortgage loans. "Prior to that time we really hadn't had the capital to get into mortgage loans," explains Zettel.

In 1975 the credit union leaped forward with a state-chartered expansion, gaining authorization to serve workers from any industries in Clinton, Raisin, and Tecumseh townships. It merged with the

The Tecumseh office, remodeled in 1980, serves members in the Tecumseh area.

Tecumseh Trim Credit Union of workers at the GM's Fisher Body plant in Raisin Township and others to create the Tecumseh Area Credit Union.

Another major expansion took place in 1983, when a merger took place with the Lenawee County Community Credit Union, serving Adrian, Madison, and Palmyra township industries. At this point the organization changed its name to TLC Credit Union, and extended its range to serve all of Lenawee County.

Growth was rapid, and a new, bigger Adrian office became necessary. The Adrian office had been across from the post office, and Zettel recalls the lot would be full at 8 a.m., with people standing in line waiting to be served.

After going countywide the organization added 200 members per month, Zettel recalls. The assets grew from $20 million in 1983 to $56 million today.

From a small office staff working 10- to 12-hour days the organization has grown to an office staff of around 50 people. Assets are growing at the rate of $400,000 per month. Construction of the new Adrian office began in March 1987, and the office opened in April 1988.

TLC Community Credit Union offers all financial services and boasts a modern in-house computer system that Zettel credits with making much of the growth possible. "I'm proud of the operation," Zettel says. "The growth has been so astronomical—it's probably 10 times larger than I would have dreamed."

McDONALD'S

When W.A. "Bill" Sigmund opened his first McDonald's restaurant in Jackson, the signs still counted hamburgers sold in thousands. Thirty-one years later he owns three restaurants, has sold five, and is among the longest-tenured franchise holders in the entire company.

In 1959 Sigmund had been with Kraft Foods for 26 years, but had wearied of constant travel. Ray Kroc had opened his first McDonald's franchise restaurant in the Chicago suburb of Des Plaines, Illinois, near Sigmund's Elmhurst home in 1955. Sigmund at first considered McDonald's as an investment, but wound up buying a franchise himself. When the chance came to open a restaurant in Jackson, Michigan, he took it.

The restaurant was a success, and Sigmund soon operated four restaurants in Jackson and one in Albion. In 1971 he opened a store at Adrian Mall. Two years later followed the McDonald's on North Main in Adrian, and in 1977 he introduced the Golden Arches to Tecumseh.

Soon after opening in Jackson, Sigmund

The McDonald's restaurant in Tecumseh features land-scaping and plantings to create a parklike setting.

hired 17-year-old Rusty Bodman to work part time. Rusty worked hard and, after a tour of duty in Vietnam, returned to work for Sigmund full time. He and Sigmund developed a close working relationship, and Bodman wound up as manager. He later managed all eight of Sigmund's restaurants, and today is president of Jenell, Inc., Sigmund's holding company.

Bodman and Sigmund have seen to it that the company is deeply involved in community activities. McDonald's supports school fund-raisers with sandwich coupons on candy-bar wrappers and makes available orange soda in special dispenser containers for all kinds of community events—as many as 400 per year. Community relations director Melissa McLemore helps with many carnivals and parties, often with Ronald McDonald at her side, and McDonald's supports Boy Scouts and other youth activities.

Perhaps the most significant of McDonald's community projects involve hospitals. McDonald's employees visit hospitals with gifts and spend time reading to young patients. Sigmund and his wife, Vi, have donated two fully equipped Ronald McDonald guest rooms for the families of seriously ill patients—especially children—at Bixby Medical Center. McDonald's supports HOPE Recreation Center and employs several developmental disabled workers.

McDonald's restaurants are major employers. When Sigmund first opened in Jackson, he had 30 employees. As the business has grown, so has employment. When he had eight restaurants, Sigmund employed as many as 1,000 people. Today, with three restaurants in Lenawee County, the company employs almost 300 people.

Sigmund is proud of the successful restaurants, and he and Bodman agree their greatest satisfaction comes from the people they work with. Former employees have gone on to success in many fields—including three who started as crew people and today are owner/operators of McDonald's restaurants. Says Bodman, "It's a business where you can grow with your own initiative."

William Sigmund stands under the Golden Arches sign at his first McDonald's restaurant in Jackson in 1959. Today Sigmund owns two McDonald's franchises in Adrian and one in Tecumseh.

COLDWELL BANKER GLOVER REAL ESTATE ASSOCIATES

Rex Glover began selling real estate in 1951 and has been at the helm of his own firm since August 1954. When Glover opened his business, he recalls that "at the time I wanted more in life than to work for someone else."

Soon after establishing his own firm he added an associate, then another one, and

Clockwise from top left: Rex Glover, founder; the Tecumseh branch office; and the Adrian office.

established a pattern of growth for the company. Today the firm has 20 sales associates.

At first he worked from his home on Kenwood Drive, but soon opened an office on South Main Street. In 1960 he moved to 155 North Main Street, then, as the firm grew, it moved in 1973 to a building he purchased at the corner of Broad and Toledo streets. In 1980 he moved his office to its present loca-

tion at 1579 West Maumee Street. Glover also operates an office in Tecumseh, at 1204 West Chicago Boulevard.

He is especially proud his agency was selected in 1986 to join the Coldwell Banker group, part of the Sears financial network. Because of the relationship Glover is able to arrange mortgages through Sears mortgage services.

The association with Coldwell Banker has been productive, Glover says, providing training for sales associates, high-quality sales aids, and referrals.

Glover has served on the Lenawee County Board of Review, and although the body is unpopular with the public he thinks that "a lot of people came to see us a good service."

Glover served four years as president of the Lenawee County Board of Realtors and is proud to have been chosen that organization's Realtor of the Year on two occasions. He is a past president of the Real Estate Alumni of Michigan, Farm and Land Institute, and the Homebuilders Association of Lenawee County. He has also been active in chamber of commerce work, and helped with the acquisition of parcels for what is now known as Wacker Silicones on Sutton Road in Raisin Township.

"The community has supported us in our continued growth and prosperity," Glover says. "We think it is a fine place to move into and raise a family."

Glover says that today the referral service through Coldwell Banker Glover, Realtors Inc., is an integral part of his business, as his staff helps people who move to Lenawee County and are referred to his agency, and tells people who are moving about referral services in their destination market.

Glover speaks warmly of his relationship with the community. As a person who has established his own agency, he recognizes that "it all is a result of the people of Lenawee County. It's a two-way street. We've given good service and they've rewarded us."

ADDISON PRODUCTS COMPANY

Air conditioner maker Addison Products Company traces its history to 1949, when it was started as the Primus Co. by three Tecumseh Products executives, with Gorton Price and S.H. Morse as its managers. They made refrigeration units for soft-drink dispensers, and the business grew. A new building was erected in 1950, and 40 people were employed.

At the end of 1951 V.C. "Cliff" Knight became general manager. He had spent more than 20 years with a leading manufacturer of refrigeration equipment in Indiana, and a half-dozen years as part owner and manager of a refrigeration company in Chicago.

Morse and Price left to start Primor in Adrian, and Knight bought 25 percent of Primus and changed its name to Addison Products Company, becoming president and chief executive officer. He quickly began making window air conditioners.

Then came a breakthrough. Knight designed the first residential "split system"— a cooling evaporator in the plenum of a warm-air furnace connected to an air-cooled condensing unit outside. By using the furnace blower to circulate cool air through ductwork, the whole house was cooled with the single

unit. The idea spread quickly, and Addison Products was soon selling units to nearly all the warm-air furnace companies in the country.

Window air conditioners and dehumidifiers were also being made, and in 1955 the firm needed more capacity. The following

year a new plant was built in Jonesville, in Hillsdale County. Located on U.S. Route 112 (now U.S. 12), the plant was a better shipping point. The Jonesville plant grew to nearly 500,000 square feet. The plant in Addison is 240,000 square feet and includes the corporate offices.

Furnace makers soon learned to make their own split systems, and that business slowed. The company boomed, making air conditioners for Saudi Arabia in the late 1970s, but that market faded as foreign competition undersold American manufacturers.

In 1960 Addison Products purchased WeatherKing, Inc., a Florida manufacturer of heat pumps and air conditioners for difficult climactic conditions, such as salt air. The WeatherKing plant in Florida is a key supplier of equipment in that region, and the WeatherKing name is carried on many of Addison's products.

In 1955 Knight's son J.A. Knight launched Heat Controller, Inc., in Jackson, as a marketer of air-conditioning units. Heat Controller, Inc., is the major OEM customer of Addison Products, selling through distributors nationwide.

In 1963 Knight purchased the remaining stock of Addison Products Company and became sole owner. He looks back upon his accomplishments with the firm with pride.

"We built fast and made money," he says, noting that for many years Addison Products Company was the biggest employer in Hillsdale County. And while the days of rapid growth are past, Knight takes pride in his firm's contributions to the industry and the area.

V.C. "Cliff" Knight has been at the helm of Addison Products since 1951. His innovation of the split air-conditioning system using a home's furnace brought the company its first great success.

LEFT: Workers assemble air-conditioning units in the Addison plant in this photo from 1964.

An aerial view of the Addison plant in 1960. The office building and lab were added later. The Addison facilities are home to the company's corporate offices, engineering, model shop, and advanced engineering and research, as well as its manufacturing and warehousing.

HATHAWAY HOUSE

RIGHT: The stately Hathaway House, built in 1851, attracts visitors from southeastern Michigan and northern Ohio with its classic midwestern cuisine and gracious atmosphere. Photo by Frederick G. Eaton

CENTER: My Little Sweet Shop and Main Street Emporium are two of the many shops that, along with white picket fences, give Main Street a quaint flavor. Photo by Mary Ward Eaton

BOTTOM: The Ellis Inn, a Victorian-era bed and breakfast, offers guests the charm of period furniture as well as the comforts of air conditioning, room phones, color television, and a continental breakfast. Photo by Mary Ward Eaton

Elegance and style blend together with a sense of history at Hathaway House in Blissfield. Built as a residence by dry goods merchant David Carpenter in 1851, the Greek-revival building was converted to a restaurant in 1962. George and Prudence Hathaway, who occupied the house from 1945 to 1960, were the last owners to reside there.

The Weeber family assumed ownership of Hathaway House in 1963, the year following its conversion to a restaurant. Brothers Art and Mike divide respective duties of business and cuisine.

Visitors to Hathaway House will notice a plaque denoting the building as a National Register of Historic Places site. It is also in the Michigan Register. Framed historic mementos, found during restoration of the house in the 1960s, adorn the foyer. Inside, diners are seated in one of six finely appointed dining rooms.

Hathaway House cuisine begins with appetizers ranging from Italian cheese stuffed filo to escargots in garlic butter. Entrees vary from shrimp and scallops Parisienne and New Zealand lobster tail to roast prime rib of beef and veal scallopini. The specialty of the house on Friday evenings is a crab and shrimp buffet. A large and varied salad bar is the hallmark of Hathaway House. "We were a pioneer with salad bars," says co-owner Art Weeber. "All our vegetables are fresh, and all our baking, including our dessert tray, is in house." Dessert offerings include chocolate toffee torte, chocolate-peanut butter pie, and chocolate mousse with raspberry sauce. Reservations are advisable, and Hathaway House is available for banquets and receptions. Catering is offered.

A more casual menu awaits diners at Main Street Stable and Tavern, adjacent to the Hathaway House. The Stable, formerly the carriage barn at the rear of the Hathaway House property, was converted to a restaurant in February 1983. An additional state historical marker is located behind the Stable, commemorating the Erie and Kalamazoo railroad tracks (the first tracks laid west of Allegheny Mountains). Barn siding on the interior walls gives the Main Street Stable a rustic feel. Seating for 60, a bar, and the kitchen area are located on the first floor. The second floor contains office space and The Loft, a large room used for banquets and private parties. Featured at The Stable is a Sunday brunch, served in The Loft. The daily menu at The Stable ranges from sandwiches to complete dinners. Soups, salads, an array of snacks and appetizers, Mexican dishes, and desserts round out the menu. Deli trays are available with 24-hour notice.

Completing the Hathaway House complex are the Main Street shops, a lane of gift and craft stores, and The Ellis Inn, a Victorian bed and breakfast. Built in 1883 by Hiram D. Ellis, the building is another renovation project of the Weebers who believe, "if there's more to offer people, there's more reason to come to Blissfield."

LENAWEE BROADCASTING COMPANY/ WLEN-FM/103.9

W LEN-FM/103.9 observes its 25th year on the air in 1990, having first broadcast June 9, 1965. Formation of the station took place in September 1964, when John W. Koehn, Norm Haft, Gaylord Baker, and Jim Hazen invested in the venture, and the broadcasting company applied for a channel.

The idea for the station was provided by Dick Lackie, Jim Wood, and Ed Fortin, all employees of another radio station in Adrian.

After the trio approached Koehn, it was decided to apply for an available FM channel—at a time when FM radio was in its infancy and was "risky business," Koehn recalls. Koehn became sole owner within a few years.

"WLEN is what is generally referred to as a full-service community-oriented radio station. The nature of the station has changed very little since we started—we are what we always intended to be.

"We have mostly local identification, local news, local sports, local weather, and local involvement. Our programming is such that our full-service concept involves programs that have been on a long time and emphasize communities in the county," Koehn says.

The "Tecumseh Spotlight" with hostess Twila Chapman, has been on the air continuously for 23 years and is the only regular daily radio broadcast from Tecumseh. The "Hispanic Show," with host Angel Millet, has Spanish language, music, news, public affairs, and community conversation for Hispanics and has aired continuously for 21 years.

Operations manager Doug Spade hosts Lenawee County's original talk show, "Partyline." A popular local personality, Spade is blind. He is active in the Leader Dog for the Blind program as well as many community fund-raising efforts, including muscular dystrophy.

A comprehensive news staff is headed by news director Mike Clement. Other programming includes an adult-contemporary/ modern country-music format, Adrian High School and All-County basketball through tournament play, "Blissfield Report" with hostess Pam Brown, "Classified," an audience call-in show that has been on the air for 18 years, "Hudson Report" with host Jeff Schutte, and "Irish Hills Headliners" with hostess Shelly Schuch.

Rounding out the WLEN-FM/103.9 team are Lenawee County's veteran announcer with 28 years on the air, WLEN's morning disc jockey Bob Butler; Julie M. Koehn, station manager; Dale Gaertner, program director; Steve Barkway, sales manager; and Betty Wilson-Payne, marketing consultant.

Founder, president, and chief executive officer of Lenawee Broadcasting Company, Koehn recalls his 21 years of broadcasting University of Michigan sports play-by-play commentary. "I started at the University of North Carolina. My last broadcast was from the University of Hawaii," he says. Koehn is proud of "the station's ability to provide community services over the years to all segments of the population. Being available to the community for its use is our business," he says.

(From left) Dale Gaertner, Mike Clement, Bob Butler, Angel Millet, Doug Spade.

(Standing, from left) Betty Wilson-Payne, Steve Barkway, and Julie Koehn. Seated is John W. Koehn.

THE DAILY TELEGRAM

The *Daily Telegram,* Lenawee County's only daily newspaper, was launched on December 3, 1892, as the *Evening Telegram,* with a pledge to "consistently admit of its supporting good men and honest measures, of whatever political complexion they may be." Although the newspaper has been through many changes in the years since that first edition, that guiding principle continues in force, according to Robert L. Krout, publisher.

The newspaper was established by Elmer E. Putnam and M.W. Redfield, who operated a small printing shop in the Wheeler block. That building at the southeast corner of Maumee and Winter streets now houses Jean Christopher Studios.

The newspaper was printed by D.W. Grandon, publisher of a twice-weekly paper called *The Messenger.* Grandon's plant was in a building on Maumee Street west of the Adrian State Savings Bank—on land that is now parking for Adrian State Bank.

The *Evening Telegram* began with circulation of 600 papers, sold from the newspaper office in the Wheeler Block, according to a letter written by Grandon shortly before his death in 1943. On another occasion Grandon wrote: "Mr. Redfield was a writer, and an unusually good one. His 'Caught On The Fly' column in later years was a feature long before columnists had really got down to business. Mr. Redfield did the writing, the local work, and Mr. Putnam furnished the money."

The paper struggled financially, however, and changed hands several times in its first months of operation. Grandon wound up as the owner, and, as the decade of the Gay 90s brought prosperity to the community, Grandon was able to make the newspaper prosper as well.

By 1907 the newspaper's circulation had increased to 5,000. That year the paper was purchased from Grandon by Stuart H. Perry. Perry came to Adrian from St. Johns with experience gained on the *Pontiac Press.*

Within five years Perry had succeeded in boosting the newspaper's circulation to 8,000. That year a new rotary press and new typesetting equipment were installed. The newspaper had long since moved into Grandon's location on West Maumee, and there it was to remain, with expansions, until 1968.

Perry was the guiding force behind the development of the *Daily Telegram* as the county's leading newspaper. As the century advanced he expanded circulation to all sections of Lenawee County, establishing motor routes to deliver the paper each day, even to remote rural locations.

Former *Telegram* publisher Gene Porter remembers Perry as an amateur astronomer with a national reputation for his knowledge of meteorites. Porter recalls that folks who found curious-looking rocks they suspected of astral origins would send them in boxes to the *Telegram* for Perry to examine and authenticate. Once in a while, Porter recalls, one would actually be a meteorite.

Perry built a team of dedicated reporters who reported on the community through war, peace, prosperity, depression, and progress. Donald L. Frazier was editor for many of those years, with Hoig Gay serving as managing editor, followed by Lorne Clemes. An institution at the newspaper for more than 50 years was Madge Millikin, society editor and writer.

When Perry died in 1957, circulation stood near 20,000, and the staff had grown beyond 50 people. Following Perry's death the newspaper was operated under a trust by his son-in-law, C. Kenneth Wesley, business

This Goss press produced the Adrian Daily Telegram *for many years, until it was replaced by a newer model in the newspaper's new office in 1967. Sometime after this 1920s-era photo, another bank of units was added on top of this press to increase page capacity.*

manager of the *Monroe Evening News,* as publisher and for a time by his grandson, Charles S. Wesley, assistant publisher.

In 1964 the newspaper was purchased by Thomson Newspapers, Inc. Four years later the newspaper moved around the corner to its present location at 133 North Winter Street, in a building that was converted from an A&P grocery store. A press with 44-page capacity was installed in a new press room built across the back of the lot.

That press was replaced in 1984 with a new Goss Community offset press, greatly improving reproduction. A year before that a computerized typesetting system had been installed, making it possible to publish more late news more accurately than before.

The *Daily Telegram* currently employs 50 people full time, with a delivery force numbering more than 200. The newspaper is served by the Associated Press with news and photos from around the nation and the world. A newsroom staff of 13 reports on news, sports, and social activities nationwide, and full-color photographs can be found on the front page nearly every day.

"We believe strongly in community service," Krout asserts. "Our support of United Way and other important positive efforts for Lenawee County helps us to carry out our role as a good citizen."

The *Daily Telegram* produces a number of special readership editions each year, led by the annual Focus on Lenawee in February and the popular Cook Book in October.

In 1988, after more than 90 years of publishing six afternoons per week, the *Daily Telegram* changed its Saturday paper to a morning edition. Then, on April 1, 1990, a new publication was launched—the *Sunday Telegram.* Featuring four news sections and expanded features, the Sunday product provides Lenawee County with local news every day of the week.

"Although Mr. Putnam and Mr. Redfield were producing a newspaper in a far different age than we face today, their idea of a nonpartisan newspaper that tells the truth and supports the people in the community who are working for good is as correct today as it was then," Krout observes. "That's what we attempt to do every day."

The former home of the Adrian Daily Telegram *was on West Maumee, adjoining the Adrian State Bank building. Passersby could watch the press run through the picture window on the right. The newspaper moved to 133 N. Winter Street in the 1960s.*

BIXBY MEDICAL CENTER

Doug McNeill, president of Bixby Medical Center, has helped to engineer a series of changes at the hospital since his arrival in 1985.

BOTTOM: Emma L. Bixby Hospital, located on Locust Street from 1911 to 1957, was facilitated by a man whose son died because Adrian lacked a hospital. The hospital, now Bixby Medical Center, moved to Adrian's northwest side in 1957.

BELOW: Bixby Medical Center is entering the 1990s with this new look. This architect's rendering shows the changes and additions, begun in 1989, that will include a 30,000-square-foot, two-story medical office building.

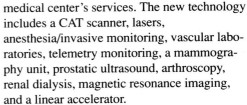

Bixby Medical Center is prepared to meet the 1990s with new technology, a new philosophy of health care delivery, and a new image that will meet the changing health care needs of Lenawee County residents.

President and chief executive officer Douglas W. McNeill is engineering the "retooling," which includes diversifying Bixby's clinical programming in order to meet the challenge of emerging trends in health care delivery.

Founded in 1911 after a man lost his son due to the lack of a hospital in Adrian, Bixby Hospital was located in a house near the center of town. The hospital moved to its present site on Riverside Avenue in 1957, and new additions were made in the mid-1960s and 1970s. Changing to a private, nonprofit organization in 1988, the new medical center will continue its growth well into the next decade.

Program and service development at Bixby have progressed significantly so that there is little reason to leave Lenawee County for medical treatment. The addition of 25 new doctors at Bixby in the past three years has strengthened the areas of family practice; obstetrics and gynecology; internal medicine; oncology; urology; orthopedics; general surgery; anesthesia; radiology; psychiatry; pulmonology; neurology; pediatrics; ear, nose and throat; and ophthalmology.

Major equipment purchases have enhanced many of the medical center's services. The new technology includes a CAT scanner, lasers, anesthesia/invasive monitoring, vascular laboratories, telemetry monitoring, a mammography unit, prostatic ultrasound, arthroscopy, renal dialysis, magnetic resonance imaging, and a linear accelerator.

The medical center has a cancer/oncology program, a psychiatric unit, the Sage Center for Substance Abuse Treatment, walk-in clinic services, physical medicine, rehabilitative services, and expanded educational programs and patient services.

McNeill refers to Bixby's cancer treatment program as "one of the major pillars of the medical center." Patients who in the past have traveled to Ann Arbor, Toledo, or Detroit to receive treatment for cancer, now find treatment closer to home. With the addition of sophisticated equipment and a staff of cancer specialists, most cancer cases in Lenawee County are now treatable at Bixby.

The medical center is also the first in the area to offer a new renal dialysis program that provides lifesaving services to the surrounding area. The program offers state-of-the-art facilities and equipment under the physician direction of a kidney specialist.

Another innovative program at Bixby is the 24-hour Ask-a-Nurse service. Registered nurses use a computer and physician-approved protocols to help callers determine the urgency of treatment. Ask-a-Nurse is also a physician-referral network, a health-information system, and is Bixby's educational program and community agency data bank. The program fields 100 telephone calls daily.

Bixby will continue to provide the health care services that the community demands. With a multimillion-dollar expansion and renovation project announced in 1989, the medical center will erect a three-story medical office building, an expanded surgery suite, an upgraded and larger critical care unit, a larger outpatient center, and expanded radiation therapy facilities. The medical center will also double its parking space to accommodate visitors to and patients of the facility.

The third-largest employer in the county and home to 110 physicians, Bixby Medical Center is ensuring quality, modern health care for the people of Lenawee County.

CLIFT PONTIAC-NISSAN-GMC

Garry Clift entered the car business in Adrian at the beginning of a recession that put scores of dealers out of business, but he has since created one of the region's leading dealerships.

Garry is the oldest of Arthur and Glenna Clift's two sons. Art and Glenna Clift moved from Toledo, Ohio, to Adrian in 1951, Art buying an interest in Adrian Glass Company. A Maple Leaf Award winner, he was a county commissioner and Kiwanis president. He led efforts to build the Kiwanis Riverside Terrace and the YMCA.

In 1976, when Garry was 22 and his brother Richard 20, their parents died when a small plane Art was piloting from a Florida vacation developed mechanical trouble and crashed in Georgia.

Garry and Richard took over the glass business, Garry leaving a job with Toyota Motor Sales. They were not enthusiastic for the glass business and sold out in 1978. Garry went to graduate school at Michigan State University for a semester, then took an auto sales job in Lansing. "I had decided I wanted to be a car dealer," he explains.

Soon after that his brother suggested he buy a dealership. When Garry asked advice of Gene Stevens, who owned Adrian's Pontiac and Datsun dealership, Stevens offered to sell.

Clift took the deal.

Clift had guessed wrong that the car slump had bottomed out. "It was just starting to go bad," he says. The first months were so difficult he feared bankruptcy. In 1981 the GMC dealer in Adrian gave his franchise to Clift.

"There were three of us selling : Ross DeKeyser, Mike Beaubien, and I," Clift recalls. To save money they would leave the showroom lights off until they saw a customer coming.

The turnaround came just in time. As sales picked up Clift invested in the business. He added more lifts in the service department and expanded to service trucks. In 1985 a large body shop was built, with state-of-the-art equipment. The office was modernized, and in 1989 a building was added for used car sales.

Now Clift Pontiac-Nissan-GMC employs 50 people, up from 12 in 1980, with the most sophisticated computer system of any dealership in the area, Clift says. The lot has been doubled.

Annual sales have quadrupled. Clift's Pontiac sales command 15 percent of his market, topping Pontiac's 11 percent in the Detroit zone and 7 percent nationwide.

Like his father, Garry Clift has been active in the community. A past chairman of the Lenawee County Chamber of Commerce, he is president of the Greater Adrian Industrial Development Corporation. He was Kiwanis Club president and is 1990 first vice-president of Lenawee United Way.

In 1989 brother Rick Clift joined the business as a sales manager. Ross DeKeyser is used car sales manager, and John Wickham, an Adrian High School classmate of Garry, is service manager.

Garry Clift (left) has built Clift Pontiac-Nissan-GMC into a thriving business in Lenawee County and is active in community affairs. His brother, Richard (right), joined him in the business in 1989 as sales manager.

LAIDLAW WASTE SYSTEMS, INC.

Laidlaw Waste Systems, Inc., operates two businesses in Lenawee County: a refuse-hauling company and a sanitary landfill in Palmyra Township east of Adrian. Based in Canada, Laidlaw is the third-largest waste services company in North America.

Laidlaw got into business in Lenawee County in 1980, but the operation it purchased is much older.

Dee Stucker opened a dump in Palmyra Township in 1964. His was the third licensed sanitary landfill in the state of Michigan. The

Laidlaw Waste Systems, Inc., provides refuse-hauling and landfill services for Lenawee County.

site was a fortunate selection because the soil has a high clay content so it is appropriate for a landfill, according to Dave Cannon, who heads the Laidlaw hauling company in Lenawee.

The landfill was served in recent years by the Weaver Trucking Company. Both were purchased in 1978 by Theta Systems, Inc., which assumed the name Lenawee Disposal. Laidlaw's introduction to Lenawee came when the corporation purchased Theta Systems.

Since making the purchase Laidlaw has made a considerable investment in the land-

fill, transforming it into a modern operation. The old landfill inherited by Laidlaw was finally sealed off in 1989, after it was covered with a mound of soil. The old site is to be landscaped even as operations begin with a state-of-the-art sanitary landfill north of the old site.

The new landfill features a clay bottom, with a double-layer rubber-composition material liner that is guaranteed by its manufacturer not to leak. The new landfill cell has a draining field for water and another drainage system for leachate, which is pumped out and hauled away to be disposed of scientifically as toxic waste.

The new $10-million landfill is expected to last for 15 years, Cannon said—and since Laidlaw owns another 20 acres at the site, the company and the county are certain to be able to meet disposal needs for many years to come. In addition, in order to comply with a Michigan law that waste be reduced by 25 percent by 1992, a recycling center has been opened at the landfill to separate glass, aluminum, and paper for recycling.

The other part of Laidlaw's business in Lenawee is waste hauling. The firm operates 15 trucks serving 1,200 commercial and 4,000 residential customers. The territory served is Lenawee County, portions of Monroe and Washtenaw counties, and Lucas County, Ohio.

"As long as Laidlaw Waste Systems, Inc., is in Lenawee County, the people of Lenawee will have a place to dispose of their garbage because Laidlaw will take care of them first," Cannon promises. "Anything we can do to improve the environment, we will do."

FLORY LANGLEY & CO., INC.

It was in 1923 that Frank Flory opened a district office for the Massachusetts Mutual Life Insurance Company in Adrian. A native of Blissfield, Flory soon established his as a top office for the firm. In 1928 he collected the first of what was to become a long string of sales awards from the firm.

It was a source of pride for Flory that during the Depression, when his farmer clients were suffering terrible times, Massachusetts Mutual shipped money by train to Lenawee County to help tide them over and keep the economy going.

Flory was also active in community activities, especially the Knights of Colum-

ored by the Lenawee County Social Services Board for his contributions to the community.

Tom continued the business and was joined in 1981 by a new partner, Richard Langley. Langley was stunned when Tom Flory died on December 22, 1982.

Like his father, Tom had been an active citizen of the community. He had been a board member for the Lenawee County Chamber of Commerce, had been a member of the Board of Associates of Siena Heights College, and had devoted his energies to the Greater Adrian Industrial Development Commission, the YMCA, and the Estate Planning Council. He had also been a member of the Lenawee Country Club.

Today Langley is owner and president of the firm, which remains a district office for Massachusetts Mutual. The organization has six agents and four sales-support and administration personnel, all working from the office in Adrian.

Massachusetts Mutual is consistently ranked among the top 10 mutual life insurance companies in the country. The firm was established in 1851 and now claims more than $22 billion in assets nationwide.

The staff of Flory Langley & Company in the Adrian office: (from left) Connie Hewitt, Ray Miller, Richard Langley, and Barb Homer.

bus. The district office grew and prospered, and in 1954 Frank's son, Tom—born the year before the firm was established—joined his father in business. The firm continued its successful pattern, and Frank Flory became a regular member of Massachusetts Mutual's Million Dollar Round Table.

In 1959 the Florys moved the district office into the First Federal Savings and Loan building in Adrian. The agency remained there until a move to present quarters in the Faulhaber Building.

Frank and Tom Flory worked together until August 8, 1967, when Frank died. He had marked his 50th wedding anniversary in 1963, and in February 1964 had been hon-

Langley specializes in closely held business opportunities and employee benefits plans, offering expertise in financial and estate planning for individuals, as well. The district office has clients in 25 states, from California to Massachusetts and from Washington to Florida, including firms with close ties to Lenawee County.

In 1989 Flory Langley & Co., Inc., had more than $50 million in retirement assets in Lenawee County. "Our goal is to double that total in five years," Langley says. In the past year the district office has expanded its space by 50 percent and added a computer area.

HERRICK MEMORIAL HEALTH CARE CENTER

Herrick Memorial Health Care Center marked its 50th anniversary in 1988. The growth and development of services since the hospital opened have been remarkable.

Tecumseh did not have a hospital in 1937. Citizens in need of hospitalization or emergency room treatment had to travel to Adrian or Ann Arbor for help.

Ray Herrick had received a warm welcome from the community to 1934, when he moved his refrigeration-compressor manufacturing business from Hillsdale, and he wanted to give something back to the community. Herrick invited 22 leading citizens to his office in August 1937 to propose a hospital. He pledged $28,000 from Tecumseh Products and other contributors. The community raised the remaining $10,000 needed to build the hospital.

A hospital association was formed, and Herrick's friend Henry Ford donated a 5.5-acre parcel to the project. A public meeting was held September 30, 1937, to involve the community in the project, and committees were formed to raise money and make plans.

On May 27, 1938, just seven months after construction began, the Tecumseh Hospital Association presented the new facility to the village. The hospital had been built with expansion in mind—a foresight that proved to be quite important.

At first Tecumseh Hospital accommodated 18 adults, 3 children, and 8 infants. The emergency room, operating room, X-ray, and obstetrical facilities were built to serve a 50-bed hospital. Upon delivering the hospital to the village the Tecumseh Hospital Association disbanded, replaced by a five-member board of directors appointed by the village.

The need to expand came quickly. The first addition was started within two years, with dedication ceremonies held in January 1941. It increased patient capacity to 37. The hospital operated at capacity throughout most of the 1940s. The hospital's directors were concerned that there was no reserve capacity to deal with emergencies, and again Ray Herrick came through, pledging enough money to expand the hospital to 55 beds in August 1951.

Three years later another expansion was undertaken, thanks to a $250,000 gift from an anonymous donor. A two-story section was built, and capacity was increased to 76 beds. A separate boiler plant was built, and maternity, surgery, and support facilities were expanded, along with creation of locker rooms for nurses and doctors working on the new floor.

It was just three years before ground was broken again in 1958 for an addition, this one to the south side of the building. A basement and two-story wing were added, raising the capacity to 100 beds. In 1966 more rooms were added to the south wing, and the X-ray, emergency, pharmacy, and laboratory facilities were enlarged. In 1968 another project was begun, which was completed in four stages by 1976, enlarging or updating emergency room, boiler room, kitchen, laboratory facilities, and creating an intensive coronary care unit, 42 new medical/surgical rooms, and various ancillary services areas.

The number of patient beds remained at 100, but the hospital had taken on the scale and the facilities of a fully equipped full-service hospital of a kind to be expected in a much larger community.

With the coming of the 1980s the hospital's role changed drastically. The need for inpatient beds declined as modern medicine

Phil Sullivan, president of Herrick Memorial Health Care Center, has been with the hospital since 1983 and at the helm since 1986.

conquered many of the debilitating illnesses that had kept patients in hospitals in years past. As the need for inpatient beds declined, Herrick Memorial turned to specialties and outpatient clinics to serve the community.

Herrick Memorial's inpatient mental health unit opened in 1980, and since then the StressCenter has served more than 1,000 patients. Other clinics and departments offering expanded outpatient and inpatient service include occupational and physical therapy, medical imaging, speech and language pathology, and respiratory therapy. The medical imaging department includes mammography, nuclear medicine, a bone densitometer machine to detect osteoporosis, ultrasound, and CAT scan.

Opening in 1989 was the latest expansion of the institution, newly renamed to reflect its new role from Herrick Memorial Hospital to Herrick Memorial Health Care Center—a modern $3.8-million wing to house the hospital's mental health services, physical therapy, and an integrated closed head injury

program.

The new center includes an apartment for functional training in adaptive living and a medical exercise and fitness center, with indoor track, courts, and aerobic components. The hospital's interdisciplinary medical teams have been augmented with new specialists to provide a comprehensive approach to treating psychiatric and physical disabilities.

At the helm during the hospital's most recent expansion and dramatic extension of services has been Phil Sullivan, president and chief executive officer. Sullivan joined the hospital in 1983 and became president three years later.

Sullivan places emphasis upon Herrick Memorial Health Care Center's role as a community hospital. "We want people to be able to come here and stay in their own community," he says. To make this possible he and the hospital board have placed great emphasis upon attracting first-rate medical staff and creating innovative programs, such as a wellness program and a Women's Health Services department.

"Ours is a full-service facility committed to providing quality health care services in the convenience of a community setting," Sullivan says. "Compassion, love, and personal attention are elements that make a community-centered hospital essential to a growing area like Lenawee County."

If Ray Herrick could see today's fulfillment of the dream he had in 1937 he would surely be proud. He'd be proud, too, to know that his family and the foundation his company made possible have continued to support the hospital he created more than 50 years ago.

Herrick Memorial enters the 1990s with a modern, new wing housing its mental health services, physical therapy unit, and closed head injury clinic, among other facilities.

Herrick Memorial Health Care Center opened in 1938 and has since undergone numerous expansions, keeping pace with the growing needs of the community.

ADRIAN DOMINICAN SISTERS

The history of the Adrian Dominican Sisters is a story of risk-taking, devotion to God and community, and amazing tenacity. In 1884 six nuns were sent from New York to establish a hospital. They began in an elm house in a cornfield at the northeast edge of Adrian.

Their heritage was from Holy Cross Convent, Regensburg, Bavaria, a contemplative congregation that in 1853 sent four nuns to teach the children of German immigrant families in America. As years passed more nuns came, opening more schools. The call to Adrian was answered from Holy Rosary Convent in New York City.

The elm house soon proved inadequate, and a red-brick structure was completed in 1886. This building, still part of Madden Hall (the motherhouse), became the center for all other buildings, which now number 16.

It was in 1892 that the Adrian hospital and its Sisters became a Province of St. Joseph, and Mother Camilla Madden arrived as provincial to apply her dynamic determination to expand and stimulate the mission of the Adrian Sisters. The beginning was small. Mother Camilla came to a community of about 30 nuns who were teaching in seven rural schools and serving in a struggling hospital.

In 1896, after four years of trying, she obtained permission from the Bishop of Detroit to establish St. Joseph's Academy. Starting the school was a risky venture, but Mother Camilla believed that Adrian's position as a rail center would allow students to come from all directions. She was right, and as the enrollment mounted the original building was extended into the east and west wings, in 1898 and 1902.

Construction of Holy Rosary chapel and the rectory was begun in 1905 and completed before 1909. The construction of other buildings followed. Girls got off the train from Chicago, Cleveland, Detroit, and other cities. Graduates returned to their parishes and praised their teachers, resulting in more growth for the congregation. Requests for new schools piled up, and every new school attracted new members.

A newspaper clipping from 1900 records an enrollment of 100 students. By 1908 enrollment was 200, and 400 a few years later. Mother Camilla sought out recognized scholars and invited them to teach at the academy.

In 1919 Mother Camilla launched St. Joseph's College. There was no building for it, so the women shared space in the successful St. Joseph's Academy. Mother Camilla had difficulty purchasing the orchard next to the academy to provide space for the college, but she managed to do it. In 1922 Sacred Heart Hall was completed. The college was founded for members of the Adrian Dominican Congregation, with an orientation toward teacher certification and the bachelor's degree. By 1922 the doors were opened to all young women. Some of these women were attracted to join the Congregation as well.

In 1923 the Adrian province separated from the motherhouse in New York and became motherhouse of the Adrian Dominican Congregation.

Before her death in 1924 Mother Camilla had extended the reach of the Adrian congregation's schools as far as Florida and New Mexico. Her policies were continued by her successors. Mother Gerald led the congregation into various and new directions, among them parish visitation, hospitals, overseas missions, care of the aging, and initiation of provinces.

In 1939 St. Joseph's College was given a new name, Siena Heights, to give it a separate identity from the celebrated academy in whose shadow it had long operated. During the 1960s, a period of reevaluation and regeneration, the college became an independent entity, with its own board of directors. Soon after it became coeducational. In 1989 the

The Maria Health Care Center carries on work begun more than 100 years ago in the old St. Joseph's Hospital. Patients in this modern facility are all nuns.

Madden Hall, which still includes portions of the first red-brick building completed in 1886, is the center of activity for the Adrian Dominican Sisters. The building is named in honor of Mother Camilla Madden, who shaped the Adrian congregation in its formative years.

Adrian Dominican Sisters served in 35 dioceses and archdioceses of the United States and in nine countries overseas.

Many and varied ministries, national and international, have developed from the traditional teaching, nursing, and social services. Education is carried out in many dimensions, including religious education, special education, adult education, tutoring, campus ministry, pastoral ministry, and care of the sick, elderly, and physically and mentally handicapped. The congregation is involved in community organization, works of peace and justice, ministries in art, law, science, journalism, public relations, communications, business, administration, housing, ways and means in assisting poor and deprived people, and special ministries in medical and health care services. St. Joseph's Academy helped the Sisters create a relationship with the people of Adrian. The first Sisters were not readily accepted by the largely Protestant community. But students of the academy and their visiting families brought life and purchasing power to the city, and acceptance followed.

Today the Sisters are a dynamic force in the community, acting as a conscience pressing for peace, justice, and progress. The Sisters have declared the motherhouse to be a Nuclear Free Zone, and once they ceremonially cut up gasoline credit cards to protest corporate involvement in South Africa.

Members of the congregation have protested U.S. policy in Central America and have demonstrated in front of the courthouse to share their views.

The teaching mission continues, with schools in Illinois, Florida, California, and points between. St. Joseph's Academy has been enhanced by the creation of the Montessori Children's House for preschoolers, and classes at the academy continue through sixth grade. The motherhouse complex includes historic Madden Hall, Holy Rosary Chapel, the Maria Health Care Center, Weber Center for meetings and seminars, and residence buildings.

In 1989, 1,400 Adrian Dominican Sisters gathered from all over the world at the motherhouse for Transformations '89, a conference to renew and rededicate the Sisters to the congregation's far-flung ministry.

The original six nuns of the Adrian Dominican Sisters came to Adrian from New York in 1884. They established St. Joseph's Hospital in this elm house in a cornfield in northeast Adrian.

LENAWEE PUBLIC SCHOOLS

The availability of quality education is a vital component of any community. In Lenawee County, 12 local school districts strive to provide the best possible opportunities for their citizens. One reason they have been able to do this is they work together—utilizing the services of the Lenawee Intermediate School District. The LISD, a regional education service district which evolved from the former county superintendent of education office in 1962, serves several roles in the county's education system. It also serves as a vital communication channel for dissemination of information regarding changes in state and federal education programs.

The LISD's first superintendent was Milton C. Porter, who moved into the newly created position from his elected post as county superintendent—a job he had held since 1947. Porter had been county superintendent through the often difficult and painful years of school consolidation, which saw the number of districts in Lenawee shrink from 187 to 12. He had also taken the first steps toward establishing special services for students with special needs.

"One day I was told to go by and see a child at one house," Porter related in a newspaper article. "I got there, and there was a child that had been in bed for two years and with no education."

After that trip, Porter hired the county's

first special-education teacher—one that visited homebound students across the county to give them an education.

By the time the LISD was established, the consolidation process was nearly complete, and the new school district set about establishing new priorities. Special education was a critical one. The program grew to involve all the public school districts in the county and in 1964 a special school, the Milton Porter Center, was built on Sutton Road for students requiring a wide range of services.

Children from all school districts, newborn through age 26, are eligible for the LISD's special education services, and more than 1,900 students are served by 130 special education professionals. Most students are considered mildly impaired and are served in one of 80 special education classrooms in the local districts. Special education faces constant change and challenge such as the move toward least restrictive environment (LRE), whereby students will be offered a continuum of educational options including the placement of some classrooms of trainable mentally impaired students in regular classroom buildings.

In 1970 the Lenawee Area Vocational-Technical Center was added to the LISD's program. The center, on M-52 at the north edge of Adrian, was created to provide young people and adults from the community with career skills. Vo-Tech offers courses from auto

Lenawee County Public School District Superintendents. Seated, from left: H.E. Cooley, J.L. Hartley, G.J. Sargeant, W.J. Ross. Standing, from left: P. Ellinger, E. Deuel, J.P. Gasidlo, J.G. Meredith, J.M. Kersh, J.L. Leary, L.C. Wilson, D.M. Harlan, N.V. Singles.

Addison Community Schools
Supt.—Jeffrey M. Kersh
Enrollment
1965—1,276
1990—1,210
Buildings
Wayne Gray Elementary School
Addison Middle School
Addison High School

Adrian Public Schools
Supt.—James L. Leary, Ed.D.
Enrollment
1965—5,928
1990—5,043
Buildings
Alexander Elementary School
Comstock Elementary School
Garfield Elementary School
Lincoln Elementary School
McKinley Elementary School
Michener Elementary School
Prairie Elementary School
Drager Middle School
Springbrook Middle School
Adrian High School

Blissfield Community Schools
Supt.—Larry C. Wilson, Ed.D.
Enrollment
1965—2,128
1990—1,594
Buildings
South Elementary School
Blissfield Middle School
Blissfield High School

Britton-Macon Area School
Supt.—John Gasidlo
Enrollment
1965—604
1990—403
Buildings
Britton Elementary & High School

Clinton Community Schools
Supt.—George J. Sargeant
Enrollment
1965—1,047
1990—1,117
Buildings
Clinton Elementary School
Clinton Middle School
Clinton High School

Deerfield Public Schools
Supt.—Paul L. Ellinger
Enrollment
1965—439
1990—430
Buildings
Deerfield Elementary School
Deerfield High School

Hudson Area Schools
Supt.—John G. Meredith, Ph.D.
Enrollment
1965—1,481
1990—1,228
Buildings
Lincoln Elementary School
Hudson Middle School
Hudson High School

Madison School District
Supt.—James L. Hartley
Enrollment
1965—1,056
1990—648
Buildings
Madison Elementary School
Madison High/Middle School

Morenci Area Schools
Supt.—Neal V. Singles
Enrollment
1965—1,147
1990—1,071
Buildings
Morenci Elementary School
Morenci Middle School
Morenci High School

Onsted Community Schools
Supt.—Eugene Deuel
Enrollment
1965—1,271
1990—1,553
Buildings
Onsted Primary Building
Onsted Middle School
Onsted High School

Sand Creek Community Schools
Supt.—Don M. Harlan
Enrollment
1965—1,052
1990—819
Buildings
Ruth McGregor Elementary School
Sand Creek High School

Tecumseh Public Schools
Supt.—H. Eugene Cooley
Enrollment
1965—3,247
1990—3,081
Buildings
Herrick Park Elementary School
Patterson Elementary School
Ridgeway Elementary School
Sutton Elementary School
Tecumseh Acres Elementary School
Tipton Elementary School
Tecumseh Junior High School
Tecumseh High School

The 12 public school districts and the LISD are working separately and cooperatively to bring about systematic, positive change. Their mission is to be innovative and responsive to the changing needs of their students as they prepare them for the twenty-first century.

mechanics and printing to accounting, horticulture, and food service to clerical and computer science. Many high school students spend half their day at their "home school" and the other half at Vo-Tech. In addition, the adult education program has grown to serve more than 2,000 adults per year. Job placement is an important component of the Vo-Tech program, and LISD superintendent William Ross says Vo-Tech helps fill around 900 job orders from employers

throughout Lenawee, Washtenaw, and Jackson counties each year.

Training programs tailored for specific industries are an LISD innovation. "People in business bring their needs to us and we try to meet them," Ross explains. "This is a fast-growing field."

The third division of the LISD provides General Services to the local schools. One of the key areas here is the Professional Development Center, which coordinates training for teachers, administrators, and support staff. The cry from local schools for expanded professional development center offerings was one of the reasons the Education Service Center building became inadequate, and in 1989 a new, $850,000 building was erected next door with funds donated privately in the community together with construction funds that had been set aside in past years.

All 12 local districts have sent teams of educators to the Professional Development Center to be trained in the Lenawee Effective Teaching Skills (LETS) program and the Cooperative Learning program. All 12 districts also work together and with the LISD consultants in the area of curriculum development.

The Lenawee Community Education Cooperative, established in the fall of 1986, is another area that demonstrates successful cooperation. This project consists of seven local districts, which have collaborated in setting up shared senior citizen, adult education, and latch-key programs.

The Cooperative Academic Program (CAP) is an example of the smaller school districts cooperating to provide advanced courses for their students which they could not afford to offer separately.

The schools are all concerned with at-risk students and the corresponding drop-out problem. Although all Lenawee schools fall below the state and national averages in drop-out statistics, they are nevertheless concerned and have all addressed the problem in some way. Throughout the county, schools are offering

In 1989 the LISD finished its new Education Service Center building on M-52 in Birdsall, alongside the site of the old building it replaced. The building was erected largely with donated funds.

preschool programs, including Head Start; developmental kindergarten classes; migrant programs; and an alternative high school.

There are programs in place throughout the county to address bilingual students and gifted and talented students. Responding to the need to keep abreast of changing technology, schools have expanded their use of computers, both in the instructional program and in management services such as financial accounting, student report cards, and student schedules.

Madison and Tecumseh schools were two of the pilot schools involved in the initial state school improvement project. Now all 12 public schools are involved to some degree in this process, which is designed to bring about systematic, positive change as schools attempt to be innovative and responsive to the changing needs of their students.

These programs and services are supported by local tax levies as well as by state funding programs and federal grants. "The Lenawee County community has been marvelously supportive of the LISD and the 12 public school districts over the years," Ross comments. "Quality education in Lenawee County has been possible because the community has been so supportive."

Such cooperation helps the schools fulfill their separate and cooperative goals and helps the LISD staff fulfill a goal inherent in its motto of being a "Partner in Education for a Changing Tomorrow" as they work with the schools in Lenawee County.

Lenawee Intermediate School District
Supt.—William J. Ross, Ph.D.
*Ass't. Supt.—Voc. Ed./General Services—
James Brown*
*Ass't. Supt.—Special Education—Stephen
Krusich*
Enrollment
1965—20,676
1990—18,197

PATRONS

The following individuals, companies, and organizations have made a valuable commitment to the quality of this publication. Windsor Publications and the Lenawee County Chamber of Commerce gratefully acknowledge their participation in *Lenawee County: A Harvest of Pride and Promise.*

Addison Products Company*
Adrian College*
Adrian Dominican Sisters*
Adrian Public Schools*
Adrian State Bank
Adrian Steel Co.*
Akzo Chemicals Inc.*
Anderson Development Co.*
Bales Trucking*
B&U Corp.*
Bank of Lenawee*
Bethany Assembly of God*
Bixby Medical Center*
Blissfield Manufacturing Co.*
Blissfield State Bank
Brazeway, Inc.*
Citizens Gas Fuel Company*
City of Adrian*
Clift Pontiac-Nissan-GMC*

Coldwell Banker Glover Real Estate Associates*
Comfort Enterprises, Inc.*
Consumers Power Co.*
The Daily Telegram*
First Federal Savings of Lenawee*
Flory Langley & Co., Inc.*
Fry Mechanical, Inc.*
Gleaner Life Insurance Society*
Gurdjian & Associates, Inc.*
Hardwoods of Michigan*
Hathaway House*
Herrick Memorial Health Care Center*
Hidden Lake Gardens*
Imperial Travel, Inc.
Inland Fisher Guide Division of General Motors*
Interamerican Zinc, Inc.*
Jacobs Plastics, Inc.
Kapnick and Company, Inc.*
Laidlaw Waste Systems, Inc.*
Lenawee Broadcasting Company/ WLEN-FM/103.9*
Lenawee Christian School and Christian Family Centre*
Lenawee Industrial Machine, Inc.*
Lenawee Public Schools*
Lenawee Tomorrow Economic

Expansion Corporation*
Libbey-Owens-Ford*
Lundy's Heating and Plumbing*
McDonald's*
Merillat Industries, Inc.*
Metalloy Corporation*
Meyers Industries*
Michigan Building Specialties*
Primore, Inc.*
Rima Manufacturing Company*
Riverbend Timber Framing, Inc.*
Siena Heights College*
Society Bank*
Southeastern Michigan Rural Electric Cooperative, Inc.*
Stevenson Lumber, Inc.*
Tecumseh Products Company*
TLC Community Credit Union*
United Savings Bank*
WABJ/Q-95 Radio*
Wacker Silicones Corporation*

*Partners in Progress of *Lenawee County: A Harvest of Pride and Promise.* The histories of these companies and organizations appear in Chapter 7, beginning on page 133

BIBLIOGRAPHY

Adrian Sesquicentennial Booklet Committee. *The Sesquicentennial History of Adrian, Michigan.* 1975.

American Association of University Women, Adrian Chapter. *Early Adrian.* 1964 (Rev. 1973).

Art Work of Lenawee and Monroe Counties. 1894.

Blissfield Area Sesquicentennial History, 1824-1974. 1974.

Bonner, Richard I., and W.A. Whitney, eds., *History and Biographical Record of Lenawee County, Michigan.* 2 vols. 1879-1880 (Reprinted 1982).

———, and John I. Knapp. *Illustrated History and Biographical Record of Lenawee County, Michigan.* 1903.

———. *Memoirs of Lenawee County, Michigan.* 2 vols. 1909.

Brablec, Carl. *Tales from the Headlands.* 1972.

Britton-Macon Area Campfire Girls and Leaders. *By-Gone Days: History of Britton, Michigan, 1830-1971.* 1971.

Bronimau, ed., *The Village of Clinton, Michigan: A History, 1829-1979.* 1981.

Cargo, Ruth, Harlan Feeman, and Fanny Hall. *The Story of a Noble Devotion.* 1945.

Carleton, Will. "Over the Hill to the Poor-House," and other poems. *Farm Ballads,* 1873.

Chandler, Elizabeth M. *Essays, Philanthropic and Moral, Principally Relating to the Abolition of Slavery in America.* 1836.

———. "Letters from a Michigan Log Cabin." *Yale Review,* 1926.

———. *Poetical Works of Elizabeth M. Chandler: With a Memoir of Her Life and Character by Benjamin Lundy.* 1836.

Clemes, Lorne. *A Century of Leadership: The Story of the Bank of Lenawee County.* 1969.

Coman, Russell. *History of Hudson.* 1976.

Comstock, Elizabeth L. *Life and Letters.* 1895.

Cook, Vicki J., ed. *A Little Bit of Yesterday: The History of Franklin Township.* 1976.

Danforth, Mildred E. *A Quaker Pioneer: Laura Haviland.* 1961.

Dawson, John Harper. *A Biography of Ray W. Herrick.* 1984.

Doty, Sile. *The Life of Sile Doty, 1800-1876: The Most Noted Thief and Daring Burglar of His Time.* 1948.

Dunbar, Willis. *All Aboard! A History of Railroads in Michigan.* 1969.

Fields, Harriet. *The Little Red School: Foundation of Lenawee Education.* 1976.

———, and Cynthia Mowery. *Lenawee Schools 1976.* 1976.

Frazier, Doris. *Lenawee County, 1823-1860.* 1965.

Fuller, George N., ed. *Historic Michigan, Vol. III: Saginaw and Lenawee Counties.* 1927.

Harrington and Keehl, eds. *125th Anniversary Booklet for Tecumseh, Michigan.* 1949.

Haviland, Laura. *A Woman's Life Work.* 1881.

Hogaboam, James J. *The Bean Creek Valley: Incidents of Its Early Settlement.* 1876 (Reprinted 1980).

Holubik, Regina, LaDonna Schlapman, and Rita Woods. *Deerfield Album, 1873-1973.* 1973.

Jeffreys, Raymond. *God Is My Landlord.* 1947.

Jones, Mary Patricia. *Elizabeth Margaret Chandler—Poet, Essayist, Abolitionist.* 1981.

Jones, Sharon M., ed. *Los Anos de Oro: Past and Present.* 1980.

Kerr, Merle L. *A History of Raisin Township from the Beginning to the Present.* 1976.

Lenawee County Historical Society, ed. *Combined Atlases of Lenawee County,*

Michigan from 1874, 1893, and 1916. 1978.

Lincoln, James, and Deborah Moore, eds., *City of Tecumseh, Mich. Sesquicentennial Booklet, 1824-1974.* 1974.

Lindquist, Charles. *A History of Trustcorp Bank, Lenawee: 1888-1988.* 1988.

May, George S. *A Most Unique Machine: The Michigan Origins of the Americam Automobile Industry.* 1975.

Men of Affairs in Adrian. 1910.

Morenci Bicentennial Committee. *Our Journey in Time: Morenci, Michigan, 1833-1976.* 1976.

Morenci Observer. *Morenci Reflections.* 1983.

Onsted Community Historical Society. *Gateway to Progress: Cambridge Township and Onsted, 1833-1976.* 1976.

Portrait and Biographical Album of Lenawee County, Michigan. 1888.

Robinson, Janet Breslaw, ed. *Los Antepasados: The Way They Were.* 1979.

Ryan, Sister Mary Philip. *Amid the Alien Corn: The Early Years of the Sisters of Saint Dominic, Adrian, Michigan.* 1967.

Sand Lake Property Owners Association. *Sand Lake: An Historical Collection.* 1981.

Sherman, Ruth E. *112 Years of Adrian Public School History, 1828-1940.* 1940.

Slick, Russell G. *Ridgeway Township: A Topical History, the Whys, Whens and Whos.* 1983.

Slocum, Alice, and Alonzo Lewis. *History of the Addison Area: Addison, Michigan, 1834-1976.* 1976.

Tecumseh Herald. *Tecumseh Products Company, 1934-1984.* 1984.

Waldron, Clara. *One Hundred Years a Country Town: The Village of Tecumseh, Michigan, 1824-1924.* 1968.

Yager, Verdie A. *Reflections on the Bean: A History of the Hudson Area in Prose and Pictures.* 1983.

INDEX